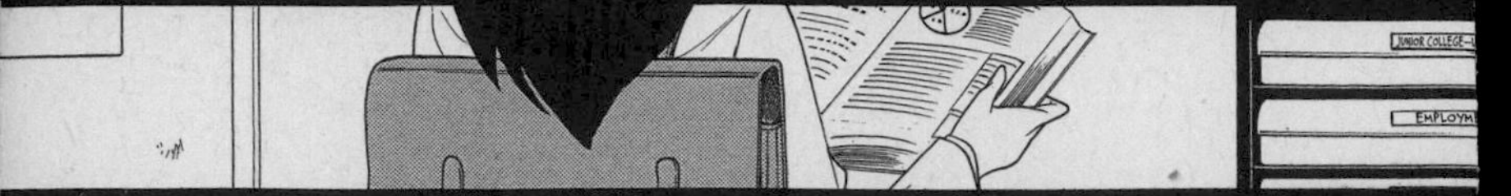

Presented by
NICO TANIGAWA

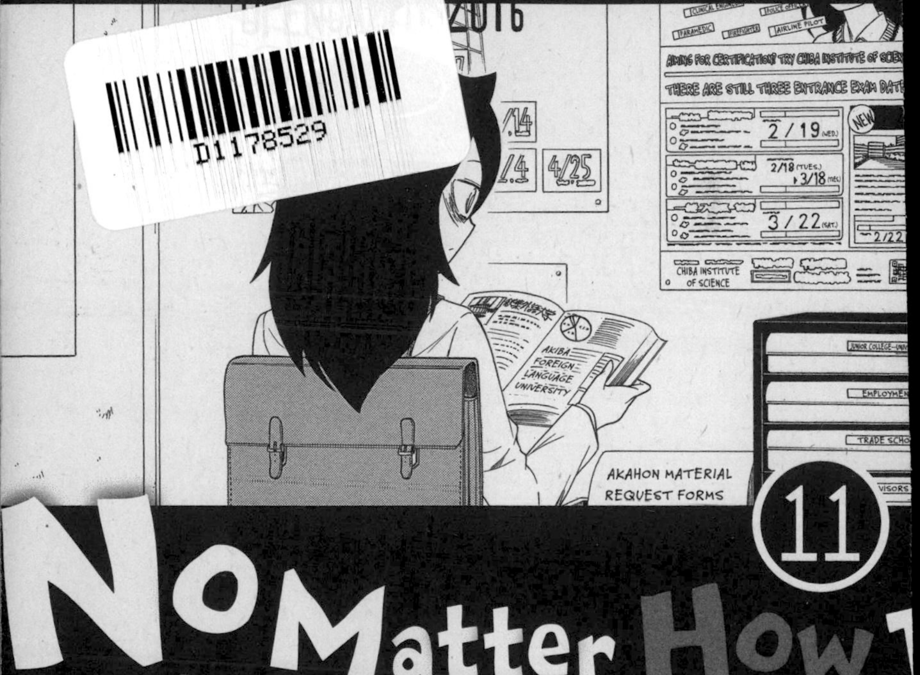

PARAMEDIC
FIREFIGHTER
AIRLINE PILOT
2/19 (WED.)
2/18 (TUES.)
3/18 (WED.)
3/22 (SAT.)
NEW
CHIBA INSTITUTE OF SCIENCE
2016
4/25
AKIBA FOREIGN LANGUAGE UNIVERSITY
AKAHON MATERIAL REQUEST FORMS

11

No Matter How I Look at It, It's You Guys' Fault I'm Not Popular!

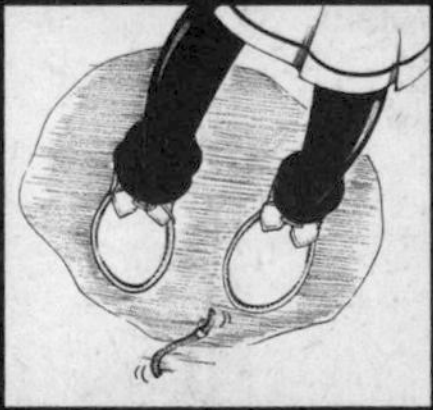

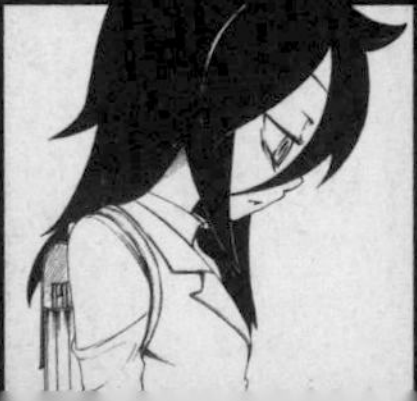

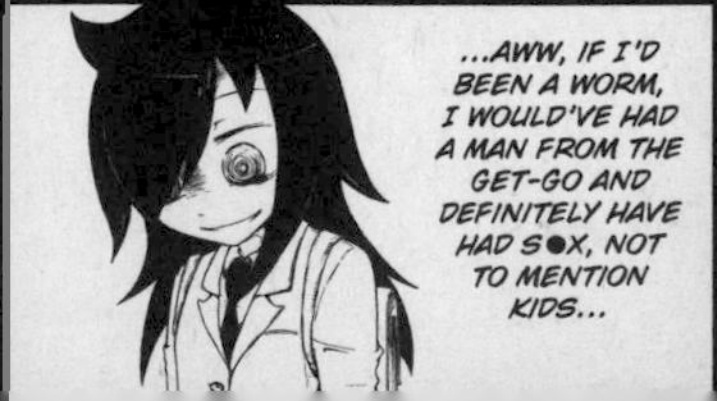
...AWW, IF I'D BEEN A WORM, I WOULD'VE HAD A MAN FROM THE GET-GO AND DEFINITELY HAVE HAD S●X, NOT TO MENTION KIDS...

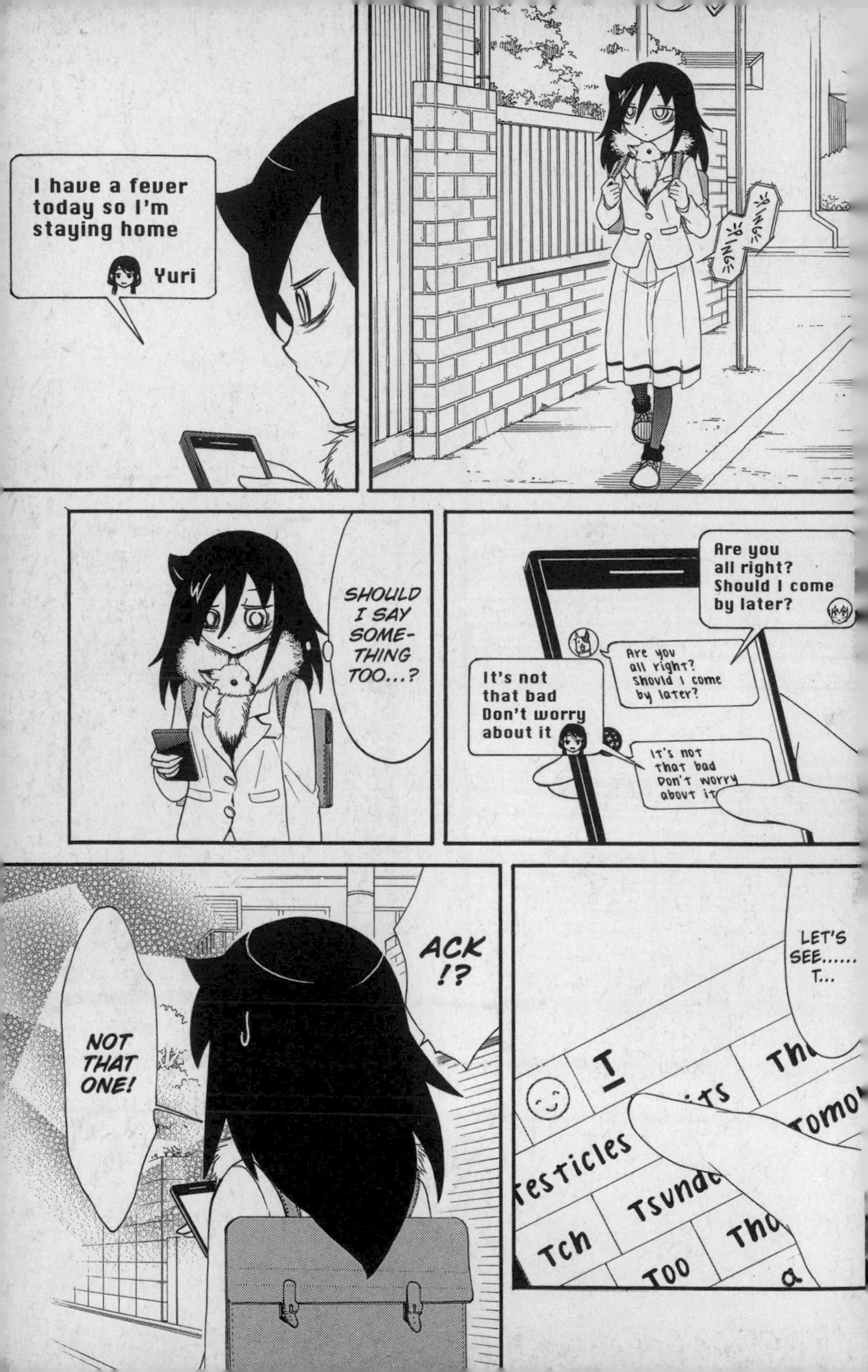
RING RING
I have a fever today so I'm staying home
Yuri
Are you all right? Should I come by later?
Are you all right? Should I come by later?
It's not that bad Don't worry about it
It's not that bad Don't worry about it
SHOULD I SAY SOMETHING TOO...?
LET'S SEE...... T...
T
Th
its
Tomo
testicles
Tsunde
Tch
Tho
Too
a
ACK !?
NOT THAT ONE!

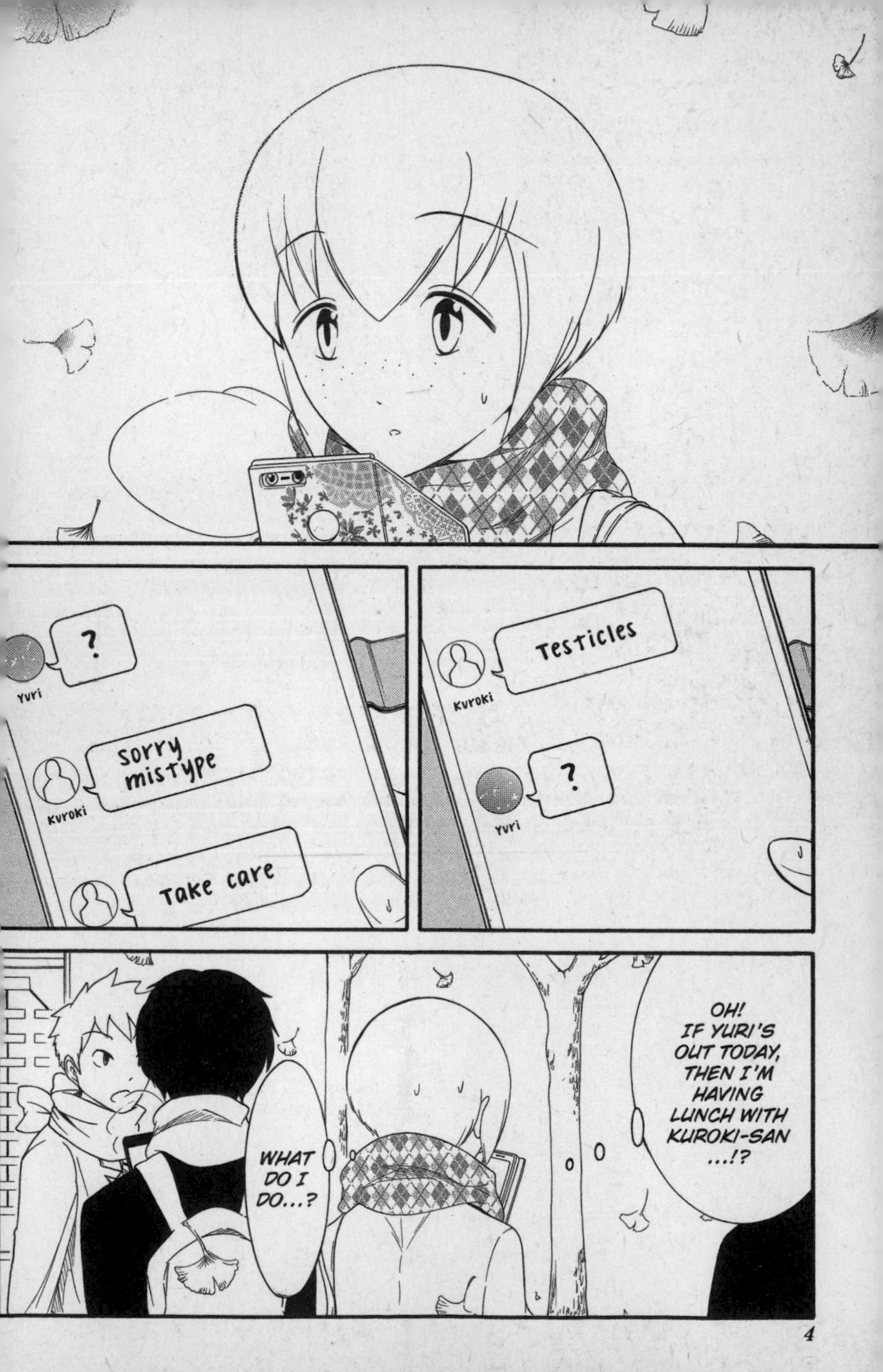
Kuroki
Testicles
?
Yuri
?
Yuri
Kuroki
sorry mistype
Take care
OH! IF YURI'S OUT TODAY, THEN I'M HAVING LUNCH WITH KUROKI-SAN ...!?
WHAT DO I DO...?

FAIL 99: I'M NOT POPULAR, SO I'M A FRIEND OF A FRIEND.

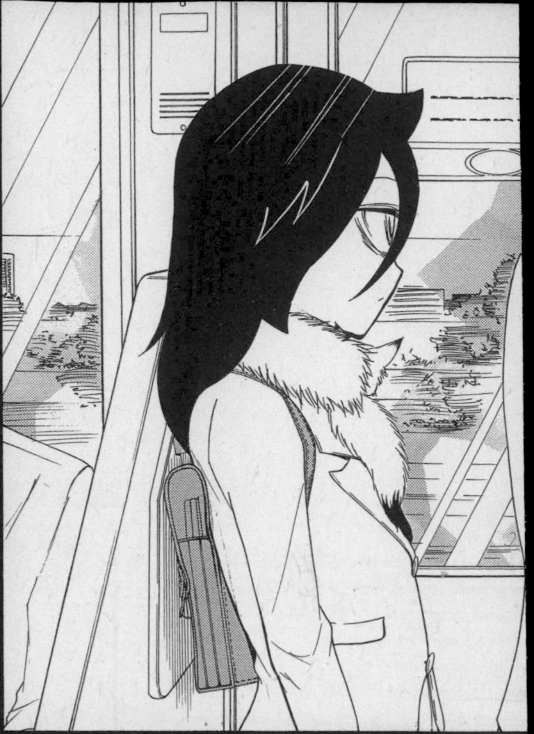

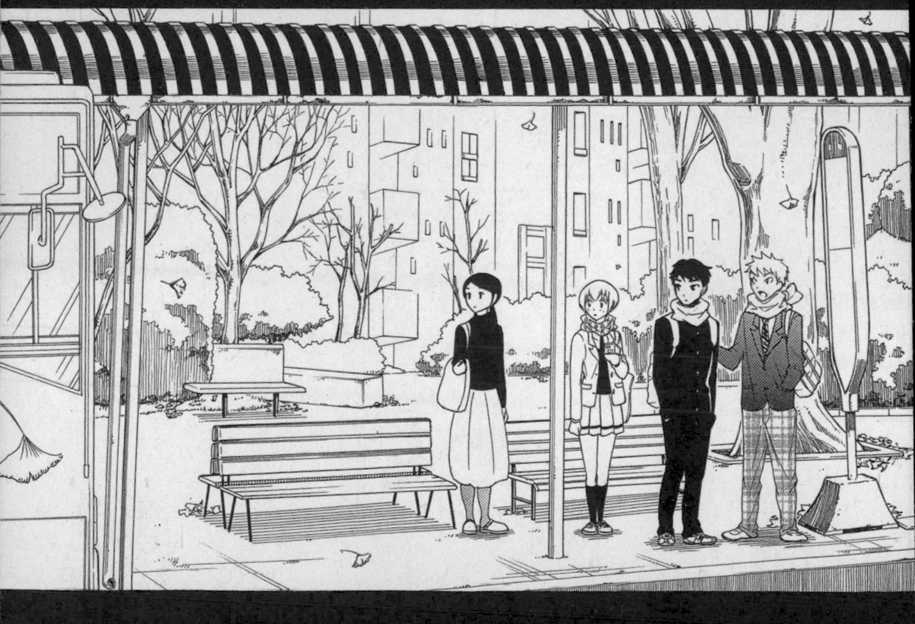

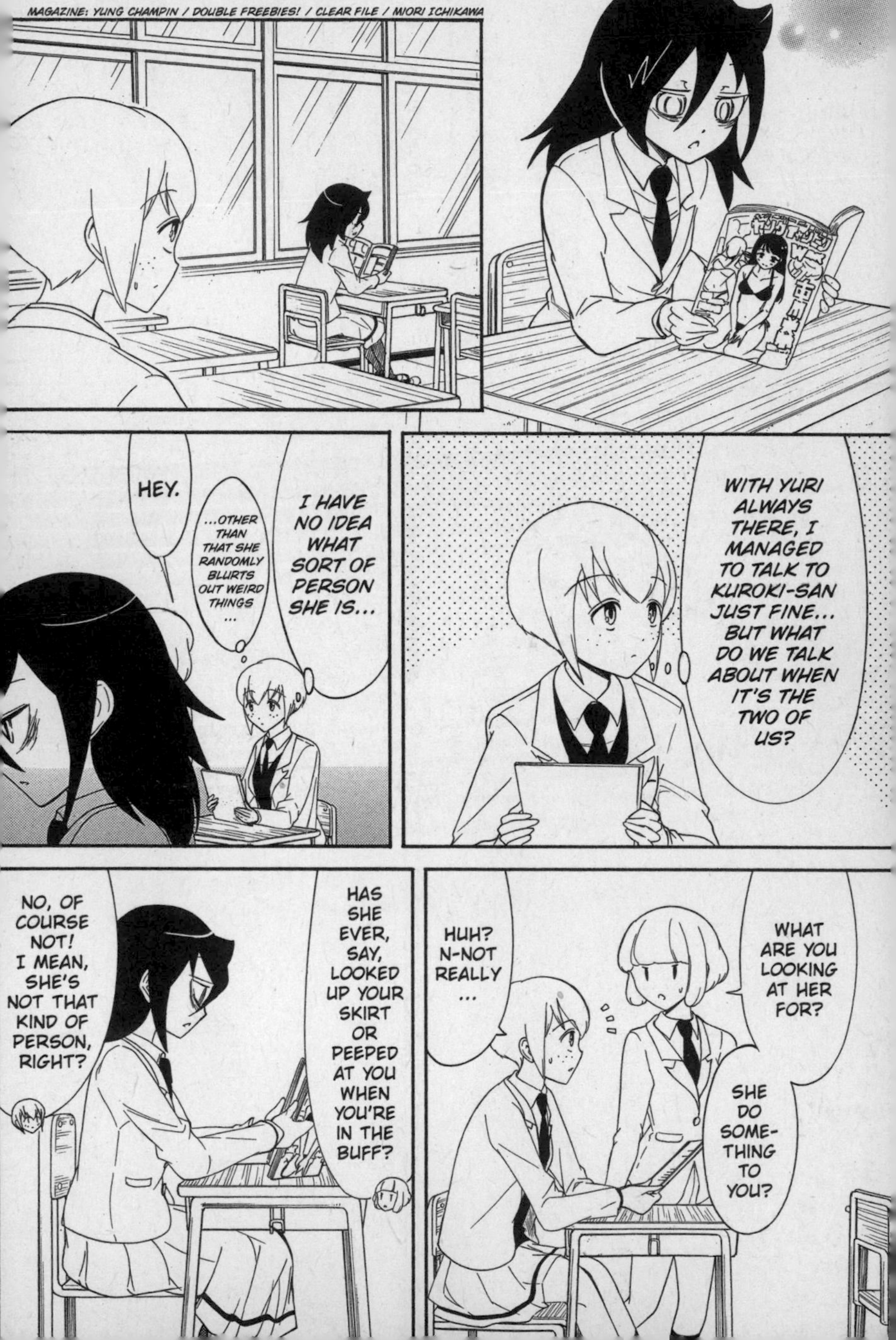
MAGAZINE: YUNG CHAMPIN / DOUBLE FREEBIES! / CLEAR FILE / MIORI ICHIKAWA
WITH YURI ALWAYS THERE, I MANAGED TO TALK TO KUROKI-SAN JUST FINE... BUT WHAT DO WE TALK ABOUT WHEN IT'S THE TWO OF US?
I HAVE NO IDEA WHAT SORT OF PERSON SHE IS...
...OTHER THAN THAT SHE RANDOMLY BLURTS OUT WEIRD THINGS...
HEY.
WHAT ARE YOU LOOKING AT HER FOR?
HUH? N-NOT REALLY...
SHE DO SOME-THING TO YOU?
HAS SHE EVER, SAY, LOOKED UP YOUR SKIRT OR PEEPED AT YOU WHEN YOU'RE IN THE BUFF?
NO, OF COURSE NOT! I MEAN, SHE'S NOT THAT KIND OF PERSON, RIGHT?

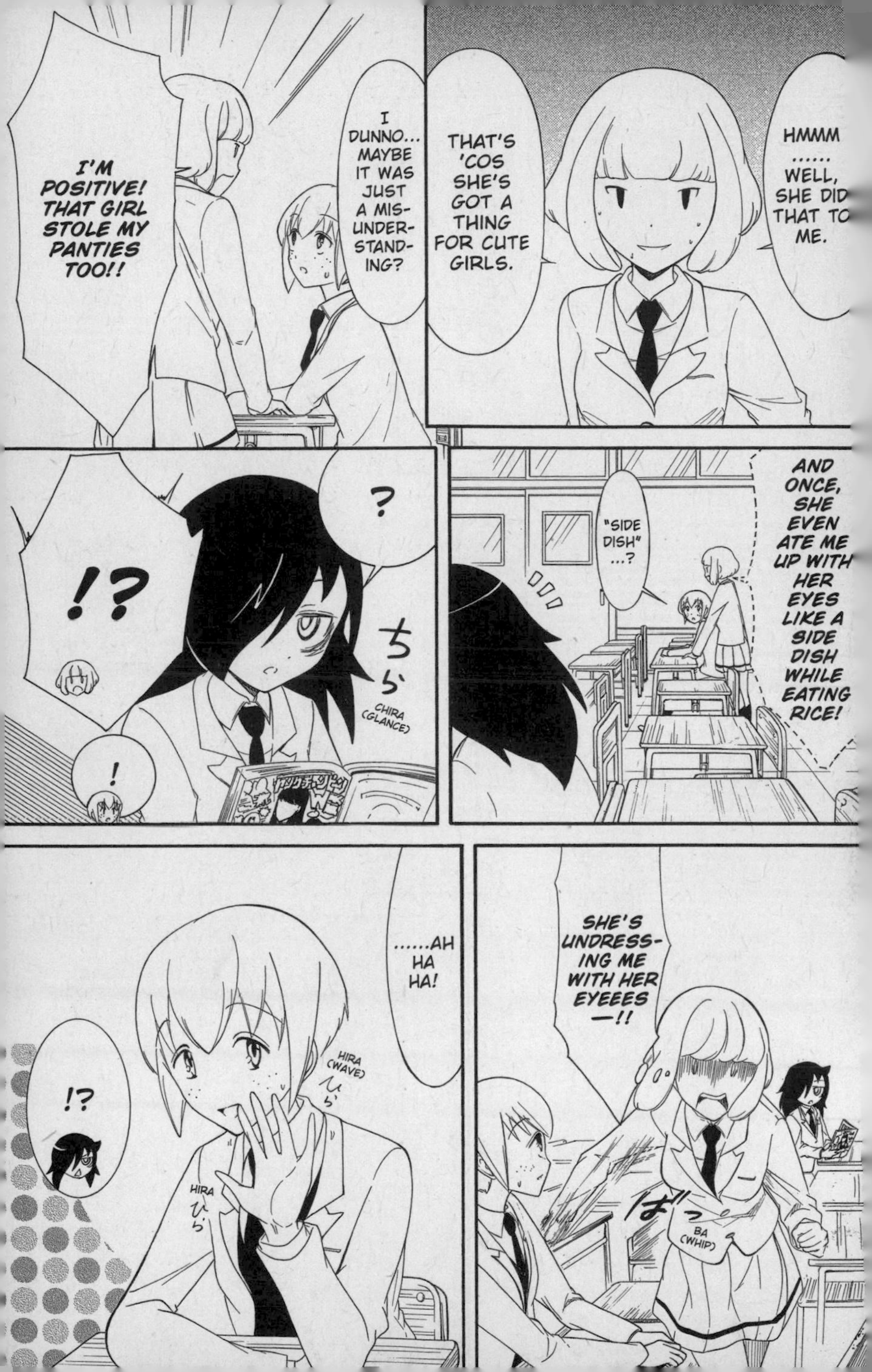
HMMM ...... WELL, SHE DID THAT TO ME.
THAT'S 'COS SHE'S GOT A THING FOR CUTE GIRLS.
I DUNNO... MAYBE IT WAS JUST A MISUNDERSTANDING?
I'M POSITIVE! THAT GIRL STOLE MY PANTIES TOO!!
AND ONCE, SHE EVEN ATE ME UP WITH HER EYES LIKE A SIDE DISH WHILE EATING RICE!
"SIDE DISH" ...?
?
ちら
CHIRA (GLANCE)
!?
!
SHE'S UNDRESSING ME WITH HER EYEEES—!!
ばっ
BA (WHIP)
......AH HA HA!
ひら
HIRA (WAVE)
ひら
HIRA
!?

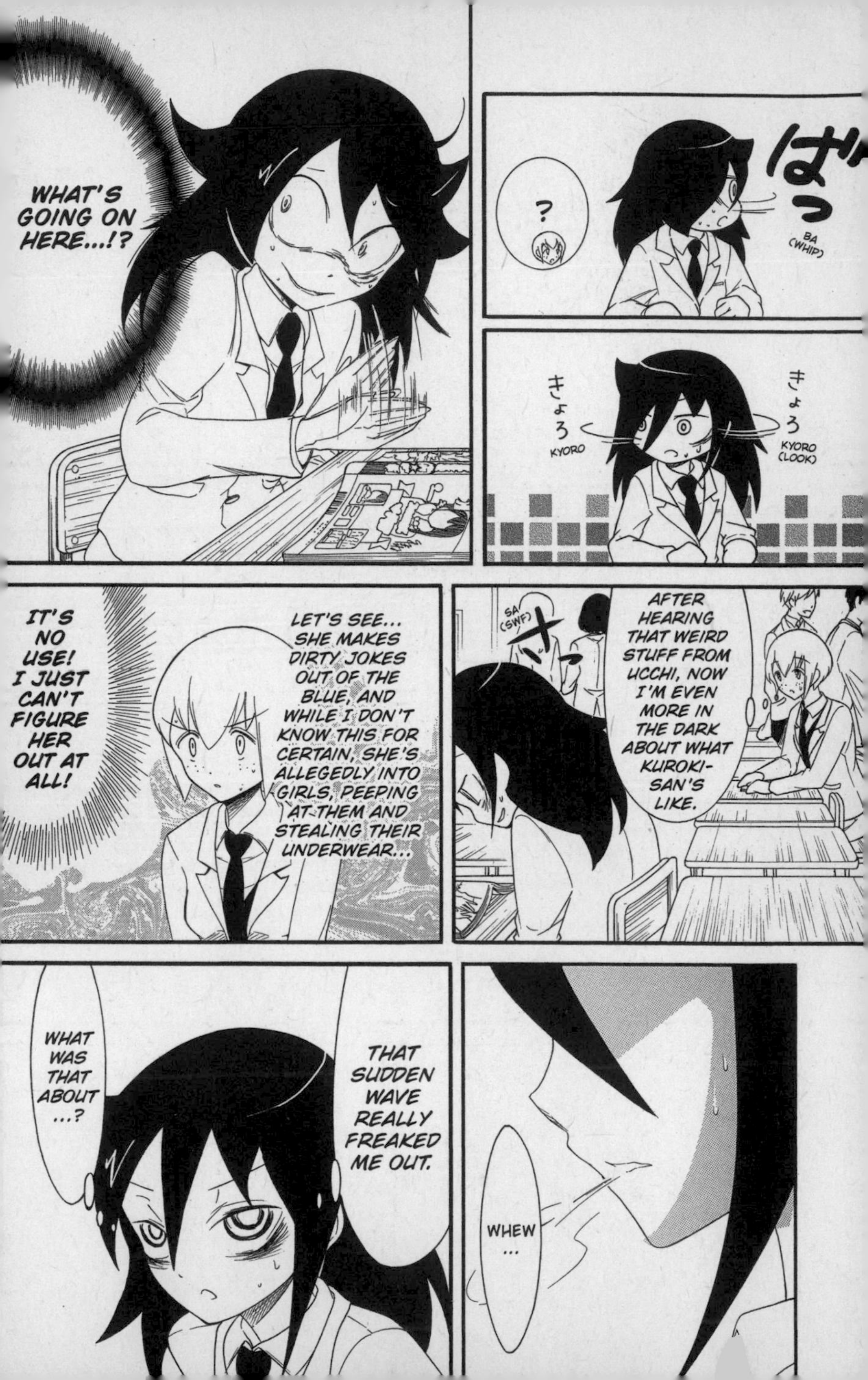
ばっ
BA (WHIP)
?
きょろ
KYORO (LOOK)
きょろ
KYORO
WHAT'S GOING ON HERE...!?
AFTER HEARING THAT WEIRD STUFF FROM UCCHI, NOW I'M EVEN MORE IN THE DARK ABOUT WHAT KUROKI-SAN'S LIKE.
さっ
SA (SWF)
LET'S SEE... SHE MAKES DIRTY JOKES OUT OF THE BLUE, AND WHILE I DON'T KNOW THIS FOR CERTAIN, SHE'S ALLEGEDLY INTO GIRLS, PEEPING AT THEM AND STEALING THEIR UNDERWEAR...
IT'S NO USE! I JUST CAN'T FIGURE HER OUT AT ALL!
WHEW...
THAT SUDDEN WAVE REALLY FREAKED ME OUT.
WHAT WAS THAT ABOUT...?

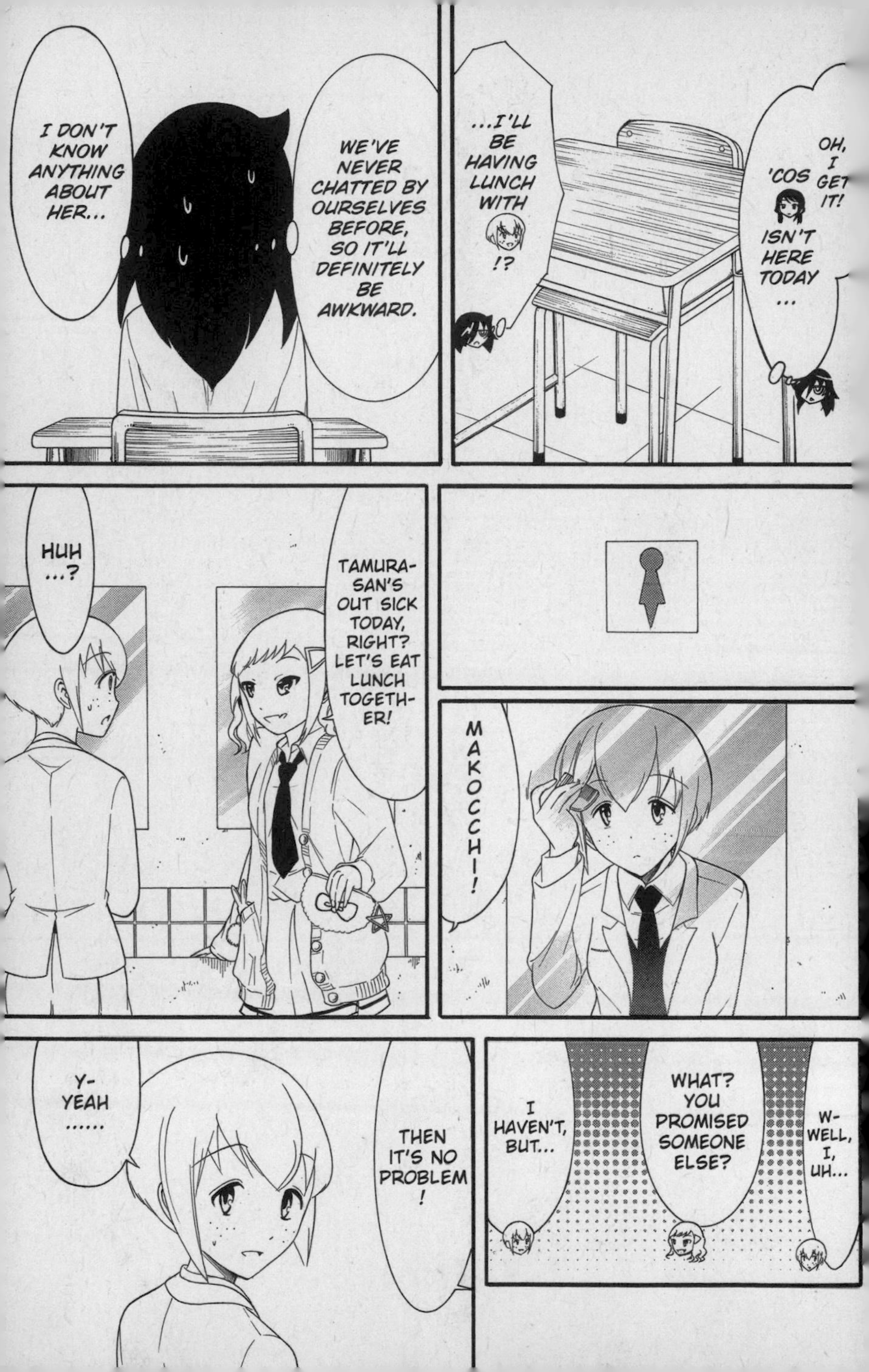
OH, I GET IT! 'COS ISN'T HERE TODAY ...
...I'LL BE HAVING LUNCH WITH !?
WE'VE NEVER CHATTED BY OURSELVES BEFORE, SO IT'LL DEFINITELY BE AWKWARD.
I DON'T KNOW ANYTHING ABOUT HER...
MAKOCCHI!
TAMURA-SAN'S OUT SICK TODAY, RIGHT? LET'S EAT LUNCH TOGETH-ER!
HUH ...?
W-WELL, I, UH...
WHAT? YOU PROMISED SOMEONE ELSE?
I HAVEN'T, BUT...
THEN IT'S NO PROBLEM !
Y-YEAH ......

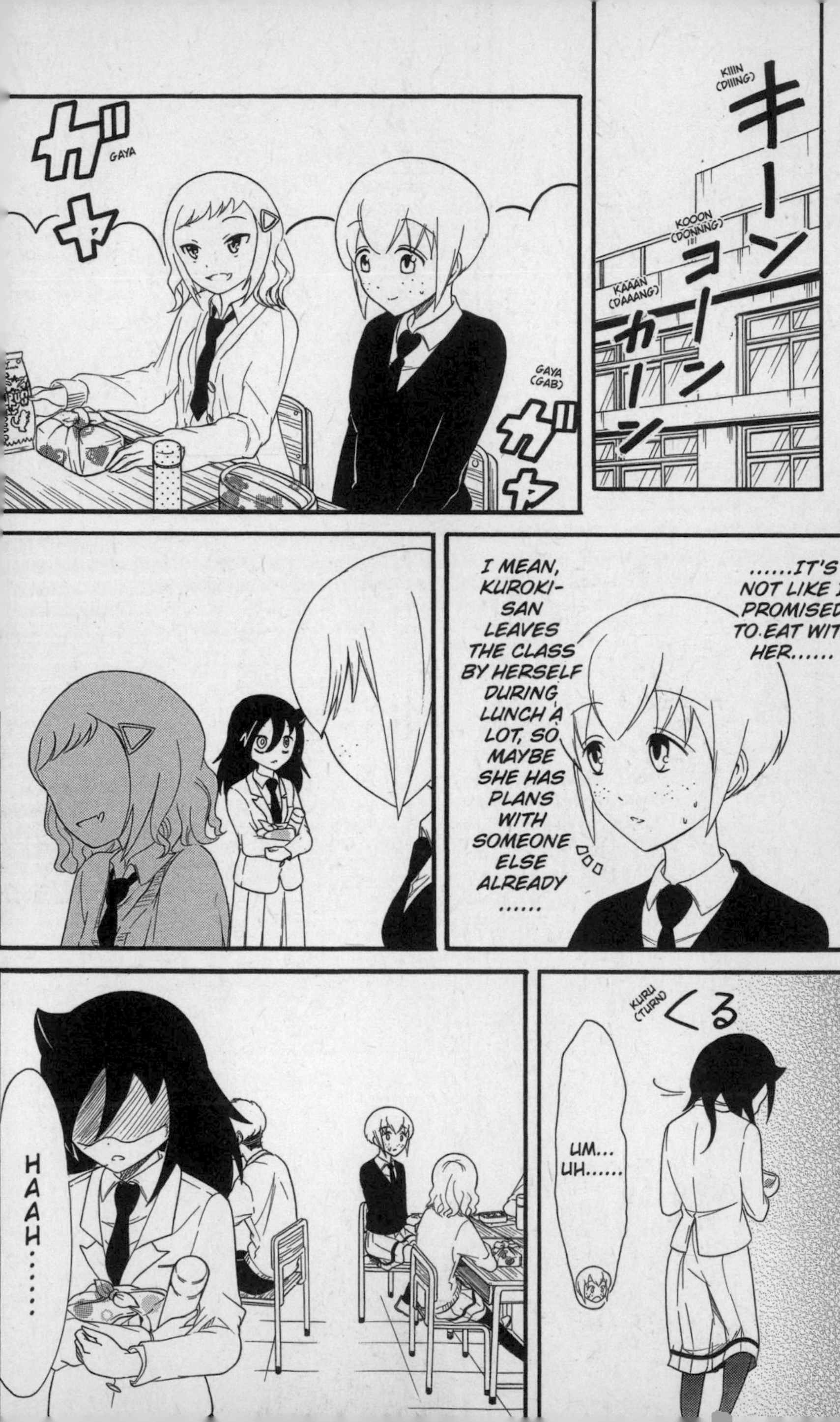
KIIIN (DIIING)
キーン
KOOON (DONNING)
コーン
KAAAN (DAAANG)
カーン
GAYA
ガヤ
GAYA (GAB)
ガヤ
......IT'S NOT LIKE I PROMISED TO EAT WITH HER......
I MEAN, KUROKI-SAN LEAVES THE CLASS BY HERSELF DURING LUNCH A LOT, SO MAYBE SHE HAS PLANS WITH SOMEONE ELSE ALREADY ......
KURU (TURN)
くる
UM... UH......
HAAH......

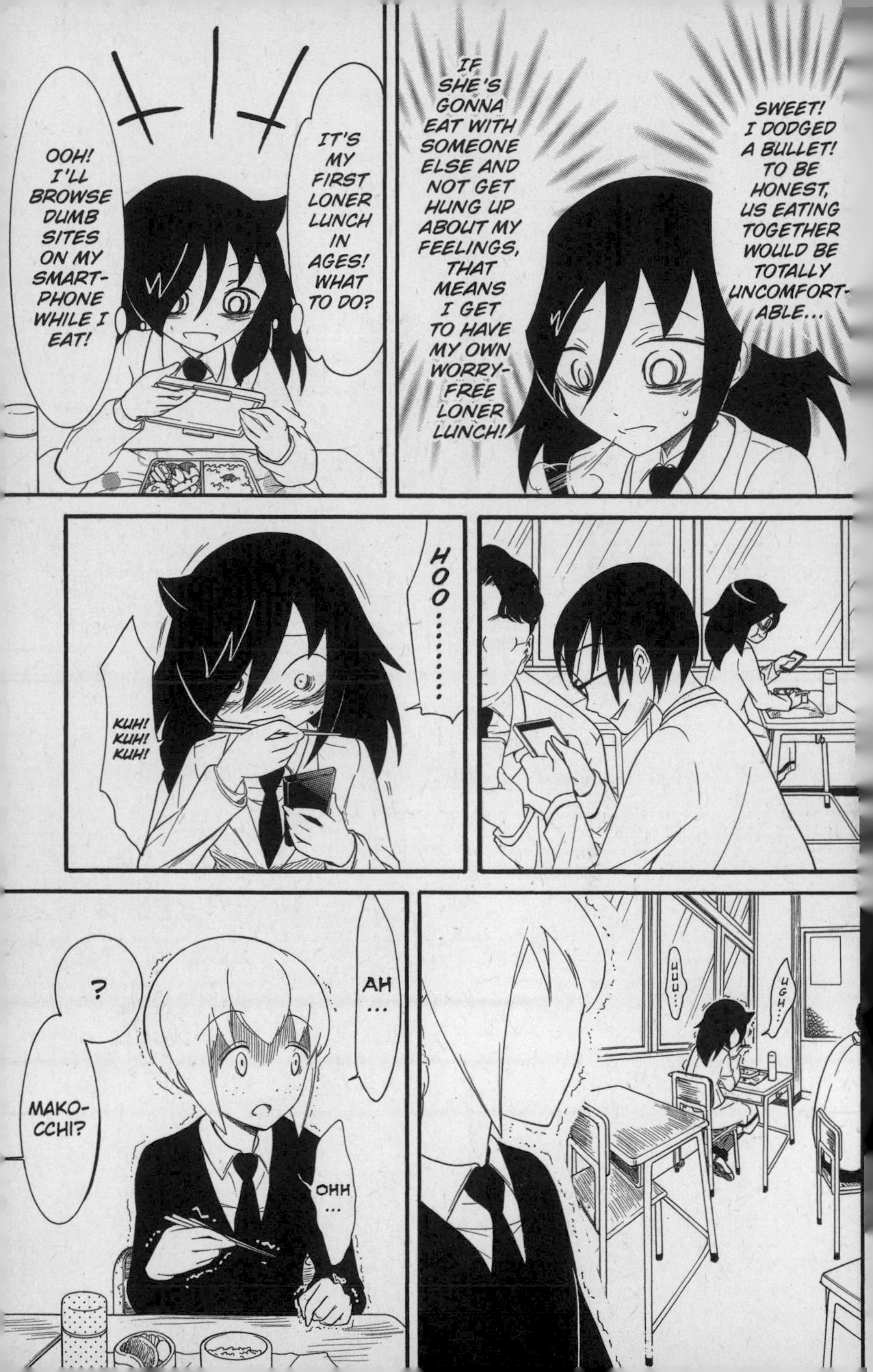
SWEET! I DODGED A BULLET! TO BE HONEST, US EATING TOGETHER WOULD BE TOTALLY UNCOMFORTABLE...
IF SHE'S GONNA EAT WITH SOMEONE ELSE AND NOT GET HUNG UP ABOUT MY FEELINGS, THAT MEANS I GET TO HAVE MY OWN WORRY-FREE LONER LUNCH!
IT'S MY FIRST LONER LUNCH IN AGES! WHAT TO DO?
OOH! I'LL BROWSE DUMB SITES ON MY SMARTPHONE WHILE I EAT!
HOO.......
KUH! KUH! KUH!
UGH...
UUU...
AH...
?
MAKOCCHI?
OHH...

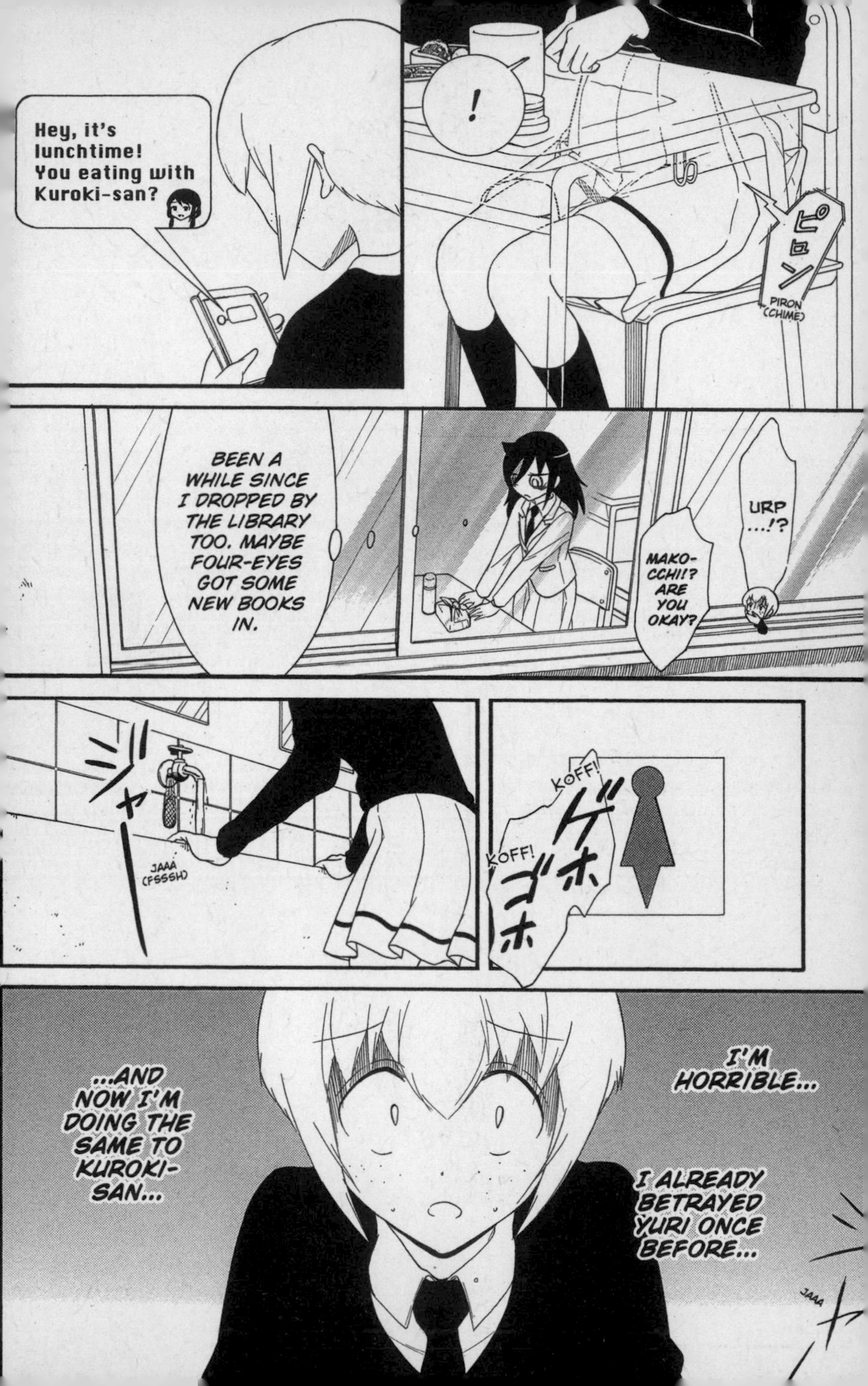
!
ピロン
PIRON (CHIME)
Hey, it's lunchtime! You eating with Kuroki-san?
URP ...!?
MAKO-CCHI!? ARE YOU OKAY?
BEEN A WHILE SINCE I DROPPED BY THE LIBRARY TOO. MAYBE FOUR-EYES GOT SOME NEW BOOKS IN.
ゲホ
KOFF!
ゴホ
KOFF!
ジャー
JAAA (FSSSH)
I'M HORRIBLE...
I ALREADY BETRAYED YURI ONCE BEFORE...
...AND NOW I'M DOING THE SAME TO KUROKI-SAN...
JAAA

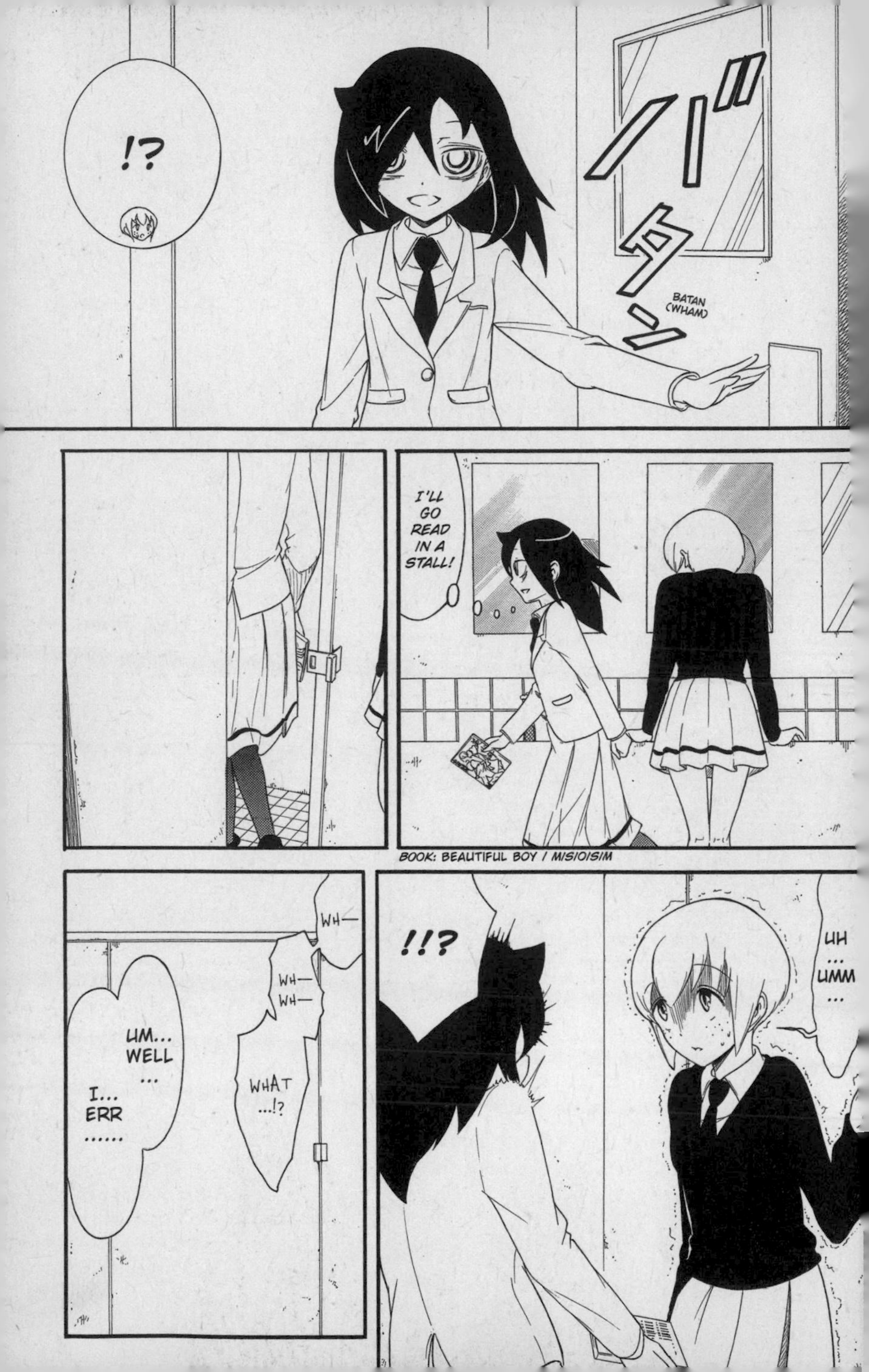
バタン
BATAN (WHAM)
!?
I'LL GO READ IN A STALL!
BOOK: BEAUTIFUL BOY / MISIOISIM
UH ... UMM ...
!!?
WH—
WH— WH—
WHAT ...!?
UM... WELL ... I... ERR ......

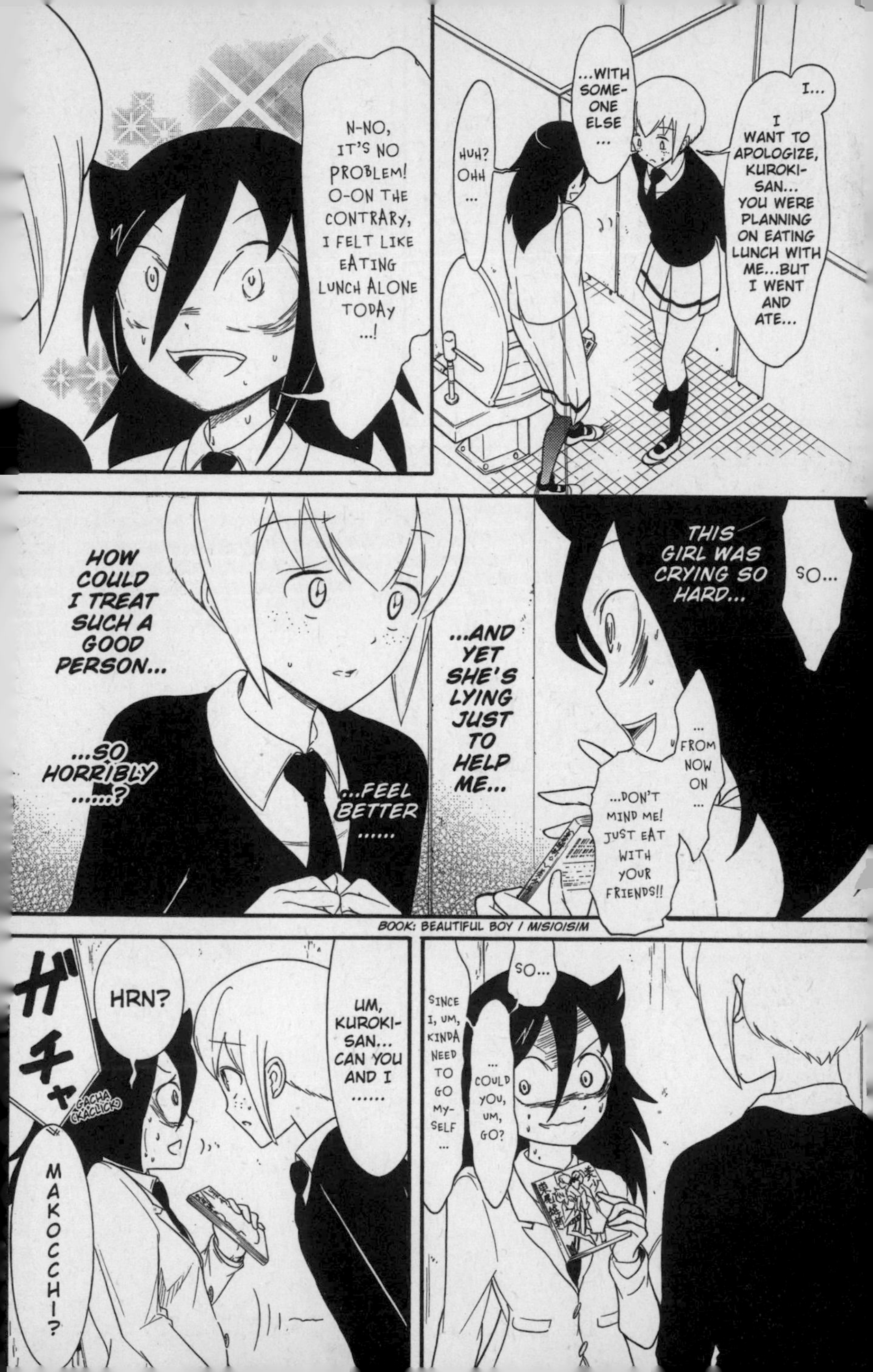
I...
I WANT TO APOLOGIZE, KUROKI-SAN... YOU WERE PLANNING ON EATING LUNCH WITH ME...BUT I WENT AND ATE...
...WITH SOMEONE ELSE...
HUH? OHH...
N-NO, IT'S NO PROBLEM! O-ON THE CONTRARY, I FELT LIKE EATING LUNCH ALONE TODAY ...!
SO...
THIS GIRL WAS CRYING SO HARD...
...FROM NOW ON...
...DON'T MIND ME! JUST EAT WITH YOUR FRIENDS!!
BOOK: BEAUTIFUL BOY / MISIOISIM
...AND YET SHE'S LYING JUST TO HELP ME...
HOW COULD I TREAT SUCH A GOOD PERSON...
...SO HORRIBLY......?
...FEEL BETTER......
SO...
SINCE I, UM, KINDA NEED TO GO MYSELF...
...COULD YOU, UM, GO?
UM, KUROKI-SAN... CAN YOU AND I ......
HRN?
ガチャ
GACHA (KACLICK)
MAKOCCHI!?

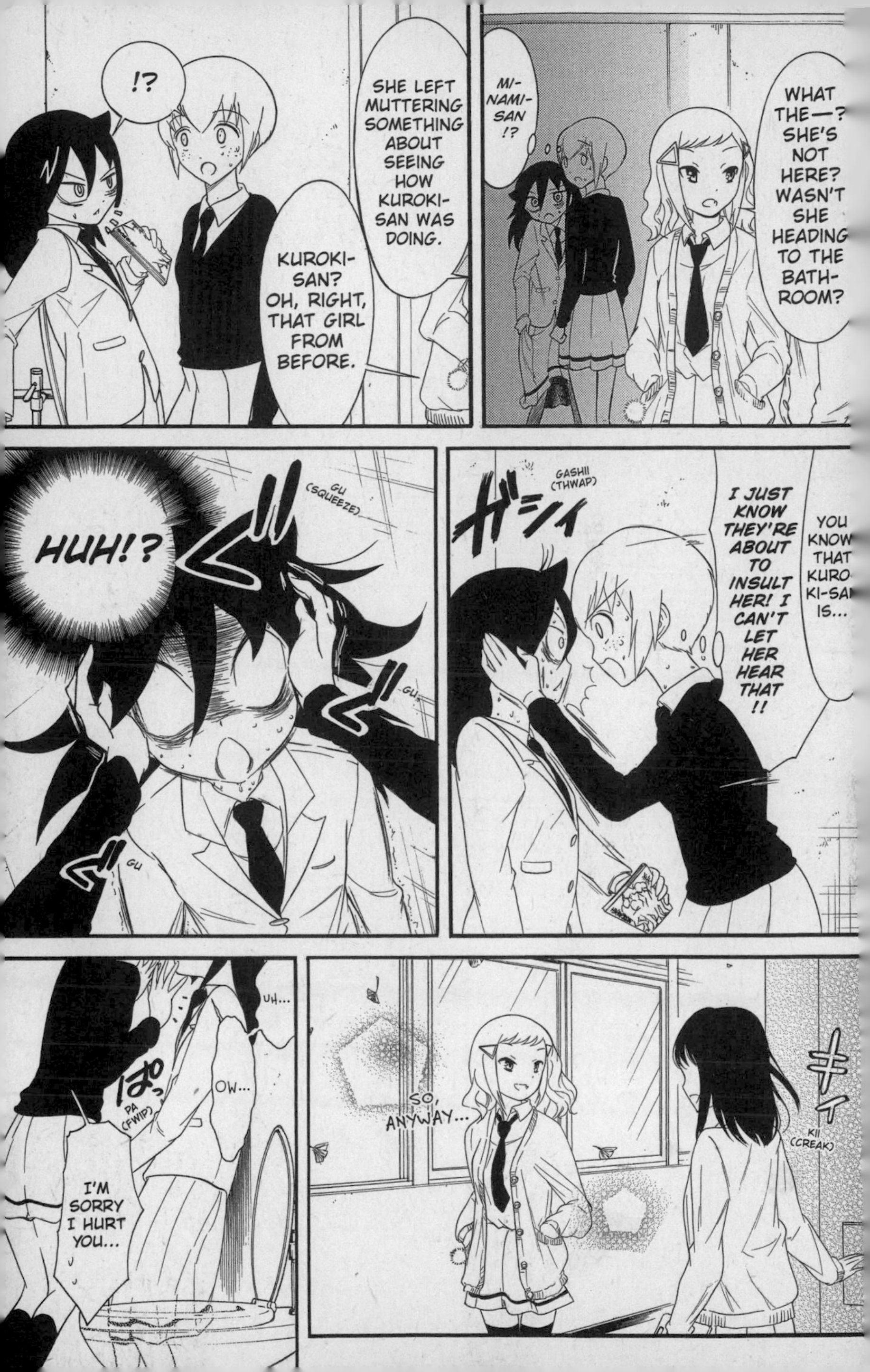
WHAT THE—? SHE'S NOT HERE? WASN'T SHE HEADING TO THE BATH-ROOM?
MI-NAMI-SAN !?
SHE LEFT MUTTERING SOMETHING ABOUT SEEING HOW KUROKI-SAN WAS DOING.
KUROKI-SAN? OH, RIGHT, THAT GIRL FROM BEFORE.
!?
YOU KNOW THAT KURO-KI-SA IS...
I JUST KNOW THEY'RE ABOUT TO INSULT HER! I CAN'T LET HER HEAR THAT !!
ガシィ
GASHII (THWAP)
GU (SQUEEZE)
HUH!?
GU
GU
ギィ
KII (CREAK)
SO, ANYWAY...
UH...
OW...
ぱっ
PA (FWIP)
I'M SORRY I HURT YOU...

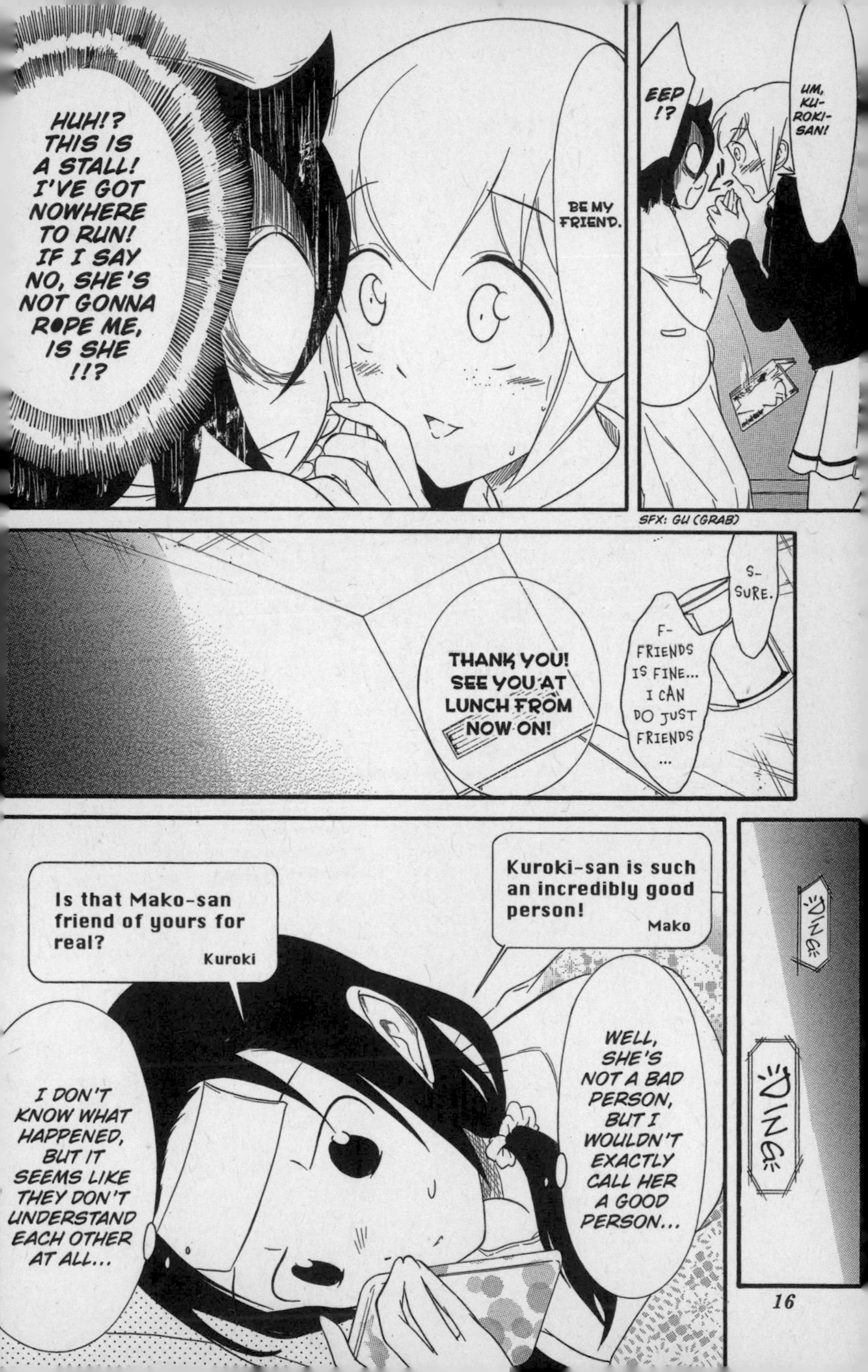
UM, KUROKI-SAN!
EEP!?
SFX: GU (GRAB)
BE MY FRIEND.
HUH!? THIS IS A STALL! I'VE GOT NOWHERE TO RUN! IF I SAY NO, SHE'S NOT GONNA ROPE ME, IS SHE!!?
S-SURE.
F-FRIENDS IS FINE... I CAN DO JUST FRIENDS...
THANK YOU! SEE YOU AT LUNCH FROM NOW ON!
DING
DING
Kuroki-san is such an incredibly good person!
Mako
Is that Mako-san friend of yours for real?
Kuroki
WELL, SHE'S NOT A BAD PERSON, BUT I WOULDN'T EXACTLY CALL HER A GOOD PERSON...
I DON'T KNOW WHAT HAPPENED, BUT IT SEEMS LIKE THEY DON'T UNDERSTAND EACH OTHER AT ALL...

No Matter How I Look at It, It's You Guys' Fault I'm Not Popular!

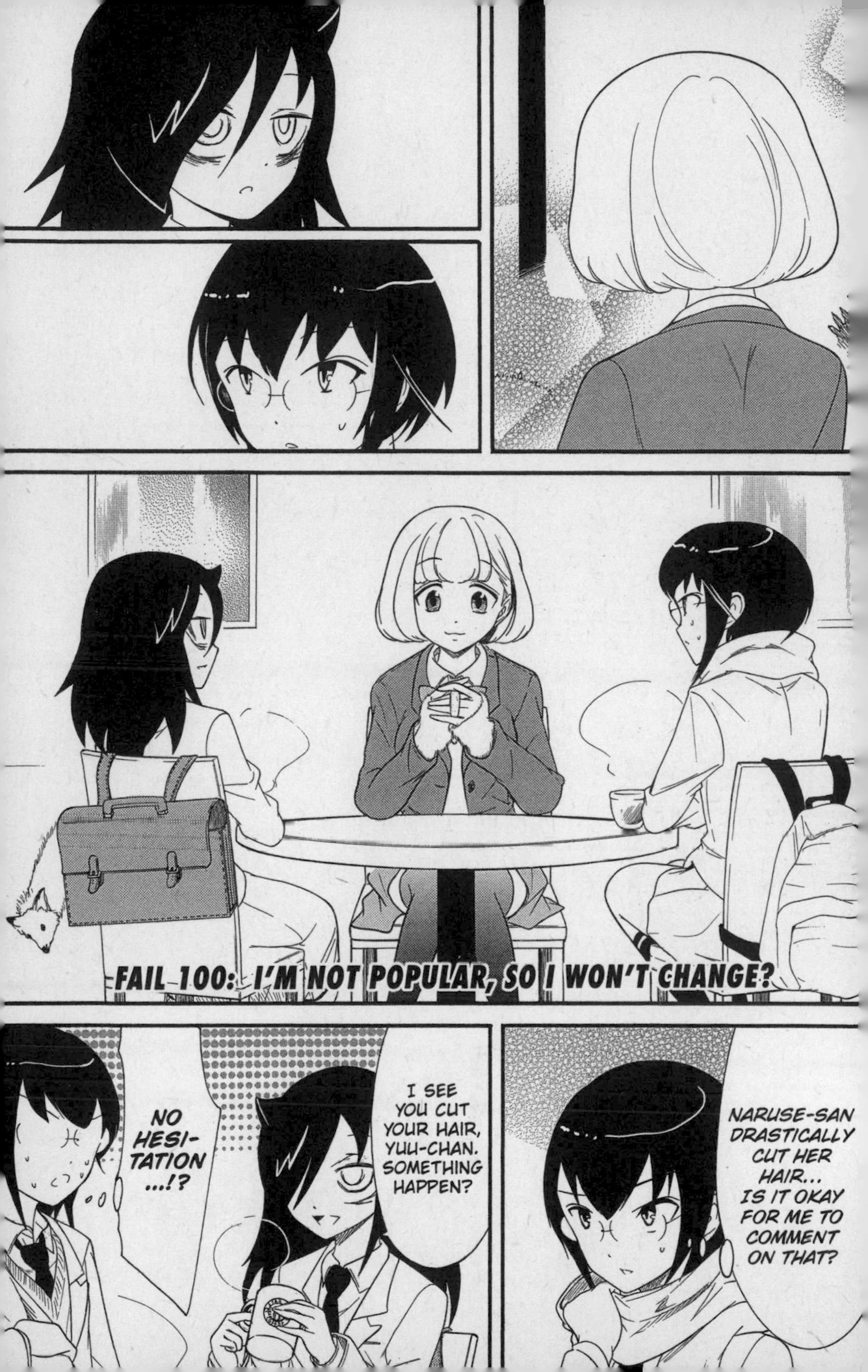
FAIL 100: I'M NOT POPULAR, SO I WON'T CHANGE?
NARUSE-SAN DRASTICALLY CUT HER HAIR... IS IT OKAY FOR ME TO COMMENT ON THAT?
I SEE YOU CUT YOUR HAIR, YUU-CHAN. SOMETHING HAPPEN?
NO HESI-TATION ...!?

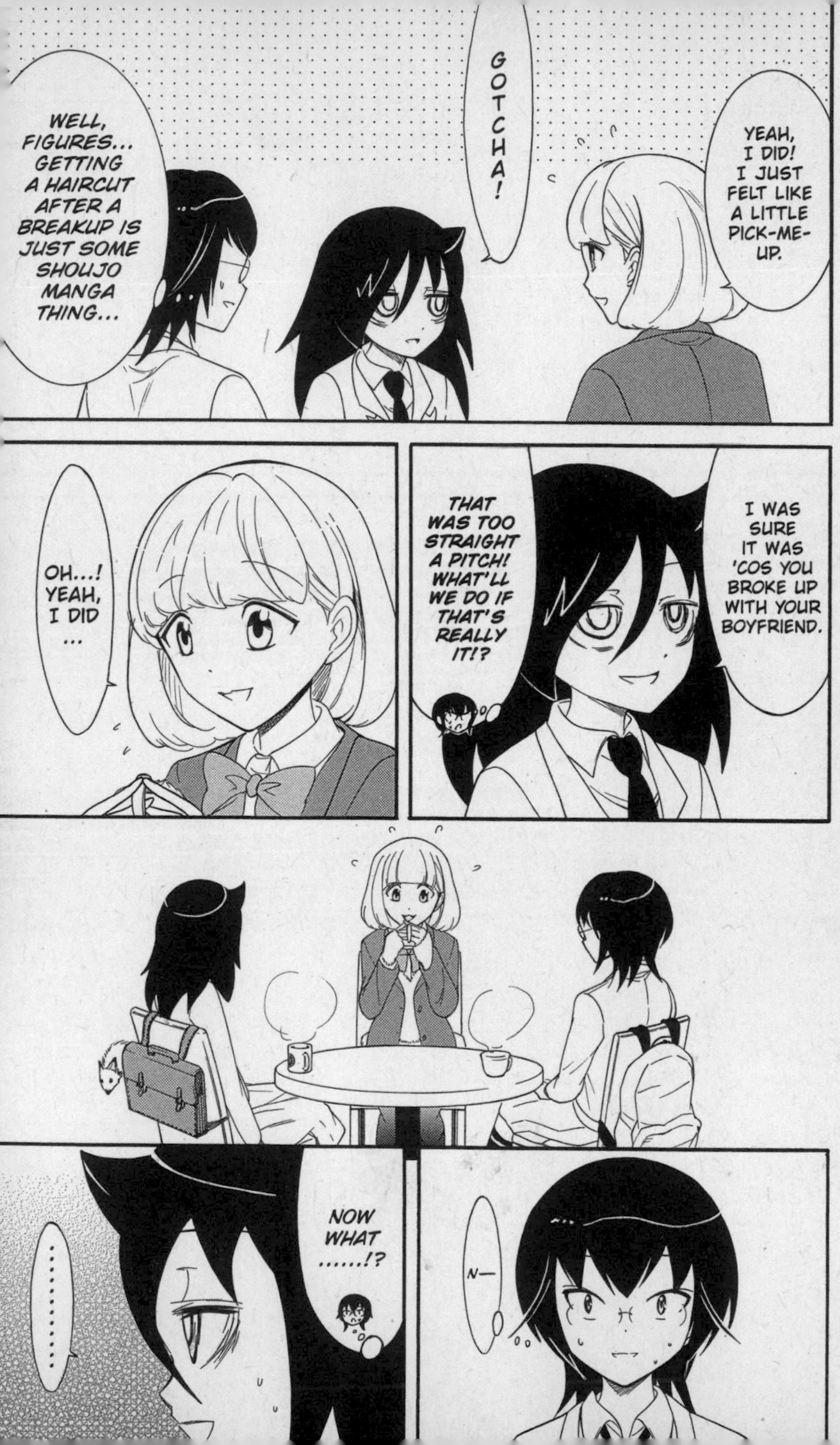
YEAH, I DID! I JUST FELT LIKE A LITTLE PICK-ME-UP.
GOTCHA!
WELL, FIGURES... GETTING A HAIRCUT AFTER A BREAKUP IS JUST SOME SHOUJO MANGA THING...
I WAS SURE IT WAS 'COS YOU BROKE UP WITH YOUR BOYFRIEND.
THAT WAS TOO STRAIGHT A PITCH! WHAT'LL WE DO IF THAT'S REALLY IT!?
OH...! YEAH, I DID ...
N—
NOW WHAT ......!?
....

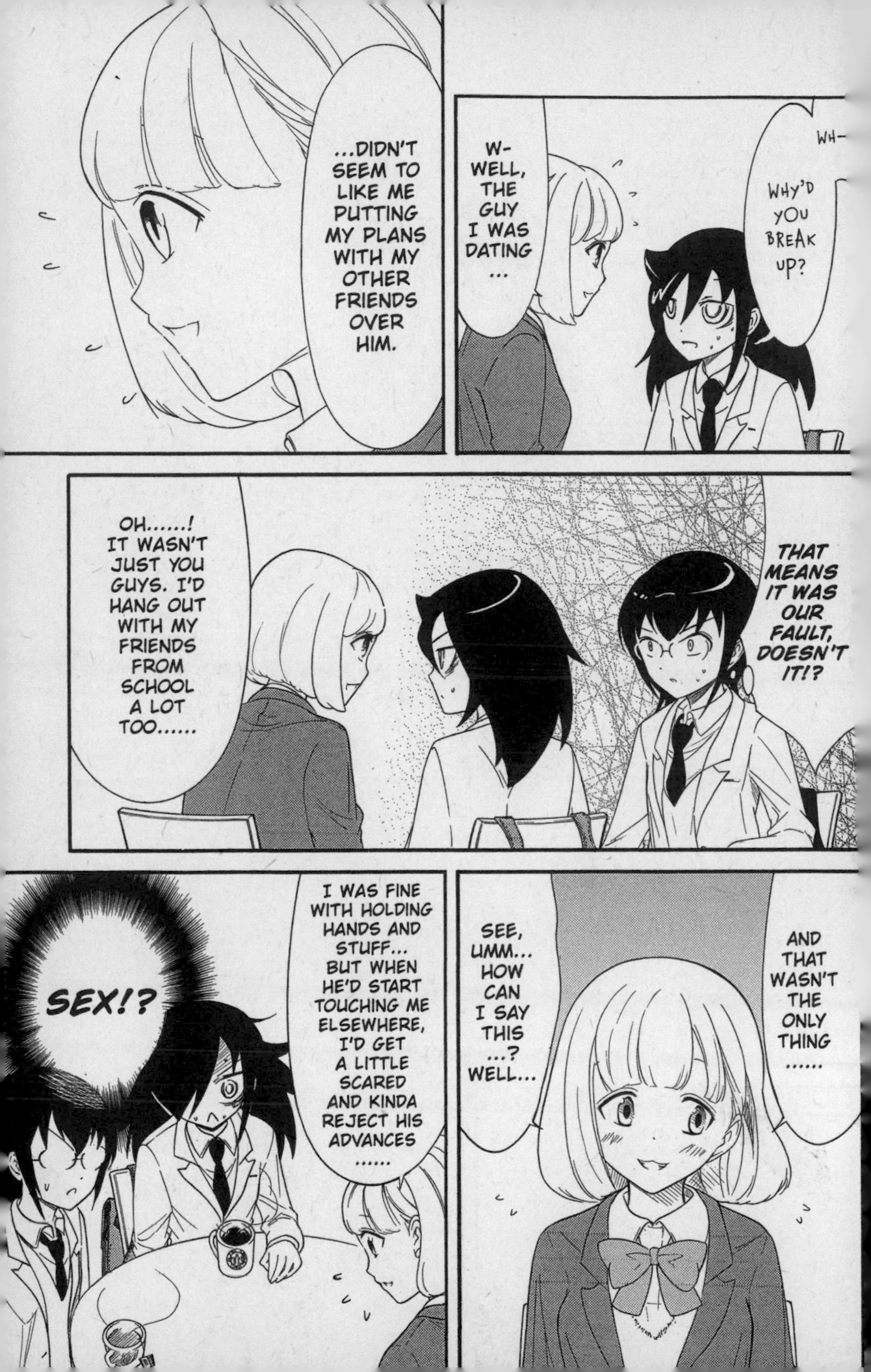
WH-
WHY'D YOU BREAK UP?
W-WELL, THE GUY I WAS DATING...
...DIDN'T SEEM TO LIKE ME PUTTING MY PLANS WITH MY OTHER FRIENDS OVER HIM.
THAT MEANS IT WAS OUR FAULT, DOESN'T IT!?
OH......! IT WASN'T JUST YOU GUYS. I'D HANG OUT WITH MY FRIENDS FROM SCHOOL A LOT TOO......
AND THAT WASN'T THE ONLY THING......
SEE, UMM... HOW CAN I SAY THIS...? WELL...
I WAS FINE WITH HOLDING HANDS AND STUFF... BUT WHEN HE'D START TOUCHING ME ELSEWHERE, I'D GET A LITTLE SCARED AND KINDA REJECT HIS ADVANCES......
SEX!?

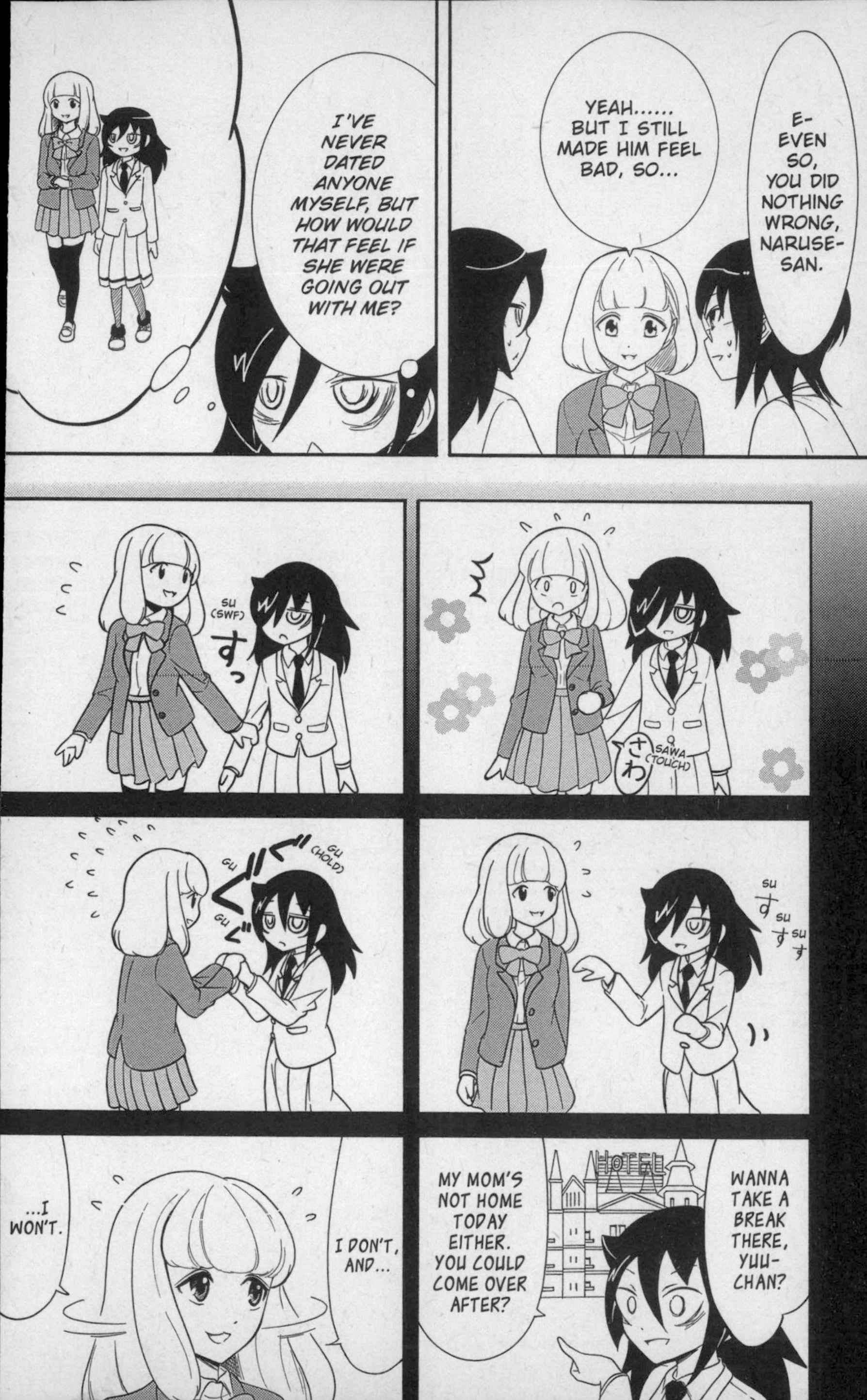
E-EVEN SO, YOU DID NOTHING WRONG, NARUSE-SAN.
YEAH...... BUT I STILL MADE HIM FEEL BAD, SO...
I'VE NEVER DATED ANYONE MYSELF, BUT HOW WOULD THAT FEEL IF SHE WERE GOING OUT WITH ME?
さわ SAWA (TOUCH)
すっ SU (SWF)
す SU
す SU
す SU
ぐ GU (HOLD)
ぐ GU
ぐ GU
WANNA TAKE A BREAK THERE, YUU-CHAN?
HOTEL
MY MOM'S NOT HOME TODAY EITHER. YOU COULD COME OVER AFTER?
I DON'T, AND...
...I WON'T.

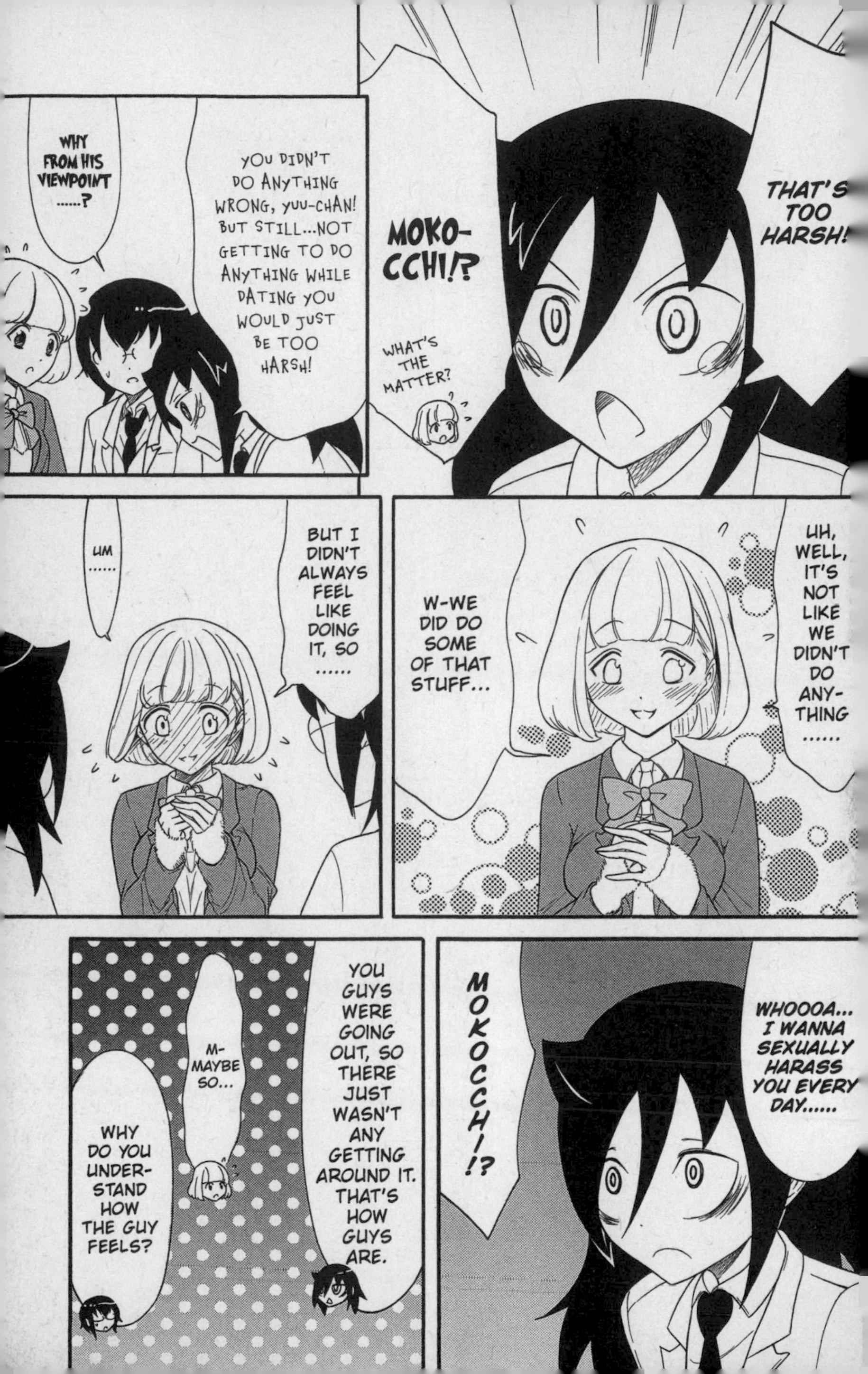
THAT'S TOO HARSH!
MOKO-CCHI!?
WHAT'S THE MATTER?
YOU DIDN'T DO ANYTHING WRONG, YUU-CHAN! BUT STILL...NOT GETTING TO DO ANYTHING WHILE DATING YOU WOULD JUST BE TOO HARSH!
WHY FROM HIS VIEWPOINT ......?
UH, WELL, IT'S NOT LIKE WE DIDN'T DO ANY-THING ......
W-WE DID DO SOME OF THAT STUFF...
BUT I DIDN'T ALWAYS FEEL LIKE DOING IT, SO ......
UM ......
WHOOOA... I WANNA SEXUALLY HARASS YOU EVERY DAY......
MOKOCCHI!?
YOU GUYS WERE GOING OUT, SO THERE JUST WASN'T ANY GETTING AROUND IT. THAT'S HOW GUYS ARE.
M-MAYBE SO...
WHY DO YOU UNDER-STAND HOW THE GUY FEELS?

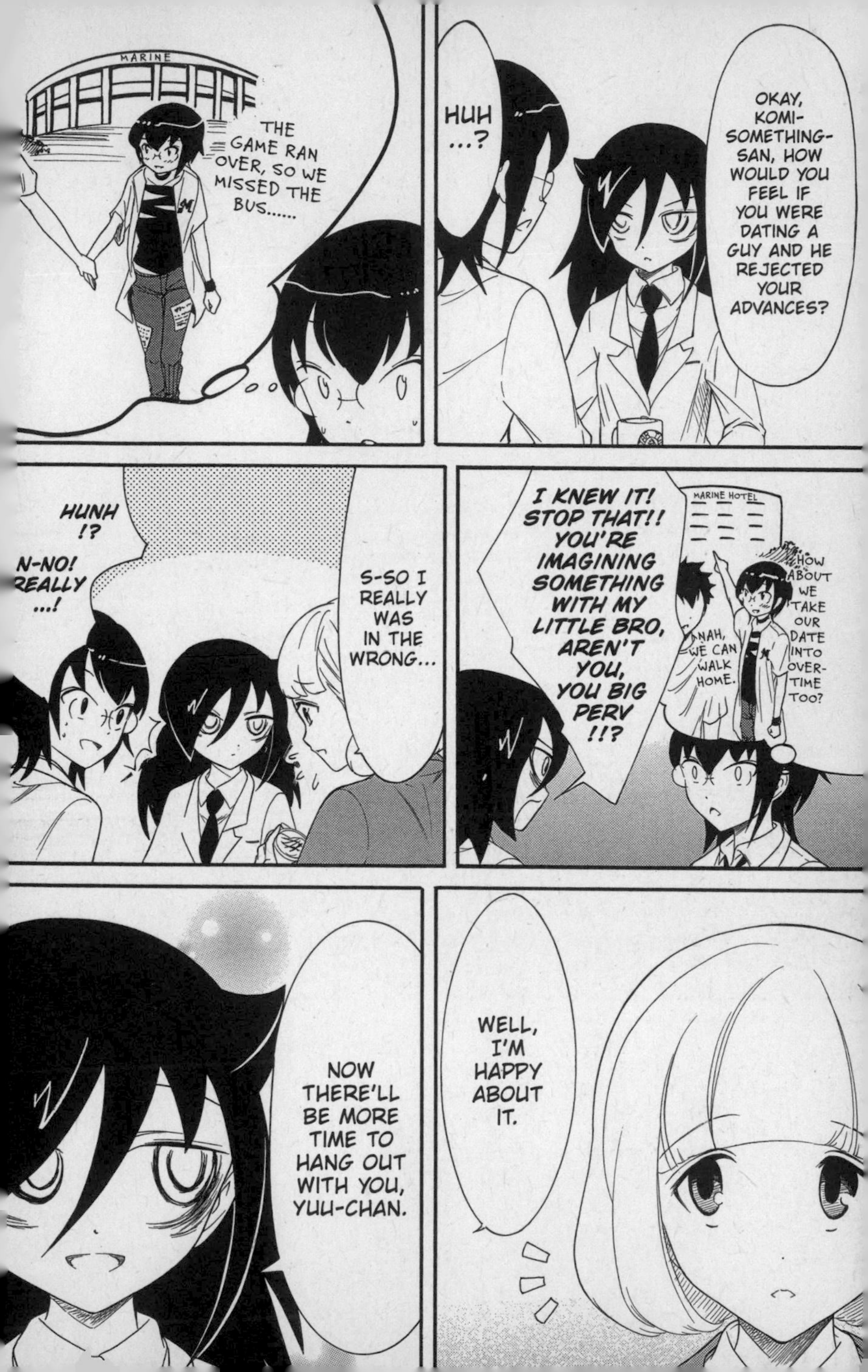
OKAY, KOMI-SOMETHING-SAN, HOW WOULD YOU FEEL IF YOU WERE DATING A GUY AND HE REJECTED YOUR ADVANCES?
HUH ...?
MARINE
THE GAME RAN OVER, SO WE MISSED THE BUS......
I KNEW IT! STOP THAT!! YOU'RE IMAGINING SOMETHING WITH MY LITTLE BRO, AREN'T YOU, YOU BIG PERV !!?
MARINE HOTEL
HOW ABOUT WE TAKE OUR DATE INTO OVER-TIME TOO?
NAH, WE CAN WALK HOME.
S-SO I REALLY WAS IN THE WRONG...
HUNH !?
N-NO! REALLY ...!
WELL, I'M HAPPY ABOUT IT.
NOW THERE'LL BE MORE TIME TO HANG OUT WITH YOU, YUU-CHAN.

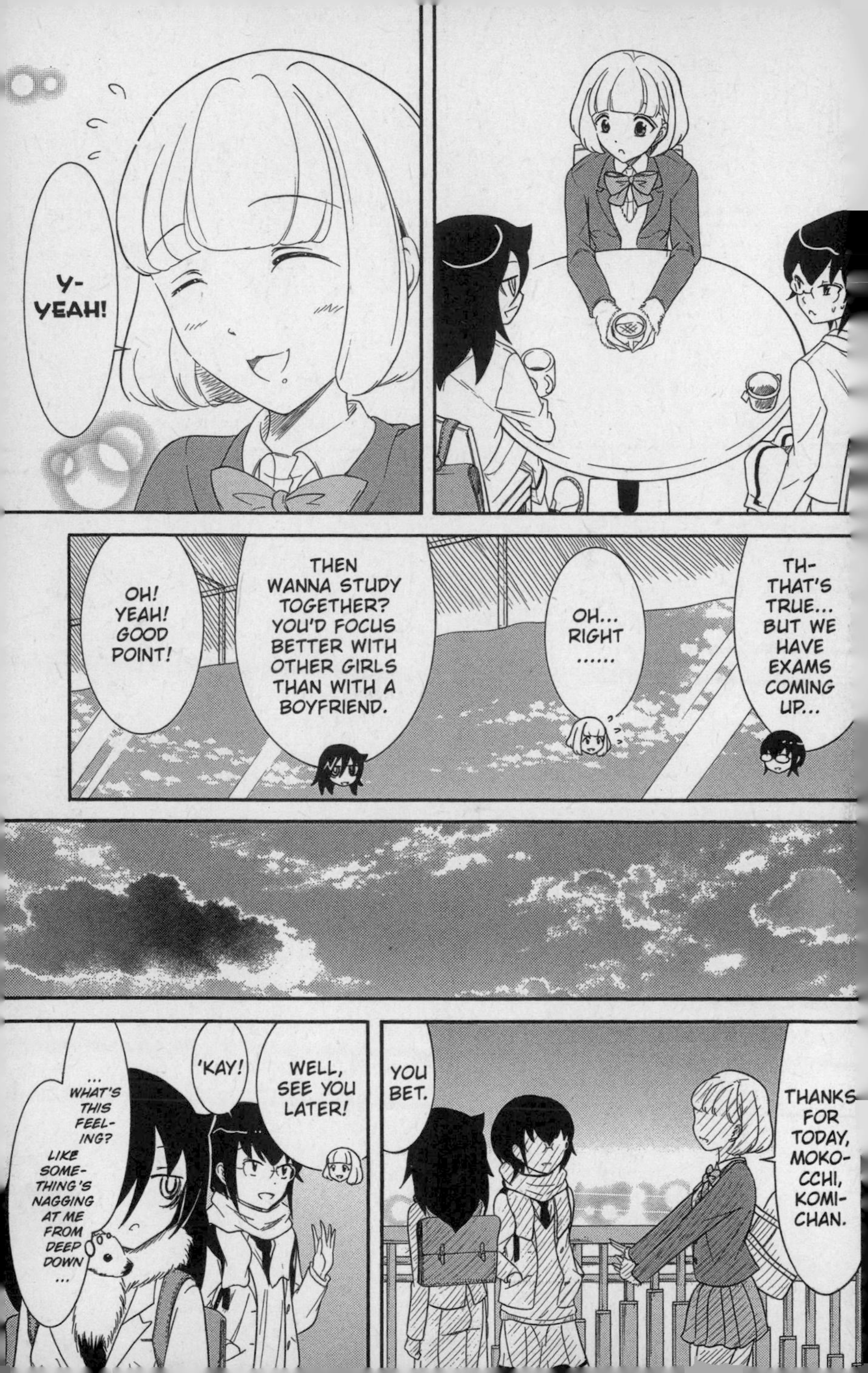
Y-YEAH!
TH-THAT'S TRUE... BUT WE HAVE EXAMS COMING UP...
OH... RIGHT ......
THEN WANNA STUDY TOGETHER? YOU'D FOCUS BETTER WITH OTHER GIRLS THAN WITH A BOYFRIEND.
OH! YEAH! GOOD POINT!
THANKS FOR TODAY, MOKOCCHI, KOMI-CHAN.
YOU BET.
WELL, SEE YOU LATER!
'KAY!
...WHAT'S THIS FEEL-ING? LIKE SOME-THING'S NAGGING AT ME FROM DEEP DOWN...

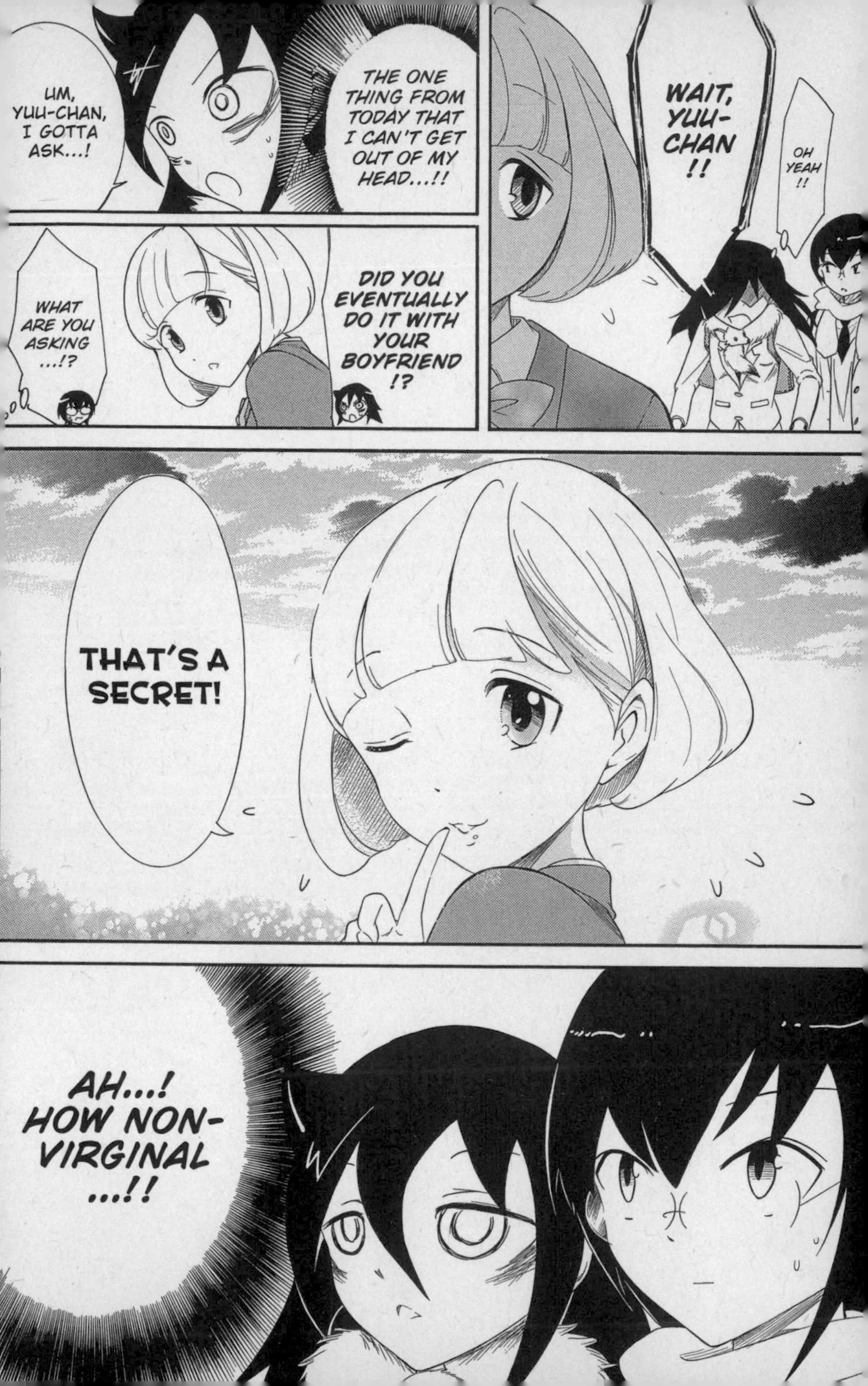
WAIT, YUU-CHAN!!
OH YEAH!!
THE ONE THING FROM TODAY THAT I CAN'T GET OUT OF MY HEAD...!!
UM, YUU-CHAN, I GOTTA ASK...!
DID YOU EVENTUALLY DO IT WITH YOUR BOYFRIEND!?
WHAT ARE YOU ASKING...!?
THAT'S A SECRET!
AH...! HOW NON-VIRGINAL...!!

No Matter How I Look at It, It's You Guys' Fault I'm Not Popular!

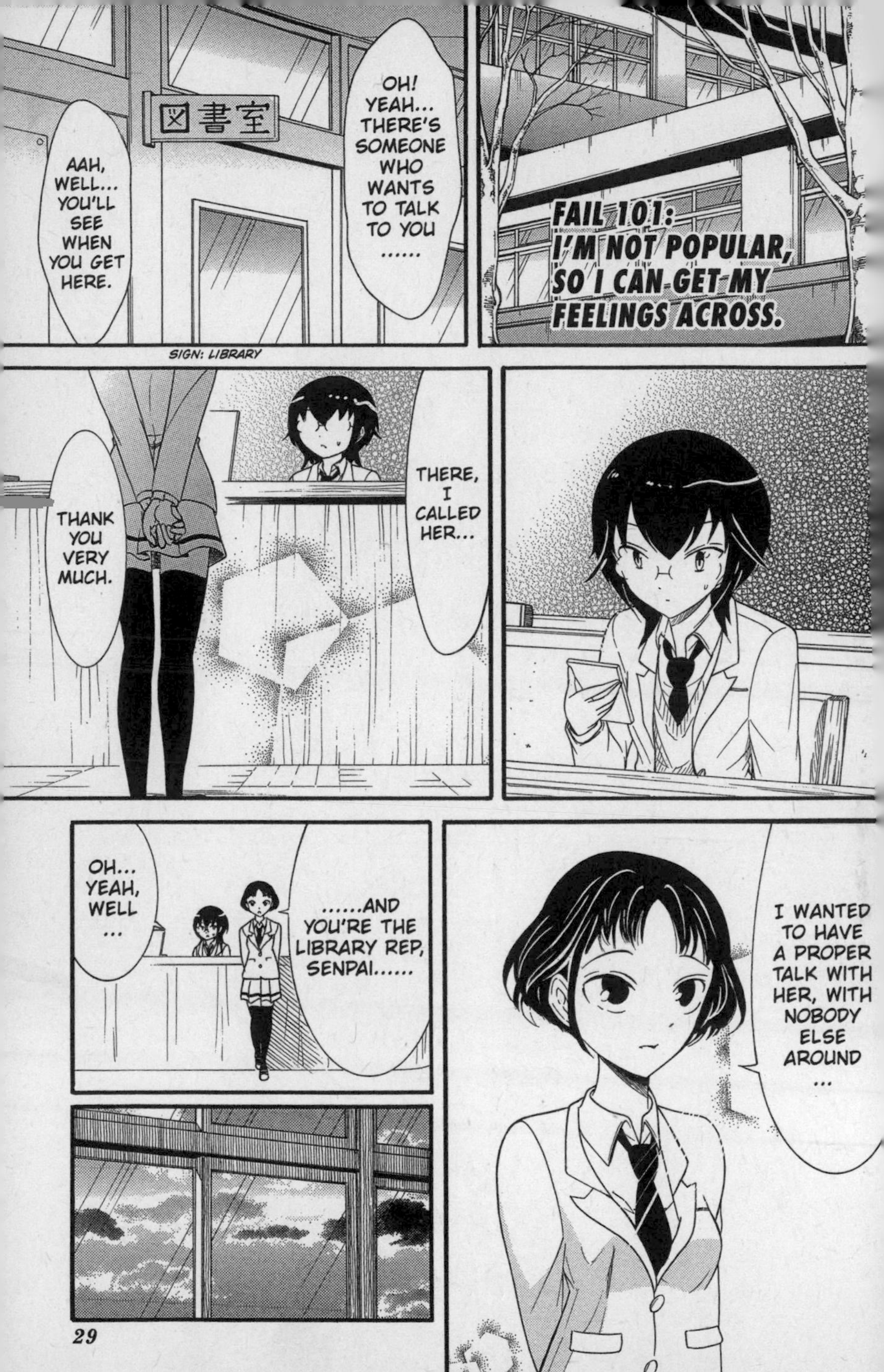
FAIL 101: I'M NOT POPULAR, SO I CAN GET MY FEELINGS ACROSS.
OH! YEAH... THERE'S SOMEONE WHO WANTS TO TALK TO YOU ......
図書室
AAH, WELL... YOU'LL SEE WHEN YOU GET HERE.
SIGN: LIBRARY
THERE, I CALLED HER...
THANK YOU VERY MUCH.
I WANTED TO HAVE A PROPER TALK WITH HER, WITH NOBODY ELSE AROUND ...
......AND YOU'RE THE LIBRARY REP, SENPAI......
OH... YEAH, WELL ...

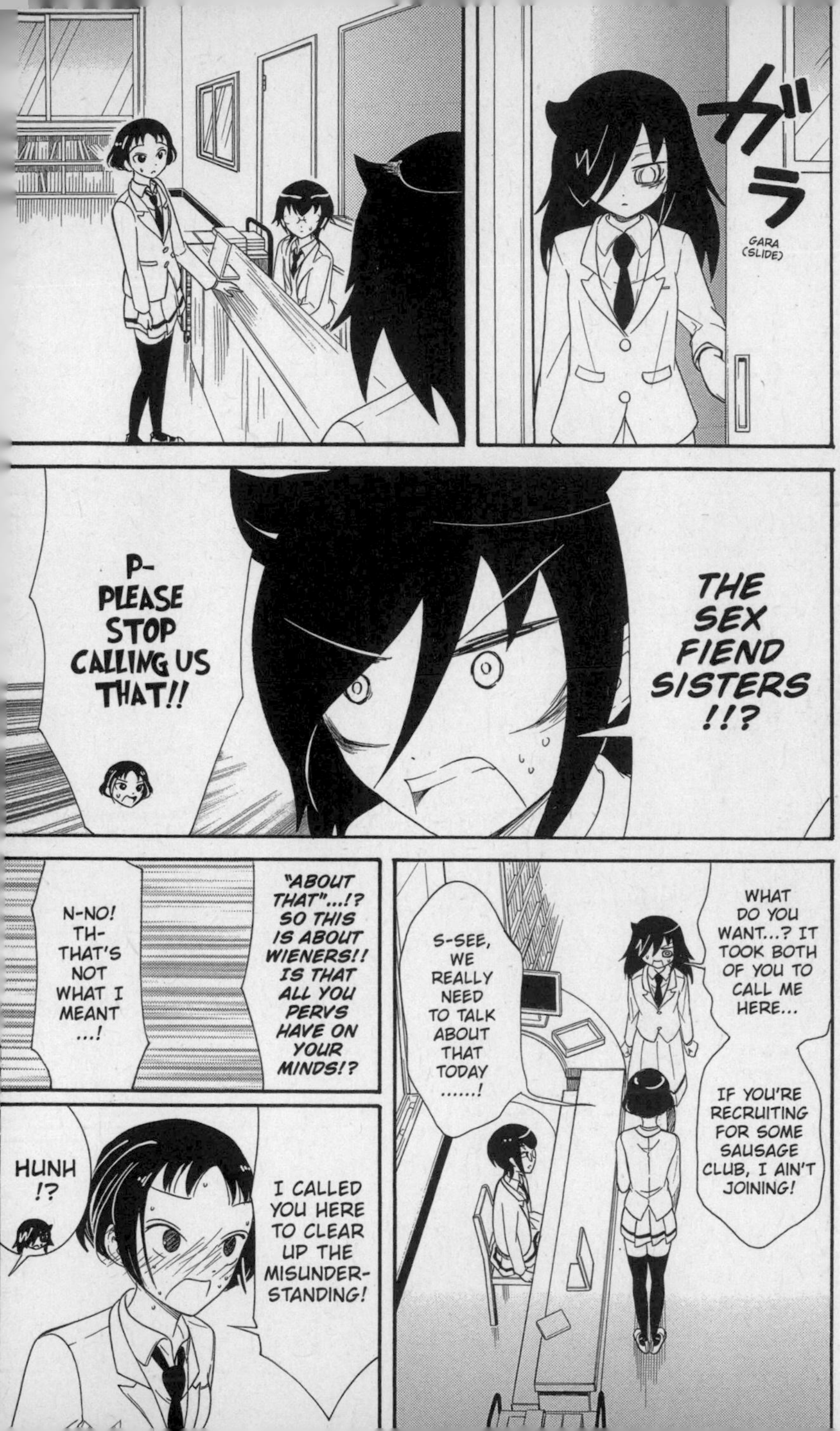
ガラ
GARA (SLIDE)
THE SEX FIEND SISTERS!!?
P-PLEASE STOP CALLING US THAT!!
WHAT DO YOU WANT...? IT TOOK BOTH OF YOU TO CALL ME HERE...
IF YOU'RE RECRUITING FOR SOME SAUSAGE CLUB, I AIN'T JOINING!
S-SEE, WE REALLY NEED TO TALK ABOUT THAT TODAY......!
"ABOUT THAT"...!? SO THIS IS ABOUT WIENERS!! IS THAT ALL YOU PERVS HAVE ON YOUR MINDS!?
N-NO! TH-THAT'S NOT WHAT I MEANT...!
I CALLED YOU HERE TO CLEAR UP THE MISUNDER-STANDING!
HUNH!?

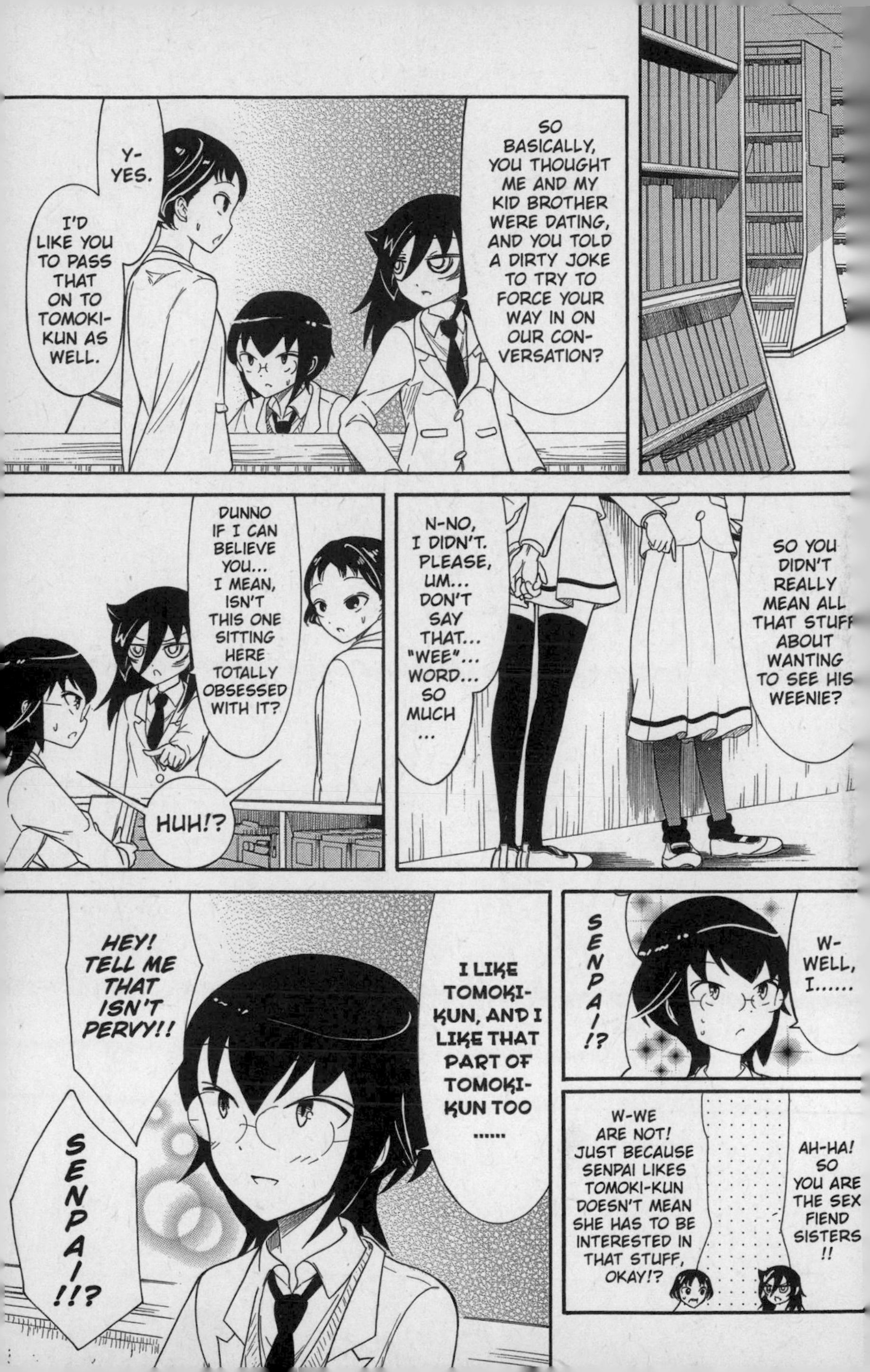
SO BASICALLY, YOU THOUGHT ME AND MY KID BROTHER WERE DATING, AND YOU TOLD A DIRTY JOKE TO TRY TO FORCE YOUR WAY IN ON OUR CON-VERSATION?
Y-YES.
I'D LIKE YOU TO PASS THAT ON TO TOMOKI-KUN AS WELL.
SO YOU DIDN'T REALLY MEAN ALL THAT STUFF ABOUT WANTING TO SEE HIS WEENIE?
N-NO, I DIDN'T. PLEASE, UM... DON'T SAY THAT... "WEE"... WORD... SO MUCH ...
DUNNO IF I CAN BELIEVE YOU... I MEAN, ISN'T THIS ONE SITTING HERE TOTALLY OBSESSED WITH IT?
HUH!?
W-WELL, I......
SENPAI!?
AH-HA! SO YOU ARE THE SEX FIEND SISTERS!!
W-WE ARE NOT! JUST BECAUSE SENPAI LIKES TOMOKI-KUN DOESN'T MEAN SHE HAS TO BE INTERESTED IN THAT STUFF, OKAY!?
I LIKE TOMOKI-KUN, AND I LIKE THAT PART OF TOMOKI-KUN TOO ......
HEY! TELL ME THAT ISN'T PERVY!!
SENPAI!!?

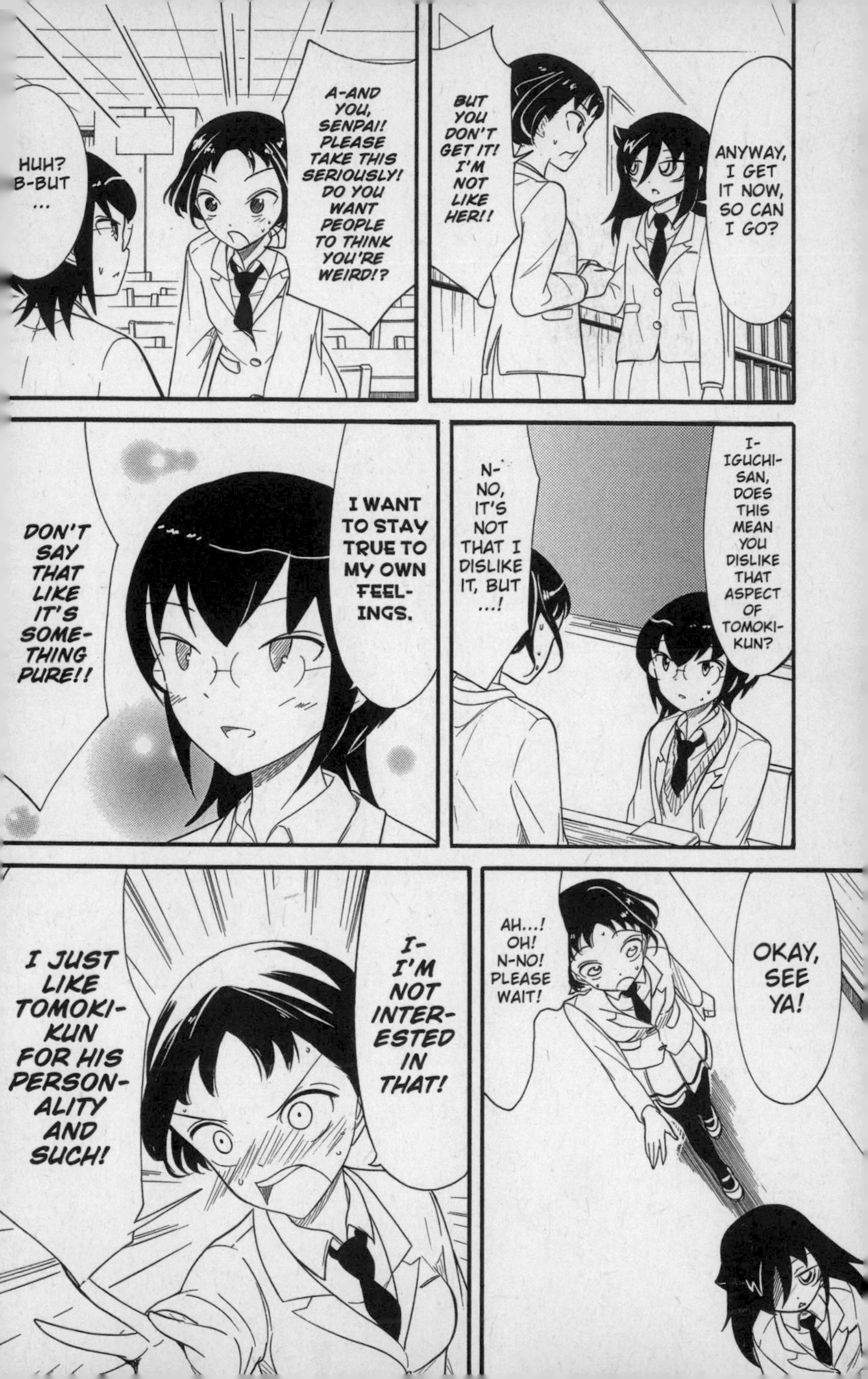
ANYWAY, I GET IT NOW, SO CAN I GO?
BUT YOU DON'T GET IT! I'M NOT LIKE HER!!
A-AND YOU, SENPAI! PLEASE TAKE THIS SERIOUSLY! DO YOU WANT PEOPLE TO THINK YOU'RE WEIRD!?
HUH? B-BUT ...
I- IGUCHI-SAN, DOES THIS MEAN YOU DISLIKE THAT ASPECT OF TOMOKI-KUN?
N-NO, IT'S NOT THAT I DISLIKE IT, BUT ...!
I WANT TO STAY TRUE TO MY OWN FEELINGS.
DON'T SAY THAT LIKE IT'S SOMETHING PURE!!
OKAY, SEE YA!
AH...! OH! N-NO! PLEASE WAIT!
I- I'M NOT INTERESTED IN THAT!
I JUST LIKE TOMOKI-KUN FOR HIS PERSONALITY AND SUCH!

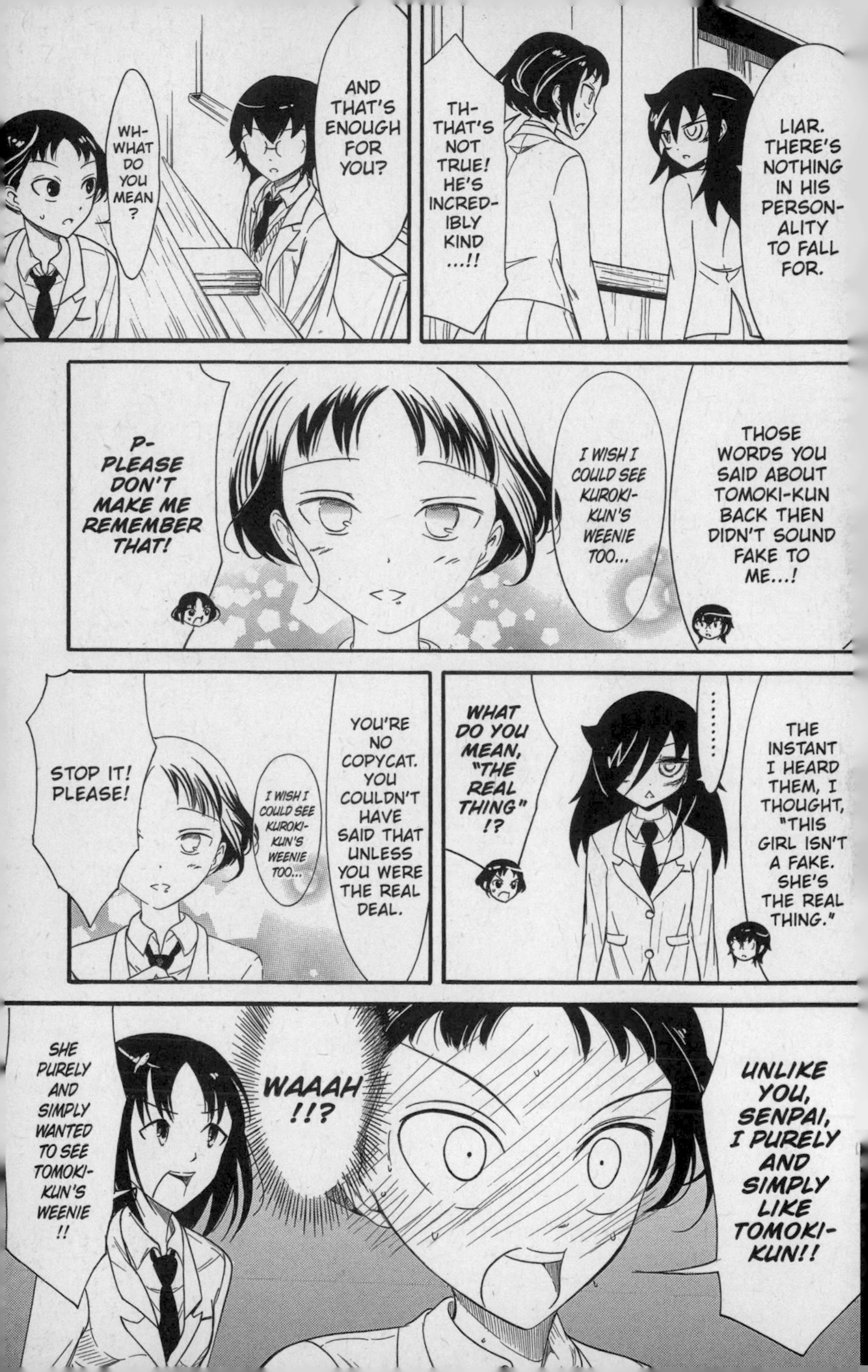
LIAR. THERE'S NOTHING IN HIS PERSONALITY TO FALL FOR.
TH-THAT'S NOT TRUE! HE'S INCREDIBLY KIND...!!
AND THAT'S ENOUGH FOR YOU?
WH-WHAT DO YOU MEAN?
THOSE WORDS YOU SAID ABOUT TOMOKI-KUN BACK THEN DIDN'T SOUND FAKE TO ME...!
I WISH I COULD SEE KUROKI-KUN'S WEENIE TOO...
P-PLEASE DON'T MAKE ME REMEMBER THAT!
THE INSTANT I HEARD THEM, I THOUGHT, "THIS GIRL ISN'T A FAKE. SHE'S THE REAL THING."
......
WHAT DO YOU MEAN, "THE REAL THING"!?
YOU'RE NO COPYCAT. YOU COULDN'T HAVE SAID THAT UNLESS YOU WERE THE REAL DEAL.
I WISH I COULD SEE KUROKI-KUN'S WEENIE TOO...
STOP IT! PLEASE!
UNLIKE YOU, SENPAI, I PURELY AND SIMPLY LIKE TOMOKI-KUN!!
WAAAH!!?
SHE PURELY AND SIMPLY WANTED TO SEE TOMOKI-KUN'S WEENIE!!

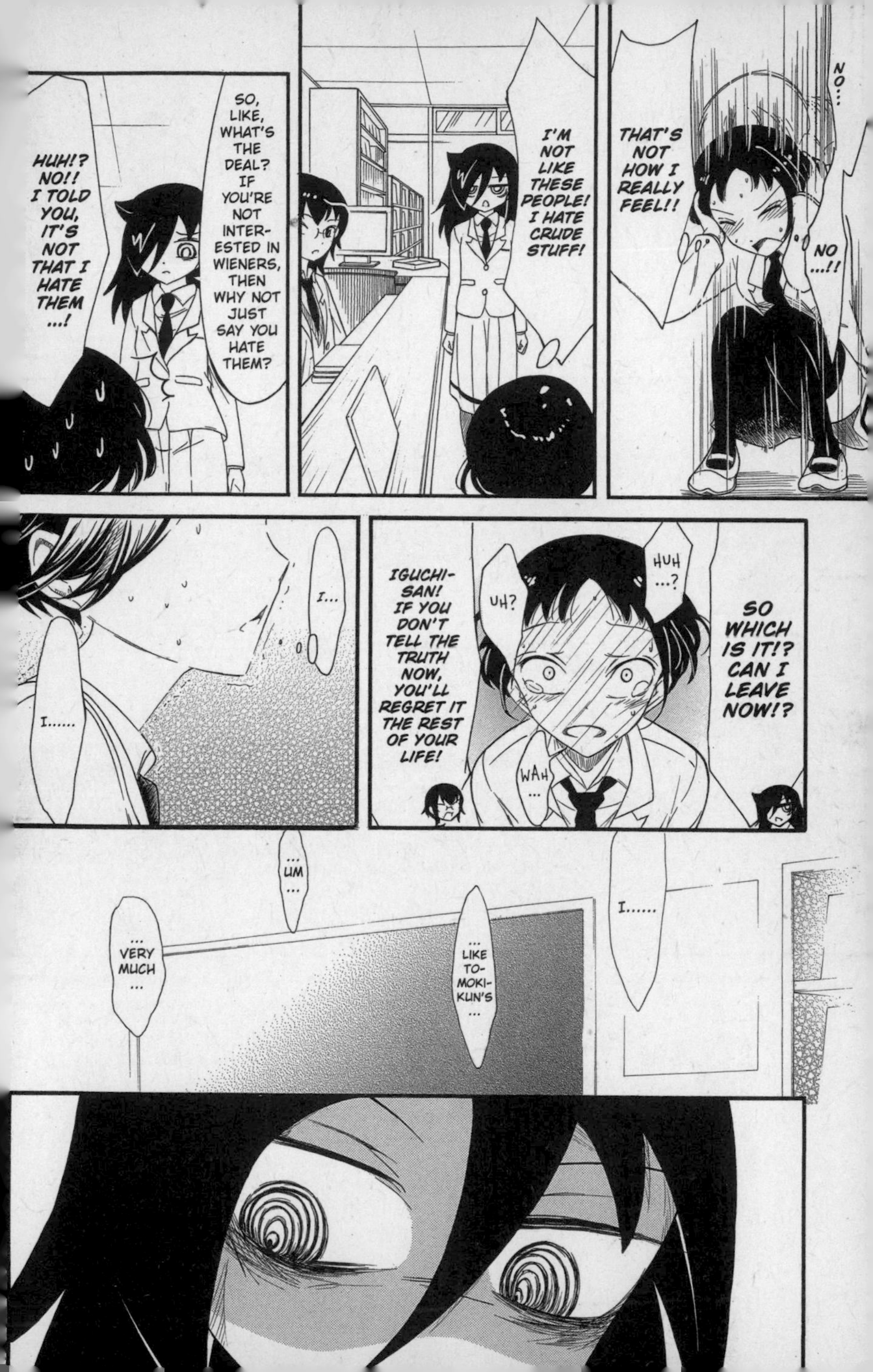
NO...
THAT'S NOT HOW I REALLY FEEL!!
NO ...!!
I'M NOT LIKE THESE PEOPLE! I HATE CRUDE STUFF!
SO, LIKE, WHAT'S THE DEAL? IF YOU'RE NOT INTER-ESTED IN WIENERS, THEN WHY NOT JUST SAY YOU HATE THEM?
HUH!? NO!! I TOLD YOU, IT'S NOT THAT I HATE THEM ...!
SO WHICH IS IT!? CAN I LEAVE NOW!?
HUH ...?
UH?
IGUCHI-SAN! IF YOU DON'T TELL THE TRUTH NOW, YOU'LL REGRET IT THE REST OF YOUR LIFE!
WAH ...
I...
I......
I......
...LIKE TO-MOKI-KUN'S...
...UM...
...VERY MUCH...

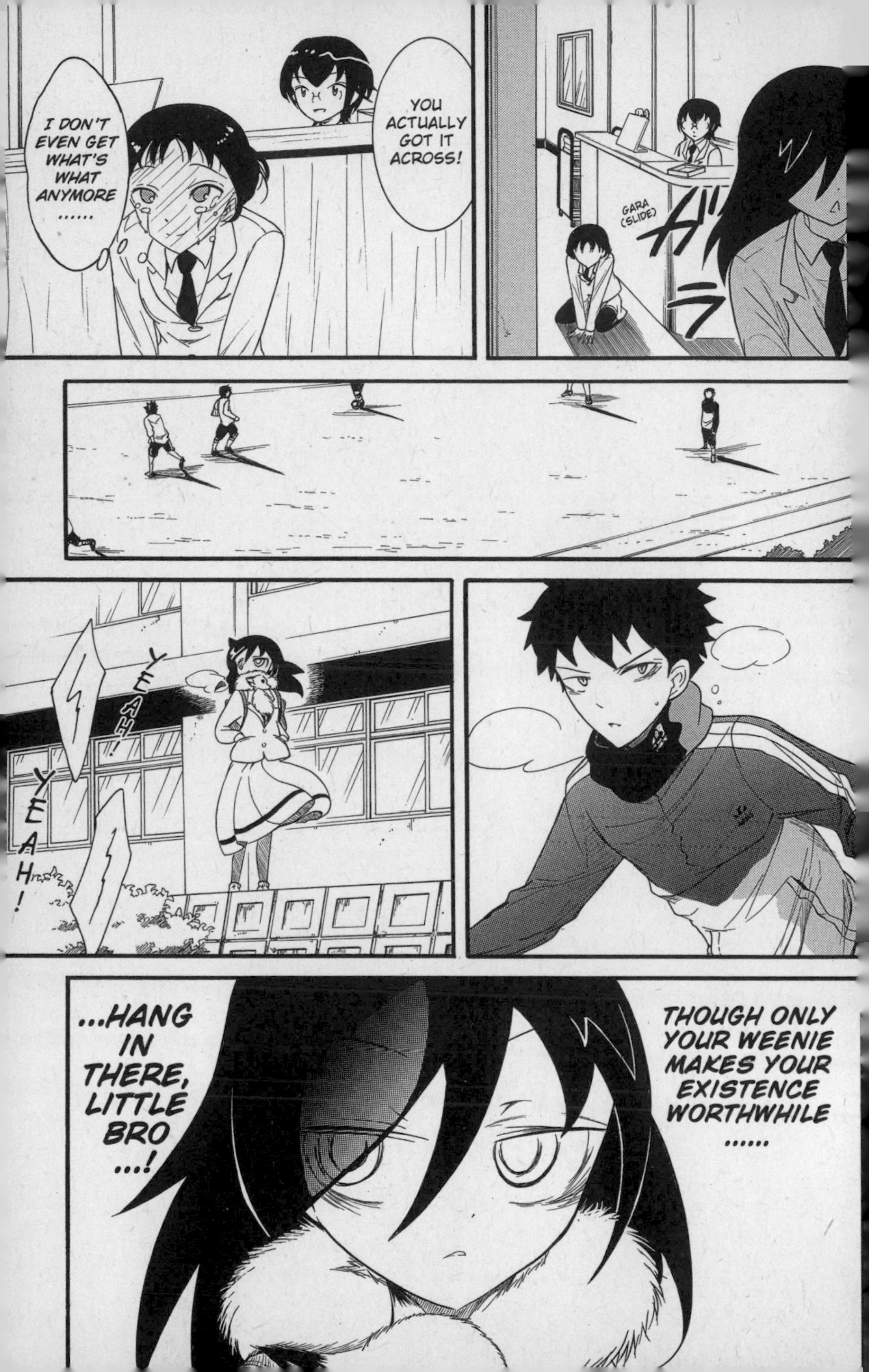

ガラ
GARA (SLIDE)
YOU ACTUALLY GOT IT ACROSS!
I DON'T EVEN GET WHAT'S WHAT ANYMORE ......
YEAH!
YEAH!
THOUGH ONLY YOUR WEENIE MAKES YOUR EXISTENCE WORTHWHILE ......
...HANG IN THERE, LITTLE BRO ...!

No Matter How I Look at It, It's You Guys' Fault I'm Not Popular!

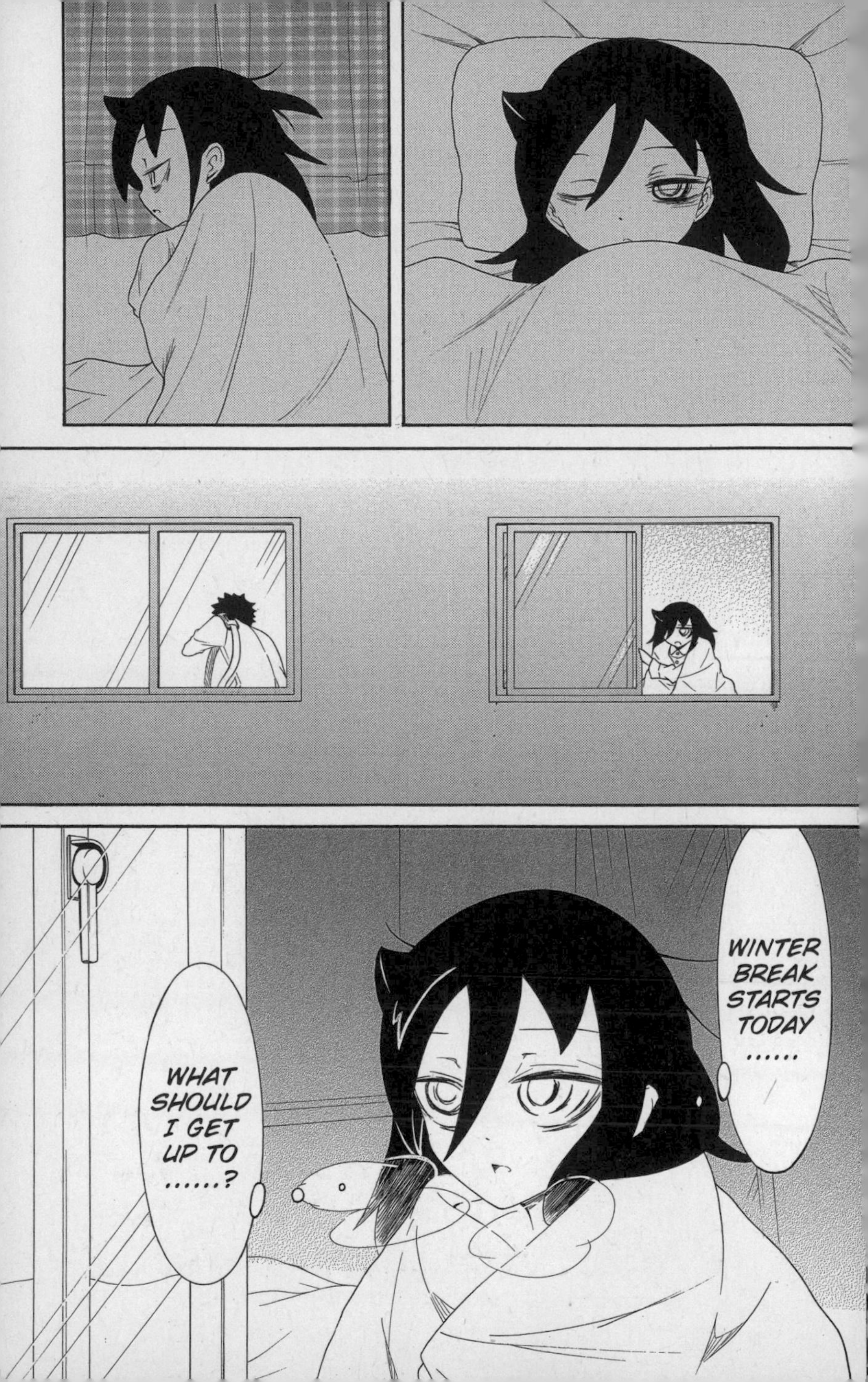
WINTER BREAK STARTS TODAY ......
WHAT SHOULD I GET UP TO ......?

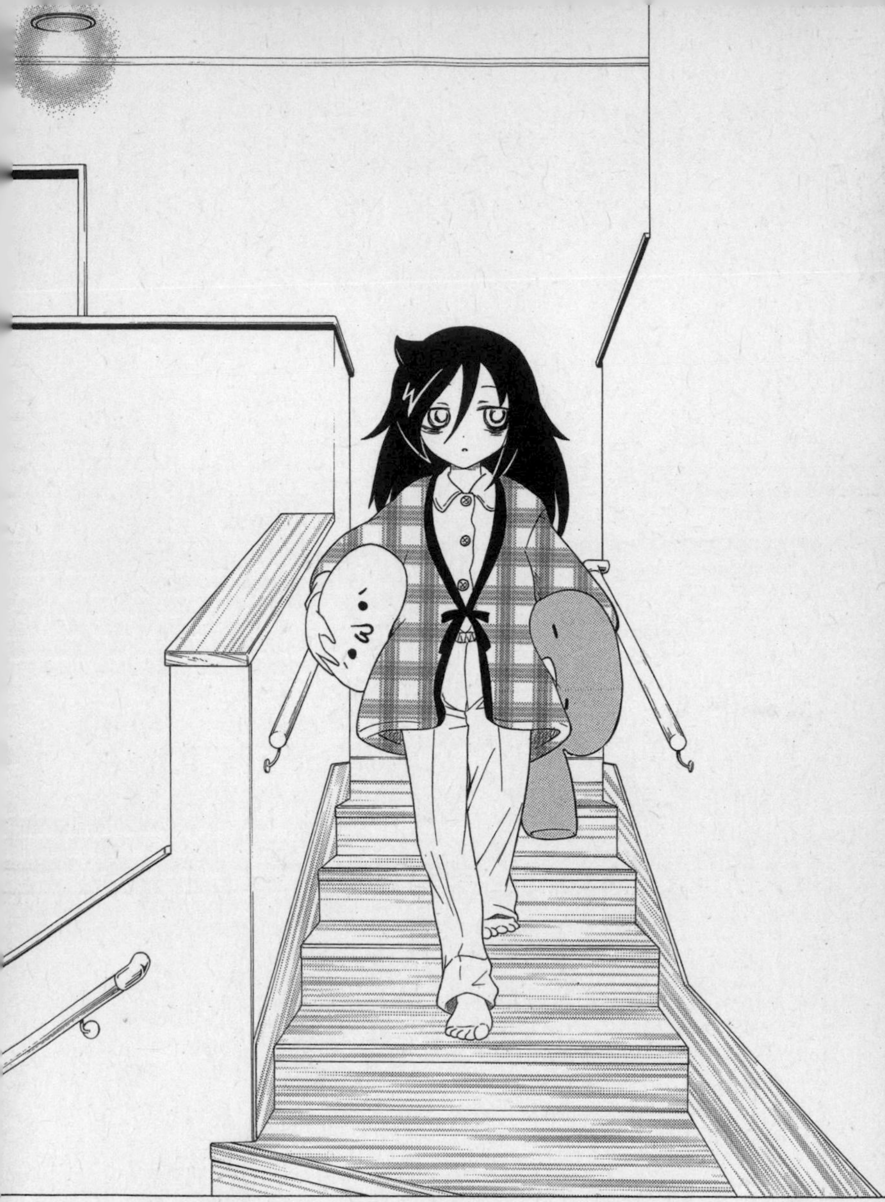

FAIL 102: I'M NOT POPULAR, SO ONE WINTER BREAK...

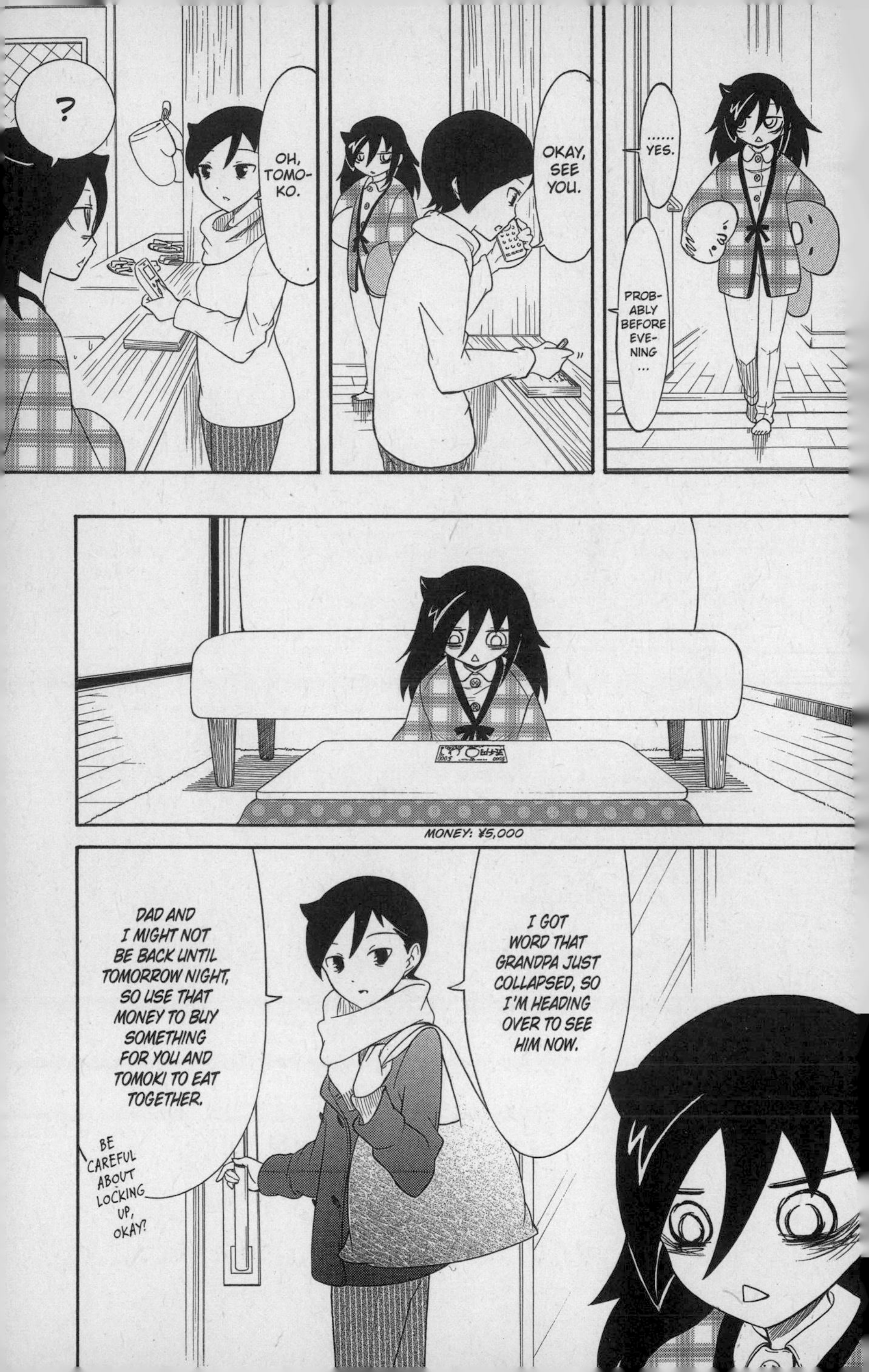
......YES.
PROBABLY BEFORE EVENING...
OKAY, SEE YOU.
OH, TOMOKO.
?
MONEY: ¥5,000
I GOT WORD THAT GRANDPA JUST COLLAPSED, SO I'M HEADING OVER TO SEE HIM NOW.
DAD AND I MIGHT NOT BE BACK UNTIL TOMORROW NIGHT, SO USE THAT MONEY TO BUY SOMETHING FOR YOU AND TOMOKI TO EAT TOGETHER.
BE CAREFUL ABOUT LOCKING UP, OKAY?

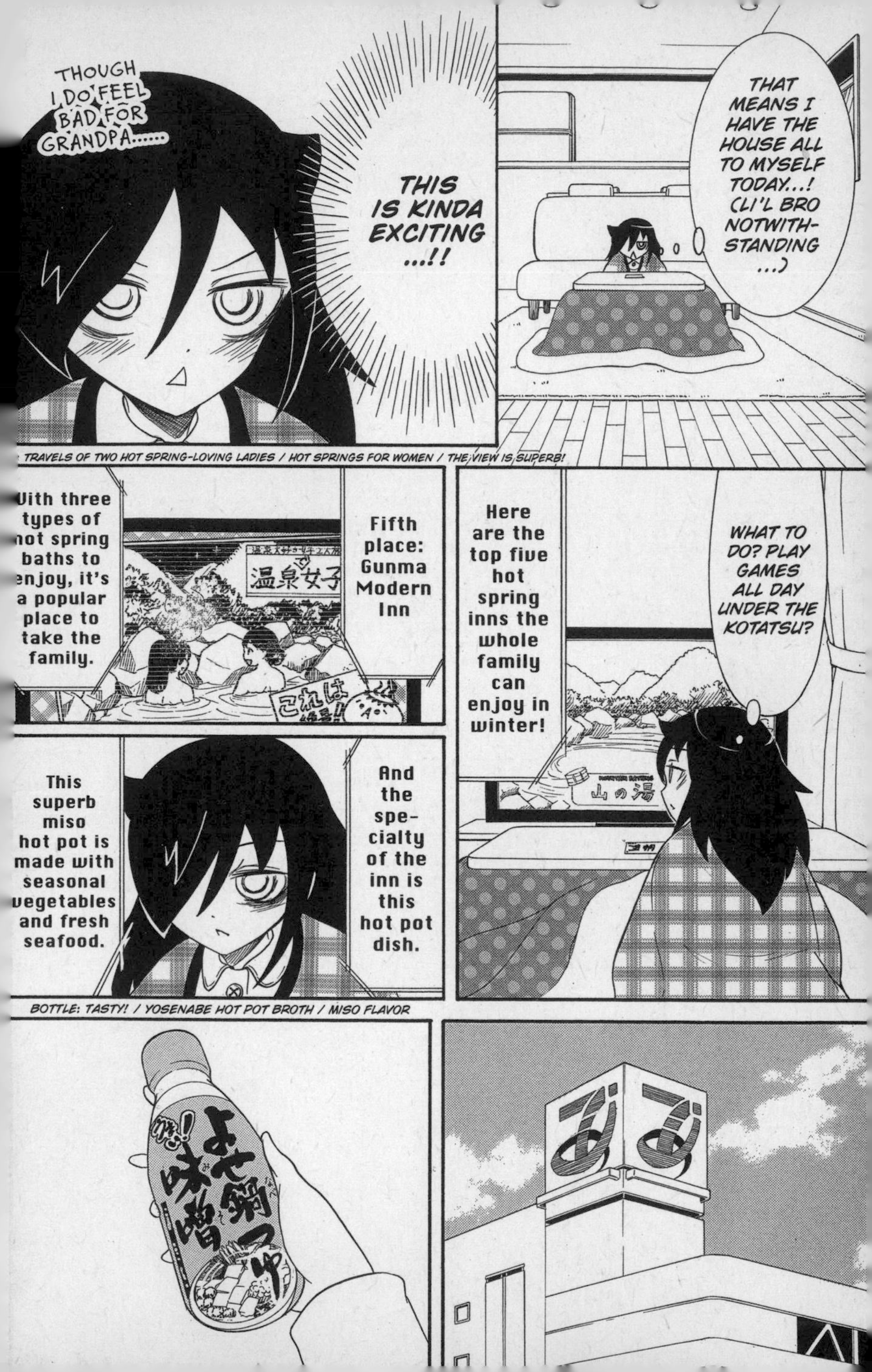
THAT MEANS I HAVE THE HOUSE ALL TO MYSELF TODAY...! (LI'L BRO NOTWITHSTANDING...)
THIS IS KINDA EXCITING ...!!
THOUGH I DO FEEL BAD FOR GRANDPA......
TRAVELS OF TWO HOT SPRING-LOVING LADIES / HOT SPRINGS FOR WOMEN / THE VIEW IS SUPERB!
WHAT TO DO? PLAY GAMES ALL DAY UNDER THE KOTATSU?
Here are the top five hot spring inns the whole family can enjoy in winter!
山の湯
Fifth place: Gunma Modern Inn
温泉女子
With three types of hot spring baths to enjoy, it's a popular place to take the family.
And the specialty of the inn is this hot pot dish.
This superb miso hot pot is made with seasonal vegetables and fresh seafood.
BOTTLE: TASTY! / YOSENABE HOT POT BROTH / MISO FLAVOR
よせ鍋つゆ
味噌

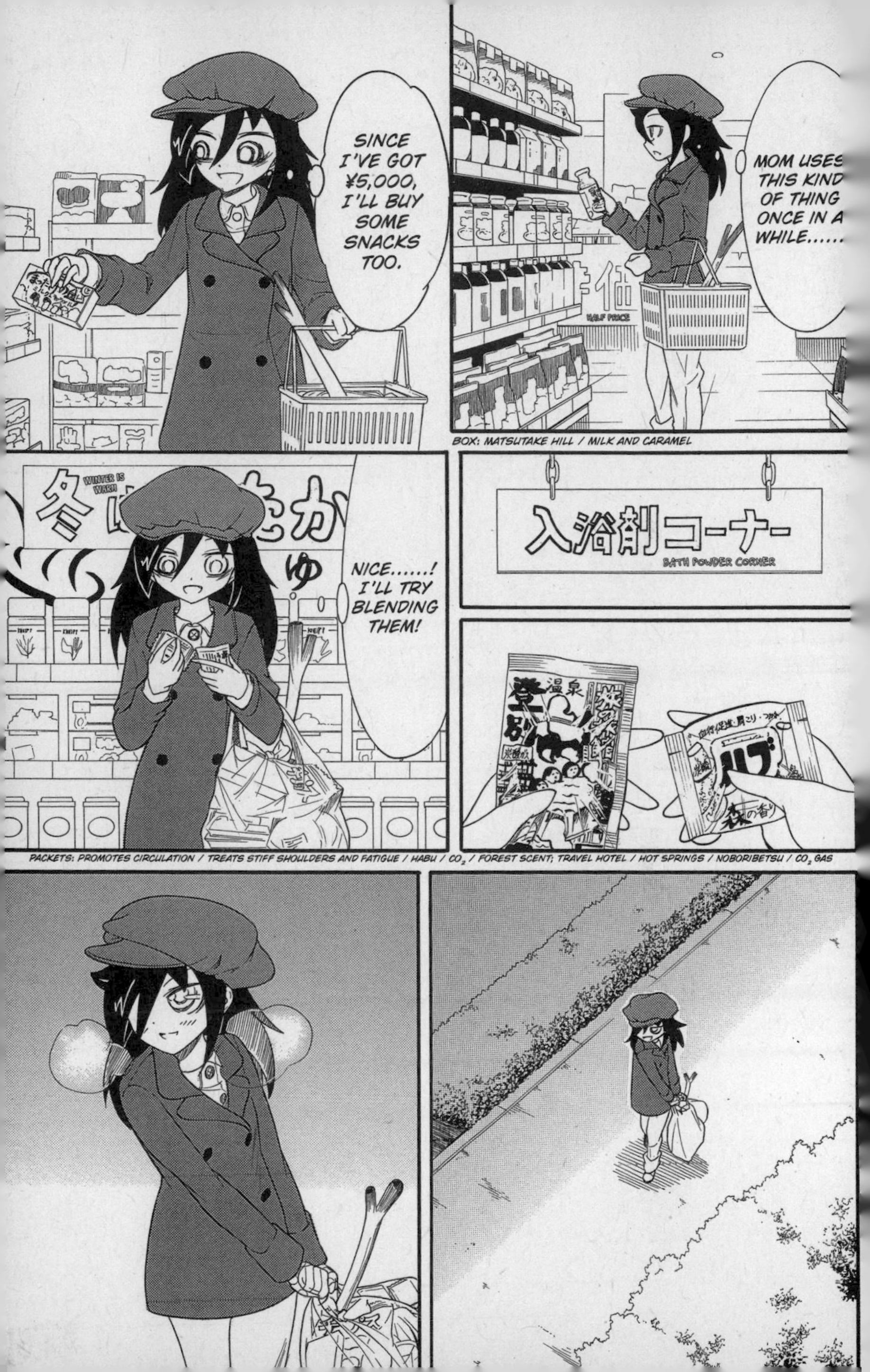
MOM USES THIS KIND OF THING ONCE IN A WHILE......
HALF PRICE
SINCE I'VE GOT ¥5,000, I'LL BUY SOME SNACKS TOO.
BOX: MATSUTAKE HILL / MILK AND CARAMEL
入浴剤コーナー
BATH POWDER CORNER
温泉
WINTER IS WARM
NICE......! I'LL TRY BLENDING THEM!
PACKETS: PROMOTES CIRCULATION / TREATS STIFF SHOULDERS AND FATIGUE / HABU / CO_2 / FOREST SCENT; TRAVEL HOTEL / HOT SPRINGS / NOBORIBETSU / CO_2 GAS

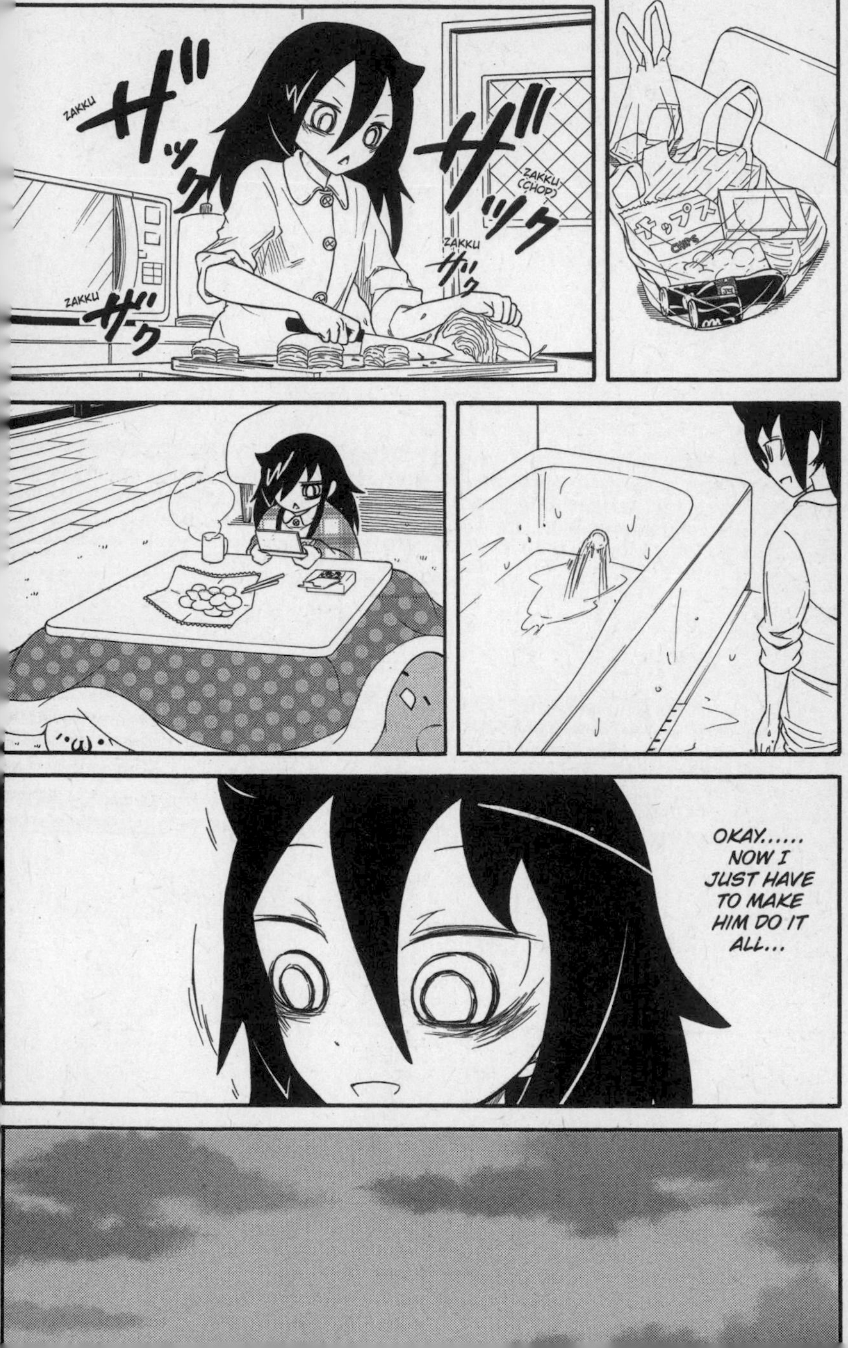
チップス
CHIPS
ZAKKU (CHOP)
ザック
ZAKKU
ザク
ZAKKU
ザック
ZAKKU
ザク
OKAY...... NOW I JUST HAVE TO MAKE HIM DO IT ALL...

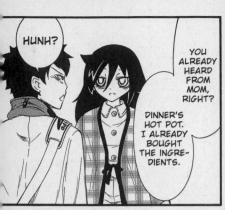

GACHA (KACHAK)
YOU ALREADY HEARD FROM MOM, RIGHT?
DINNER'S HOT POT. I ALREADY BOUGHT THE INGREDIENTS.
HUNH?
YOU GO GET IT READY SO WE CAN EAT AFTER I GET OUT OF THE BATH.
HEY ......
DOBON (PLOP)
DOBON
MY BODY IS READY... FOR BUBBLES ......
SHUWA (FIZZ)
SHUWA
MAYBE I'LL TRY...
...STRADDLING THE BATH BOMBS......

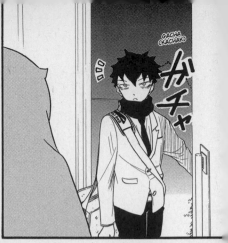

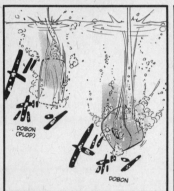

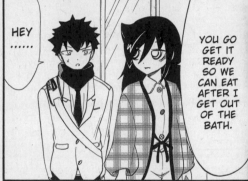

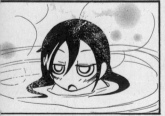

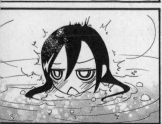

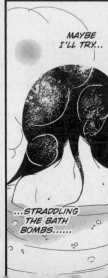

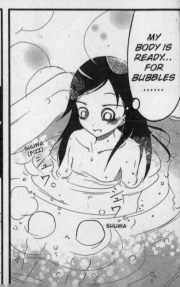

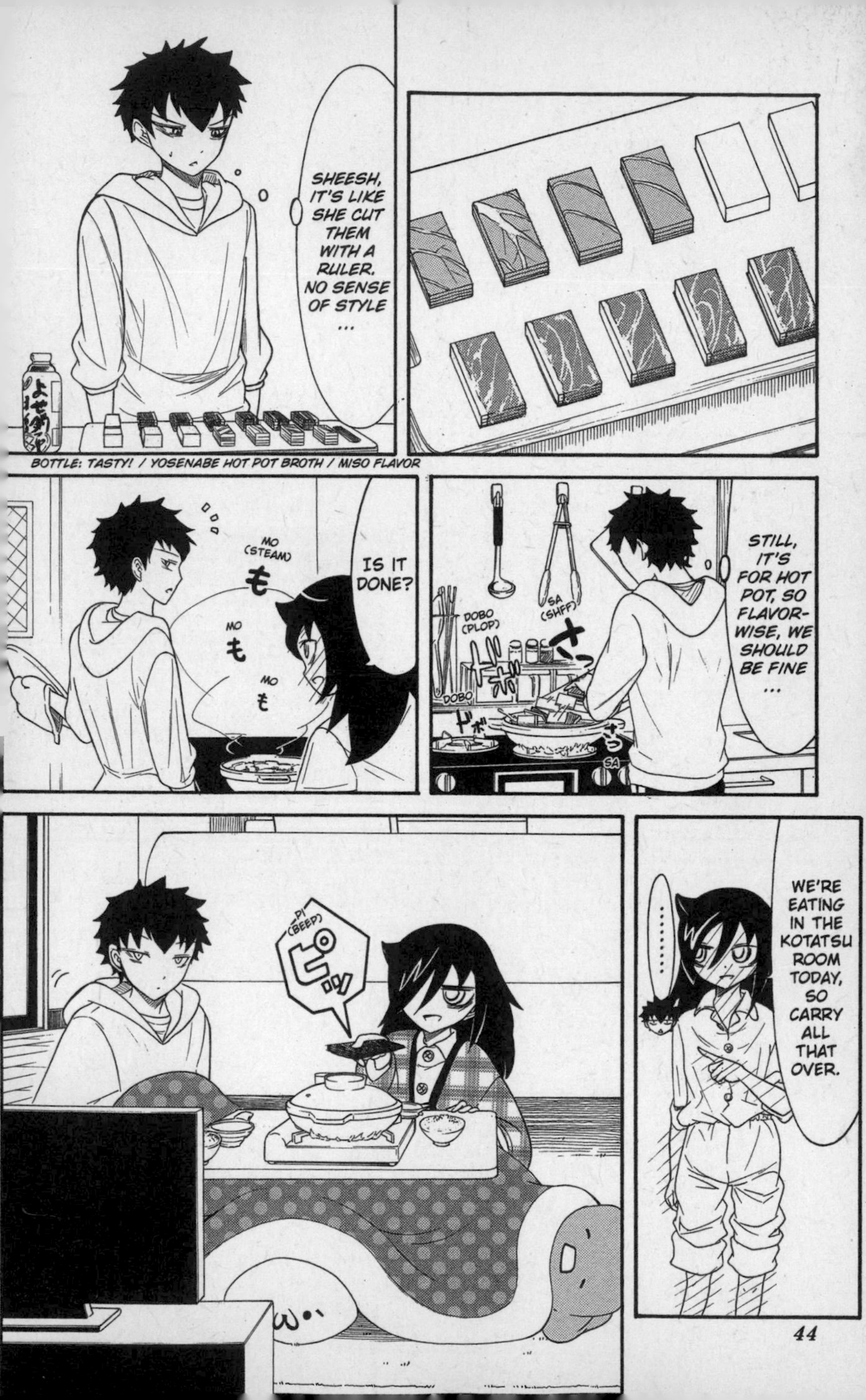
SHEESH, IT'S LIKE SHE CUT THEM WITH A RULER. NO SENSE OF STYLE ...
DOBO (PLOP)
SA (SHFF)
STILL, IT'S FOR HOT POT, SO FLAVOR-WISE, WE SHOULD BE FINE ...
DOBO
SA
IS IT DONE?
MO (STEAM)
MO
MO
WE'RE EATING IN THE KOTATSU ROOM TODAY, SO CARRY ALL THAT OVER.
......
PI (BEEP)
BOTTLE: TASTY! / YOSENABE HOT POT BROTH / MISO FLAVOR

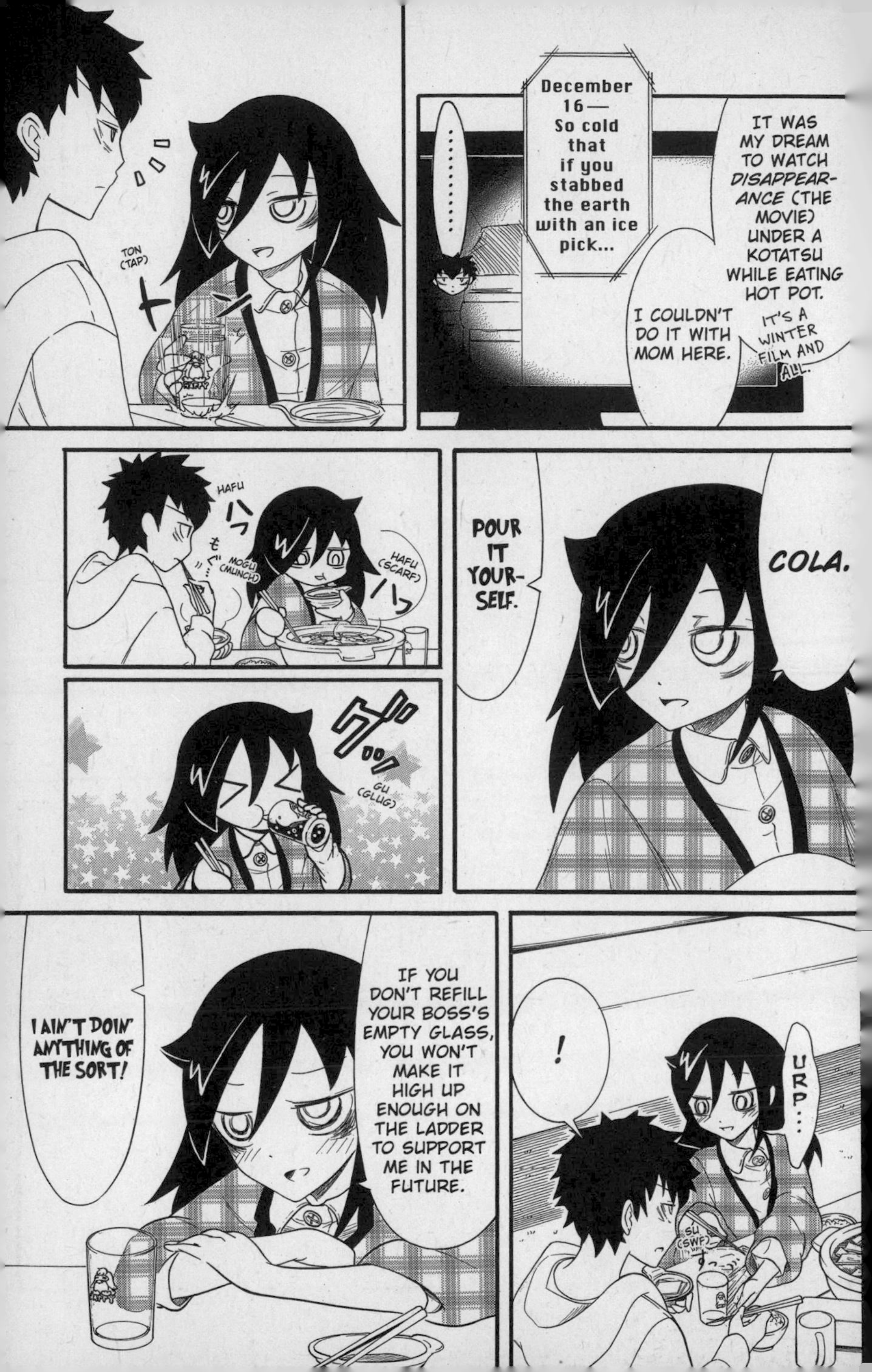
December 16— So cold that if you stabbed the earth with an ice pick...
......
IT WAS MY DREAM TO WATCH *DISAPPEARANCE* (THE MOVIE) UNDER A KOTATSU WHILE EATING HOT POT.
IT'S A WINTER FILM AND ALL.
I COULDN'T DO IT WITH MOM HERE.
TON (TAP)
COLA.
POUR IT YOURSELF.
ハフ
HAFU
もぐ
MOGU (MUNCH)
ハフ
HAFU (SCARF)
グッ
GU (GLUG)
URP...
!
SU (SWF)
IF YOU DON'T REFILL YOUR BOSS'S EMPTY GLASS, YOU WON'T MAKE IT HIGH UP ENOUGH ON THE LADDER TO SUPPORT ME IN THE FUTURE.
I AIN'T DOIN' ANYTHING OF THE SORT!

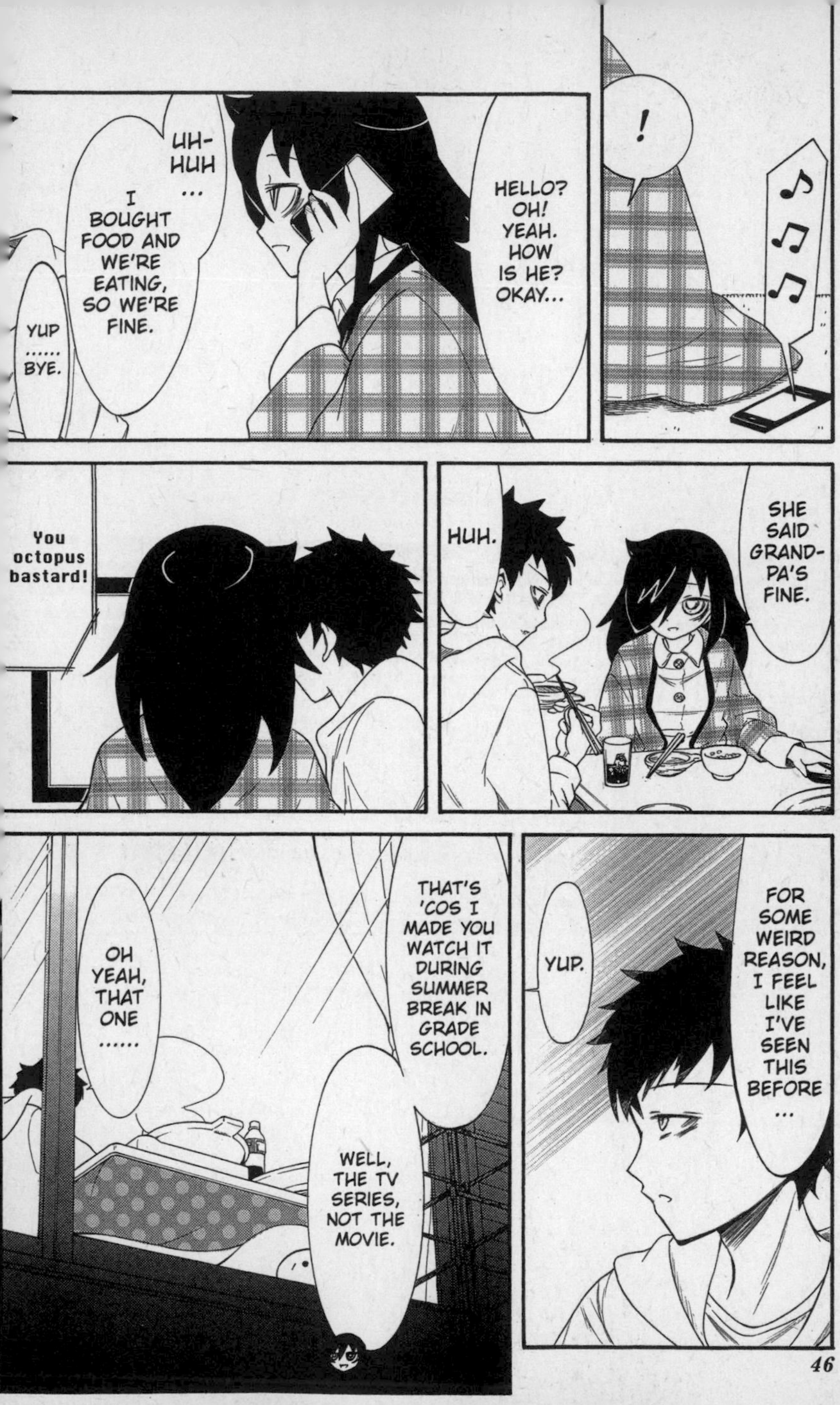
!
...
HELLO? OH! YEAH. HOW IS HE? OKAY...
UH-HUH ...
I BOUGHT FOOD AND WE'RE EATING, SO WE'RE FINE.
YUP ...... BYE.
SHE SAID GRAND-PA'S FINE.
HUH.
You octopus bastard!
FOR SOME WEIRD REASON, I FEEL LIKE I'VE SEEN THIS BEFORE ...
YUP.
THAT'S 'COS I MADE YOU WATCH IT DURING SUMMER BREAK IN GRADE SCHOOL.
OH YEAH, THAT ONE ......
WELL, THE TV SERIES, NOT THE MOVIE.

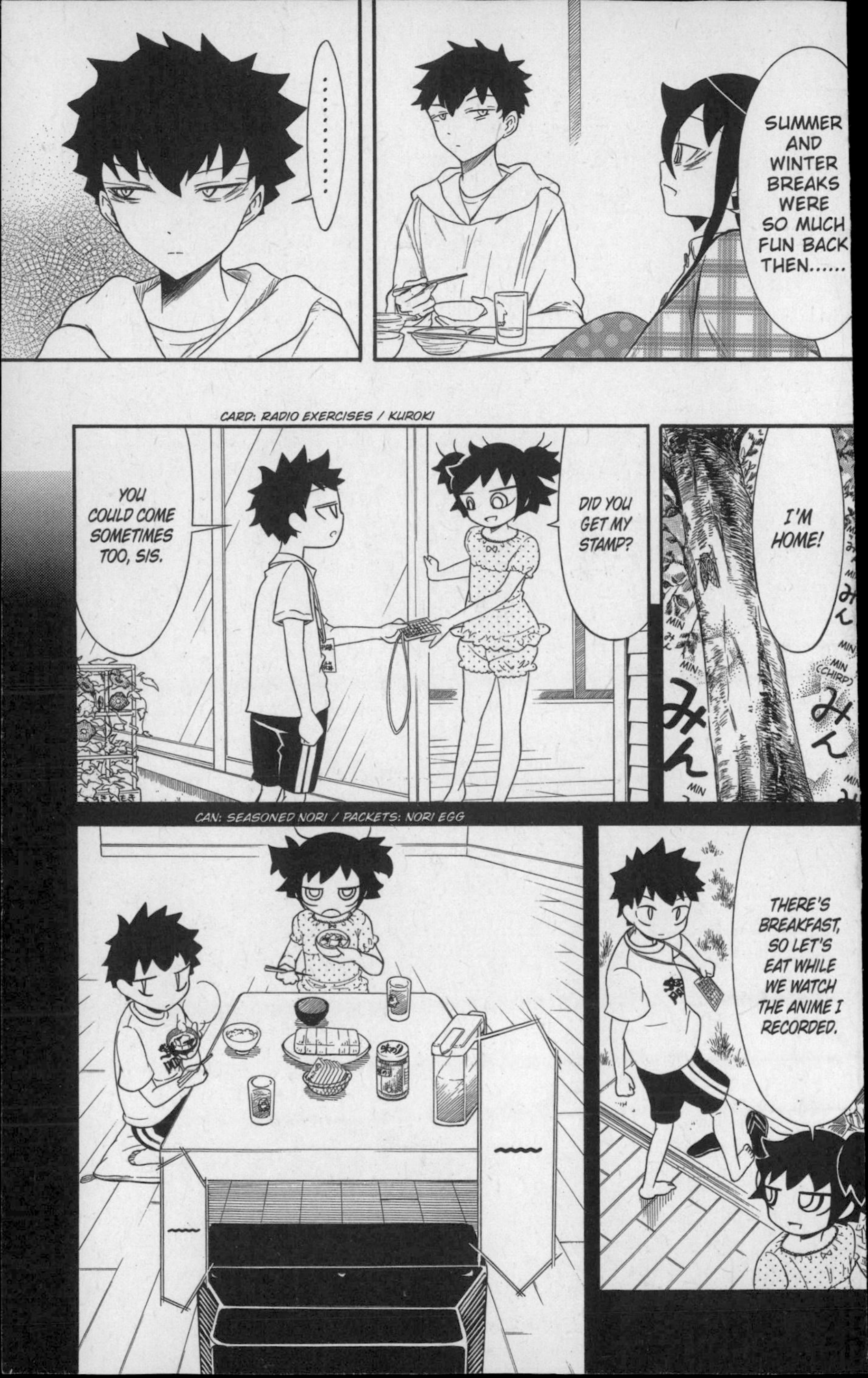
SUMMER AND WINTER BREAKS WERE SO MUCH FUN BACK THEN......
......
CARD: RADIO EXERCISES / KUROKI
I'M HOME!
みん MIN
みん MIN
MIN (CHIRP)
みん MIN
みん MIN
DID YOU GET MY STAMP?
YOU COULD COME SOMETIMES TOO, SIS.
CAN: SEASONED NORI / PACKETS: NORI EGG
THERE'S BREAKFAST, SO LET'S EAT WHILE WE WATCH THE ANIME I RECORDED.

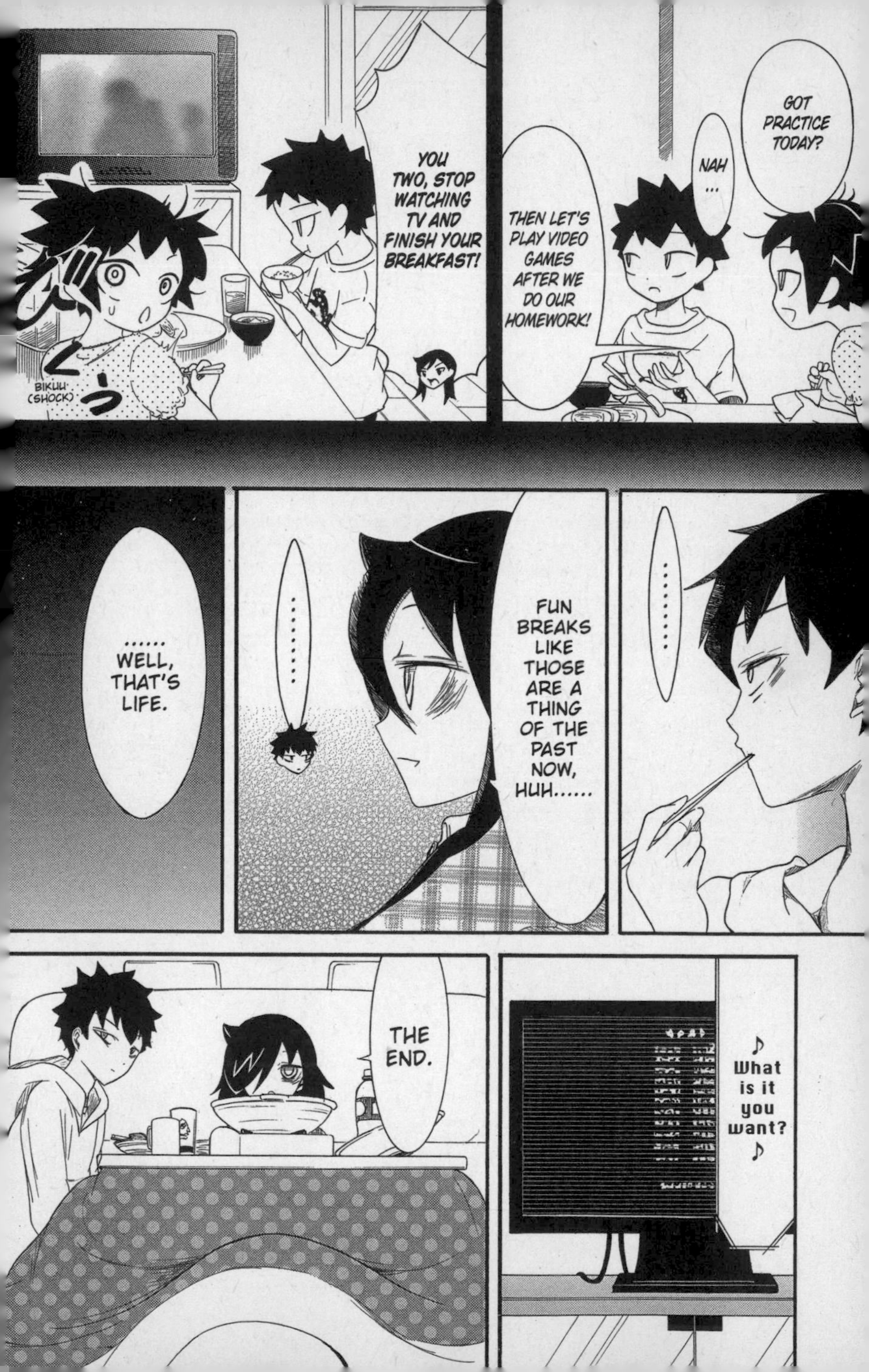
GOT PRACTICE TODAY?
NAH ...
THEN LET'S PLAY VIDEO GAMES AFTER WE DO OUR HOMEWORK!
YOU TWO, STOP WATCHING TV AND FINISH YOUR BREAKFAST!
BIKUU (SHOCK)
......
FUN BREAKS LIKE THOSE ARE A THING OF THE PAST NOW, HUH......
......
...... WELL, THAT'S LIFE.
♪ What is it you want? ♪
THE END.

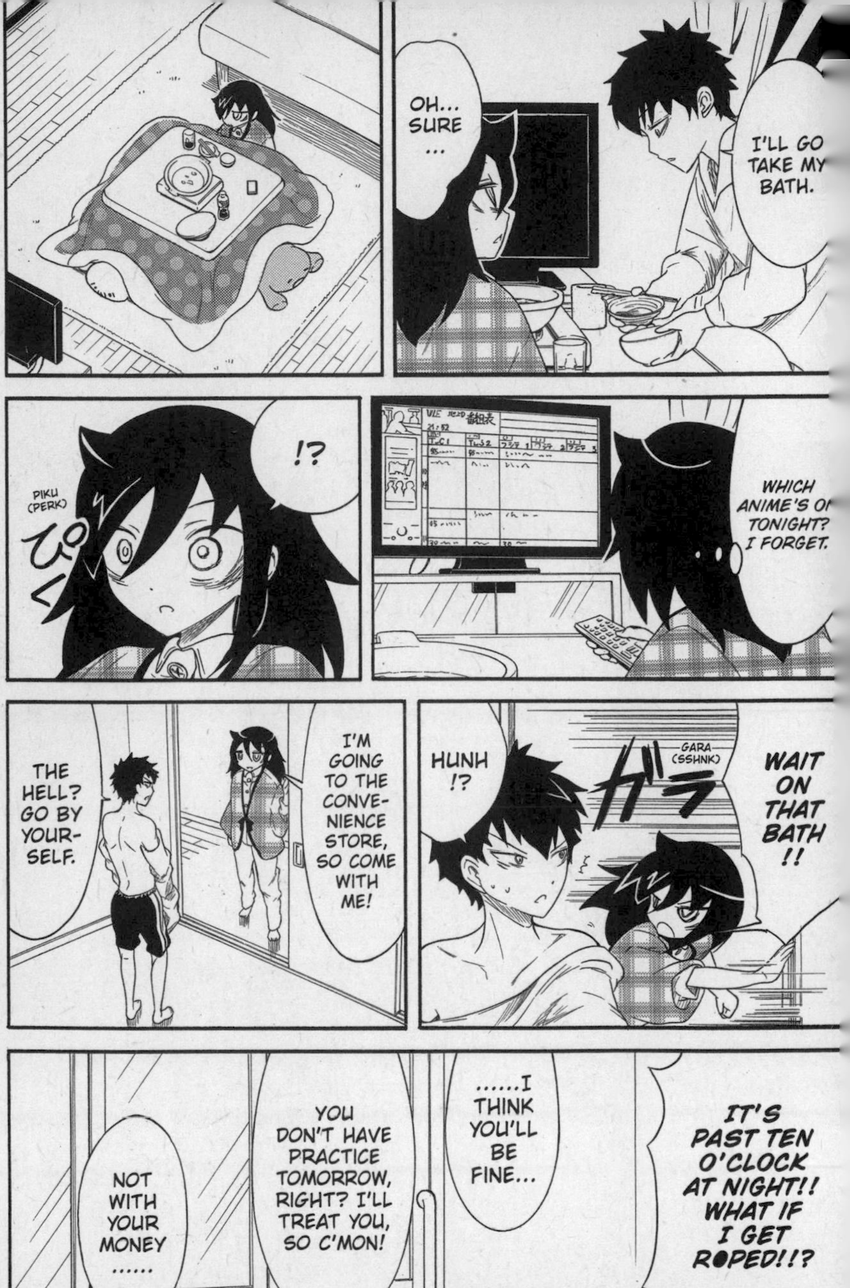
I'LL GO TAKE MY BATH.
OH... SURE ...
WHICH ANIME'S ON TONIGHT? I FORGET.
!?
PIKU (PERK)
ぴく
WAIT ON THAT BATH!!
GARA (SSHNK)
ガラ
HUNH !?
I'M GOING TO THE CONVE-NIENCE STORE, SO COME WITH ME!
THE HELL? GO BY YOUR-SELF.
IT'S PAST TEN O'CLOCK AT NIGHT!! WHAT IF I GET ROPED!!?
......I THINK YOU'LL BE FINE...
YOU DON'T HAVE PRACTICE TOMORROW, RIGHT? I'LL TREAT YOU, SO C'MON!
NOT WITH YOUR MONEY ......

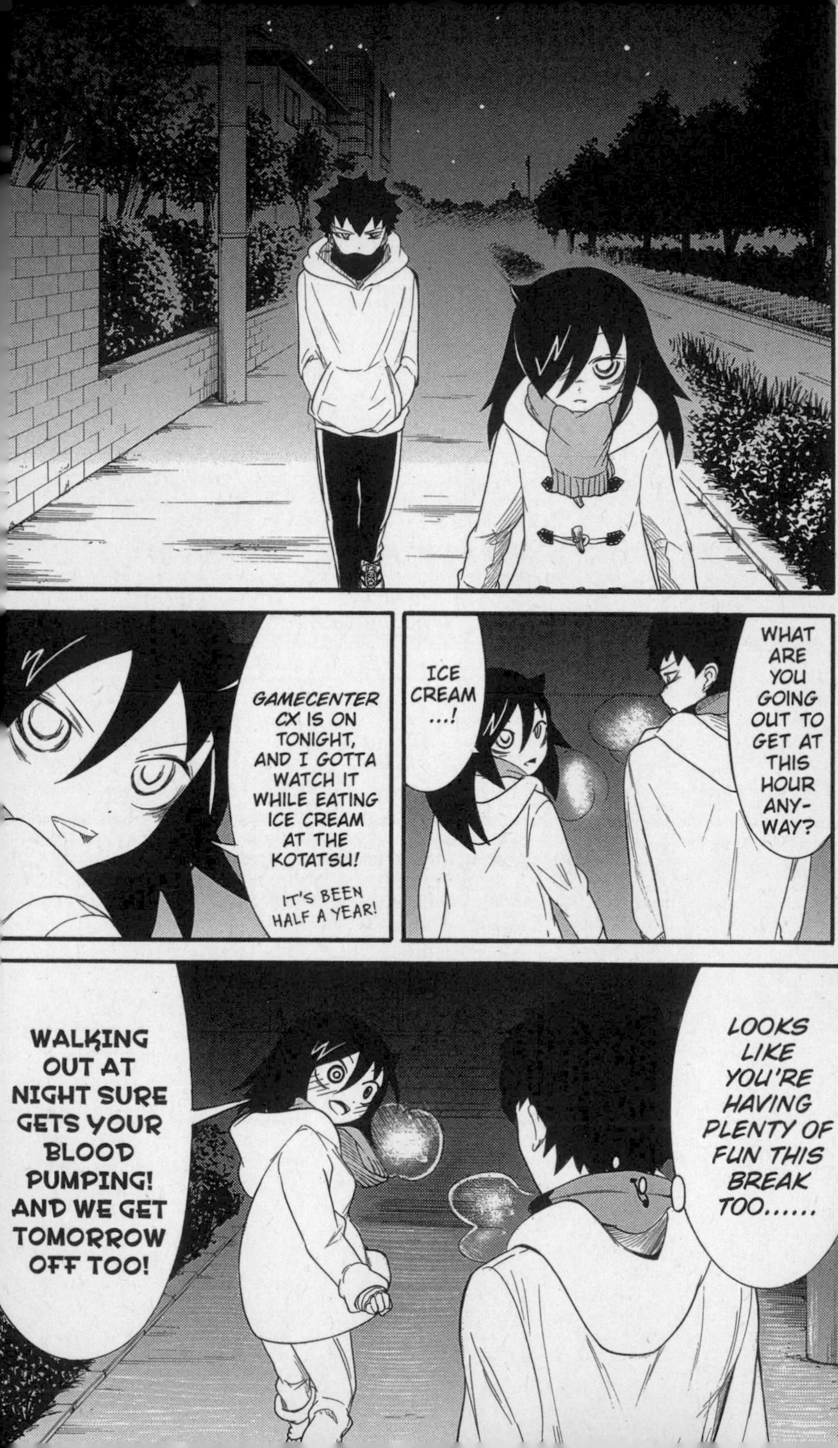
WHAT ARE YOU GOING OUT TO GET AT THIS HOUR ANYWAY?
ICE CREAM ...!
GAMECENTER CX IS ON TONIGHT, AND I GOTTA WATCH IT WHILE EATING ICE CREAM AT THE KOTATSU!
IT'S BEEN HALF A YEAR!
LOOKS LIKE YOU'RE HAVING PLENTY OF FUN THIS BREAK TOO......
WALKING OUT AT NIGHT SURE GETS YOUR BLOOD PUMPING! AND WE GET TOMORROW OFF TOO!

No Matter How I Look at It, It's You Guys' Fault I'm Not Popular!

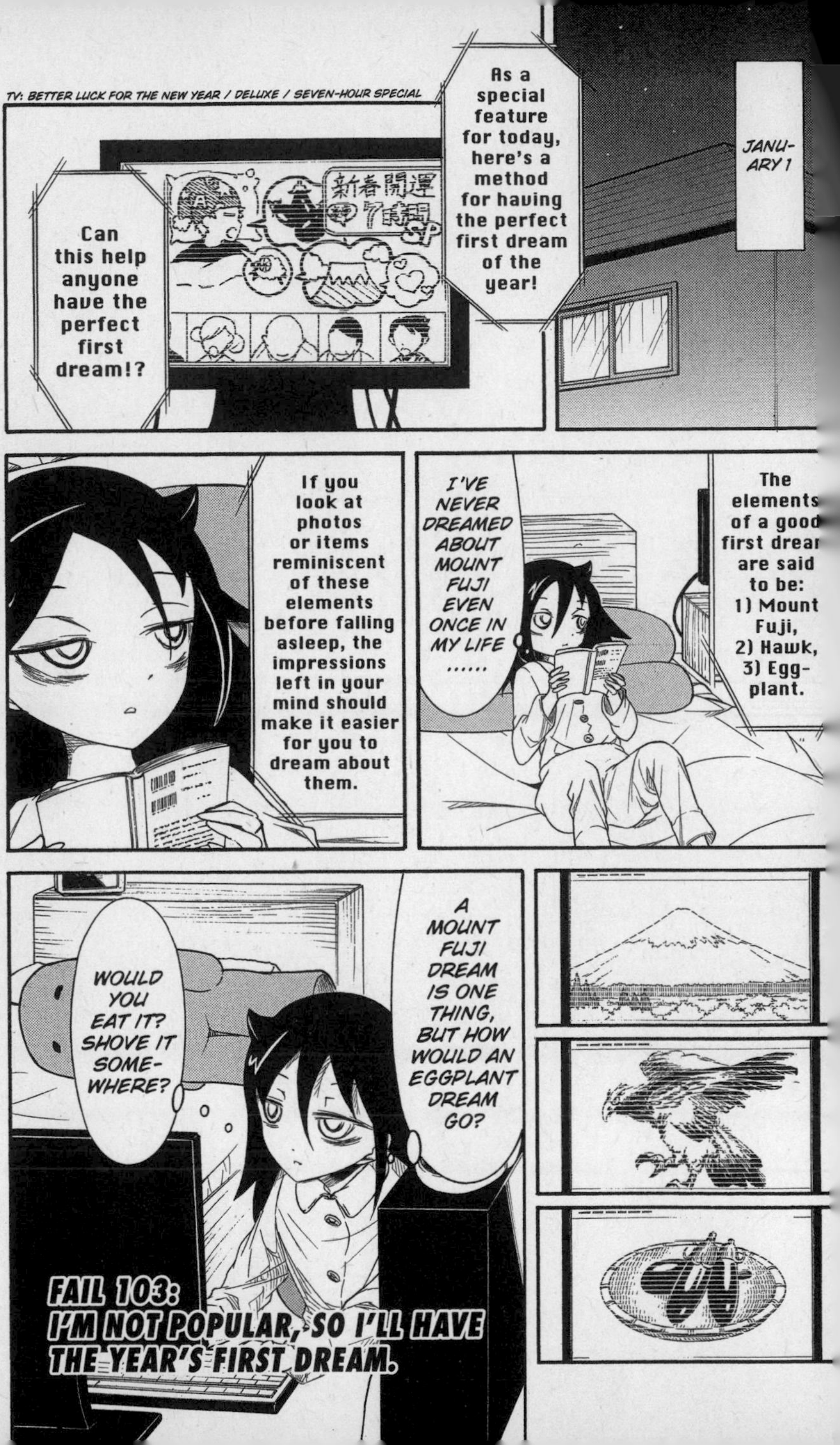
JANU-ARY 1
As a special feature for today, here's a method for having the perfect first dream of the year!
TV: BETTER LUCK FOR THE NEW YEAR / DELUXE / SEVEN-HOUR SPECIAL
Can this help anyone have the perfect first dream!?
The elements of a good first drea are said to be: 1) Mount Fuji, 2) Hawk, 3) Egg-plant.
I'VE NEVER DREAMED ABOUT MOUNT FUJI EVEN ONCE IN MY LIFE ......
If you look at photos or items reminiscent of these elements before falling asleep, the impressions left in your mind should make it easier for you to dream about them.
A MOUNT FUJI DREAM IS ONE THING, BUT HOW WOULD AN EGGPLANT DREAM GO?
WOULD YOU EAT IT? SHOVE IT SOME-WHERE?
FAIL 103:
I'M NOT POPULAR, SO I'LL HAVE THE YEAR'S FIRST DREAM.

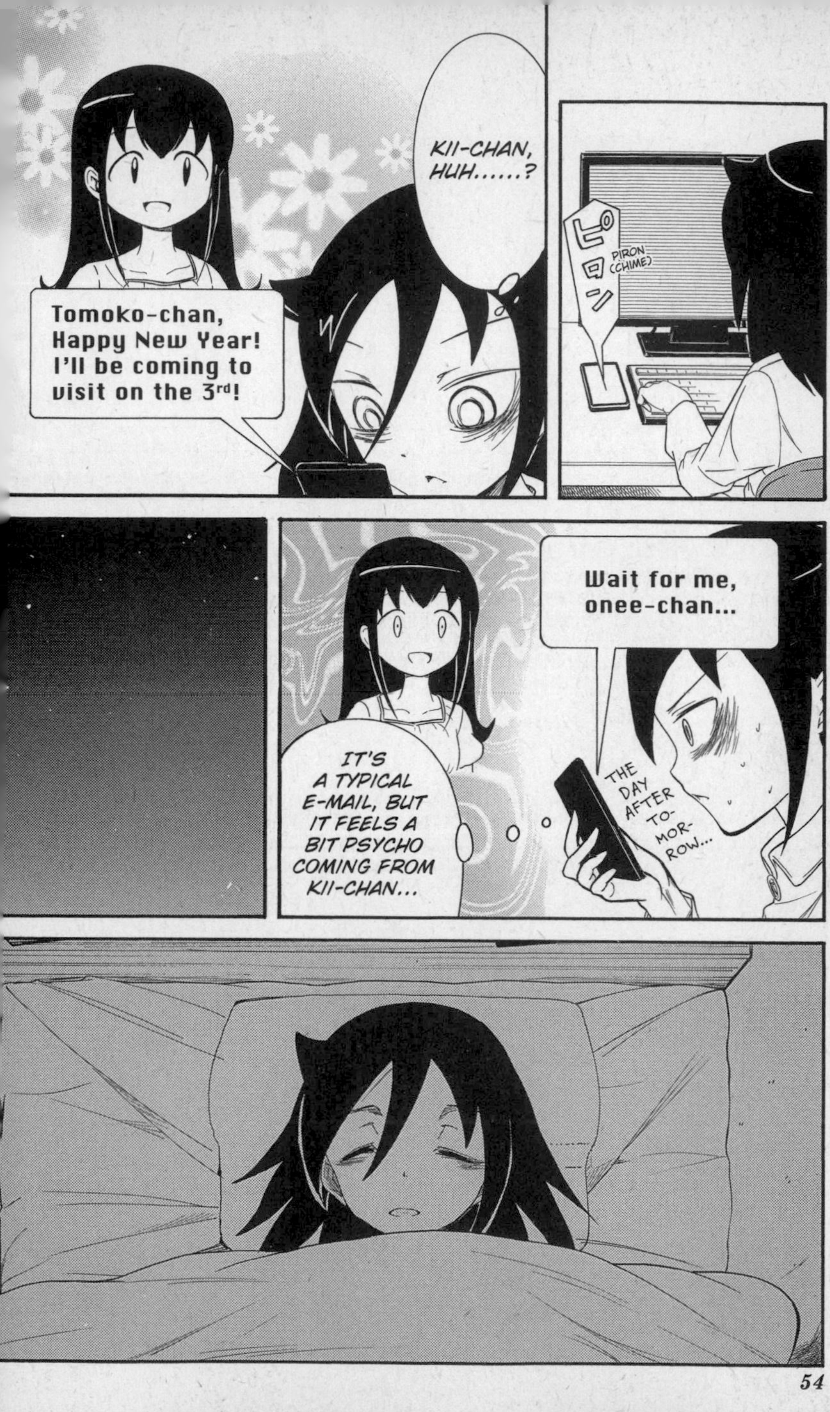
ピロン
PIRON (CHIME)
KII-CHAN, HUH......?
Tomoko-chan, Happy New Year! I'll be coming to visit on the 3rd!
Wait for me, onee-chan...
THE DAY AFTER TO-MOR-ROW...
IT'S A TYPICAL E-MAIL, BUT IT FEELS A BIT PSYCHO COMING FROM KII-CHAN...

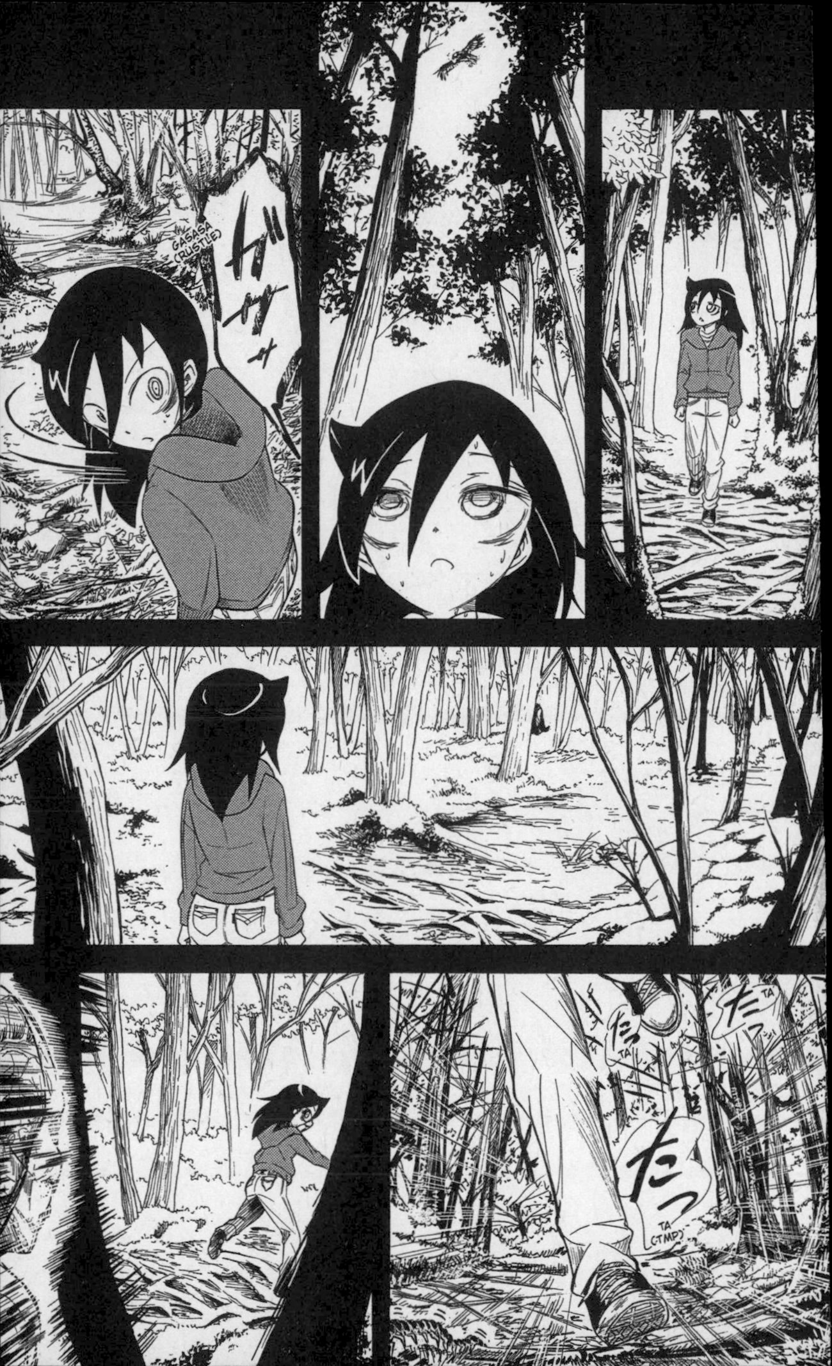
ガサッ
GASASA (RUSTLE)
たっ
TA
たっ
TA
たっ
TA (STMP)

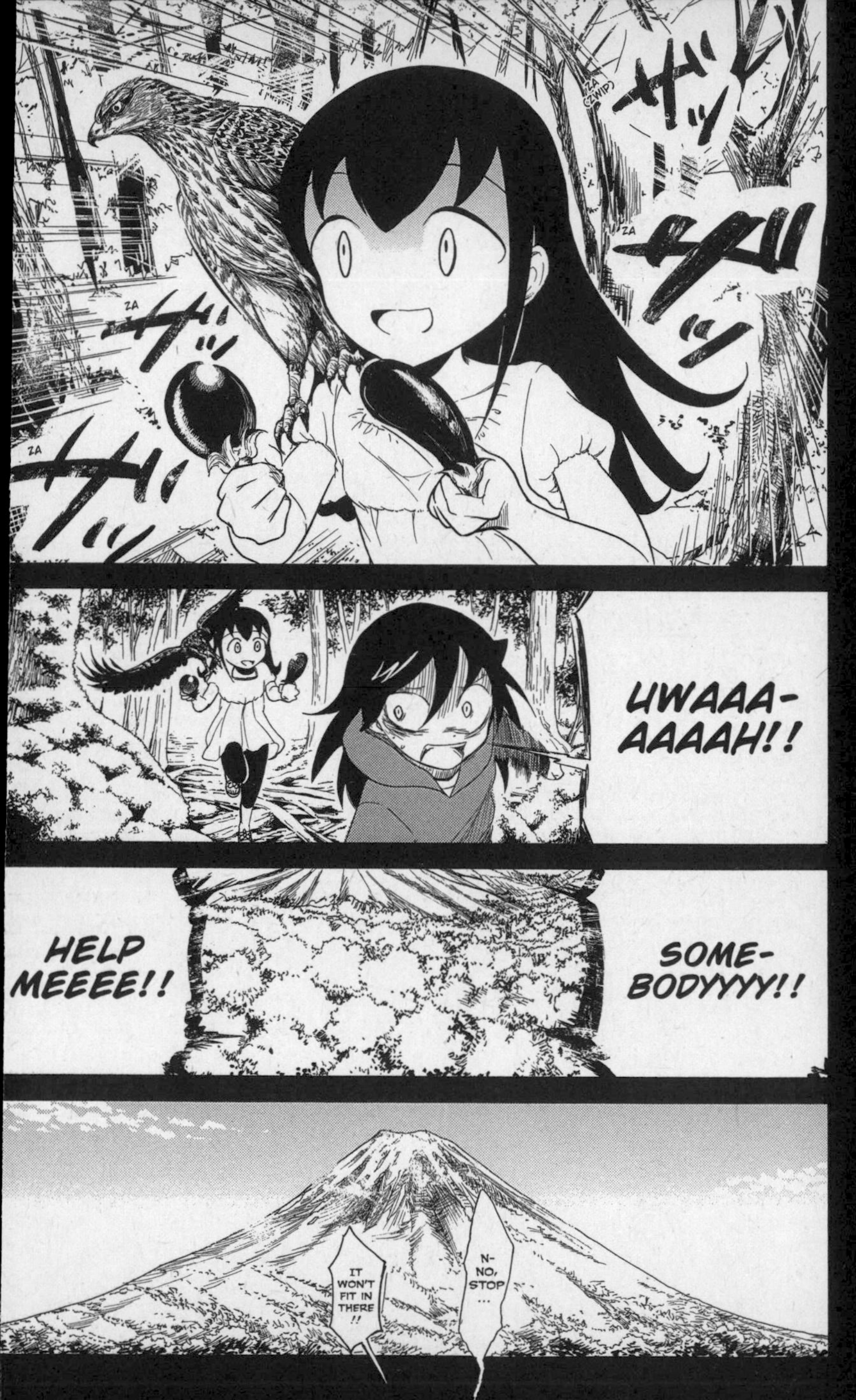
ZA (ZWIP)
ZA
ZA
ZA
UWAAA-AAAAH!!
SOME-BODYYYY!!
HELP MEEEE!!
N-NO, STOP ...
IT WON'T FIT IN THERE !!

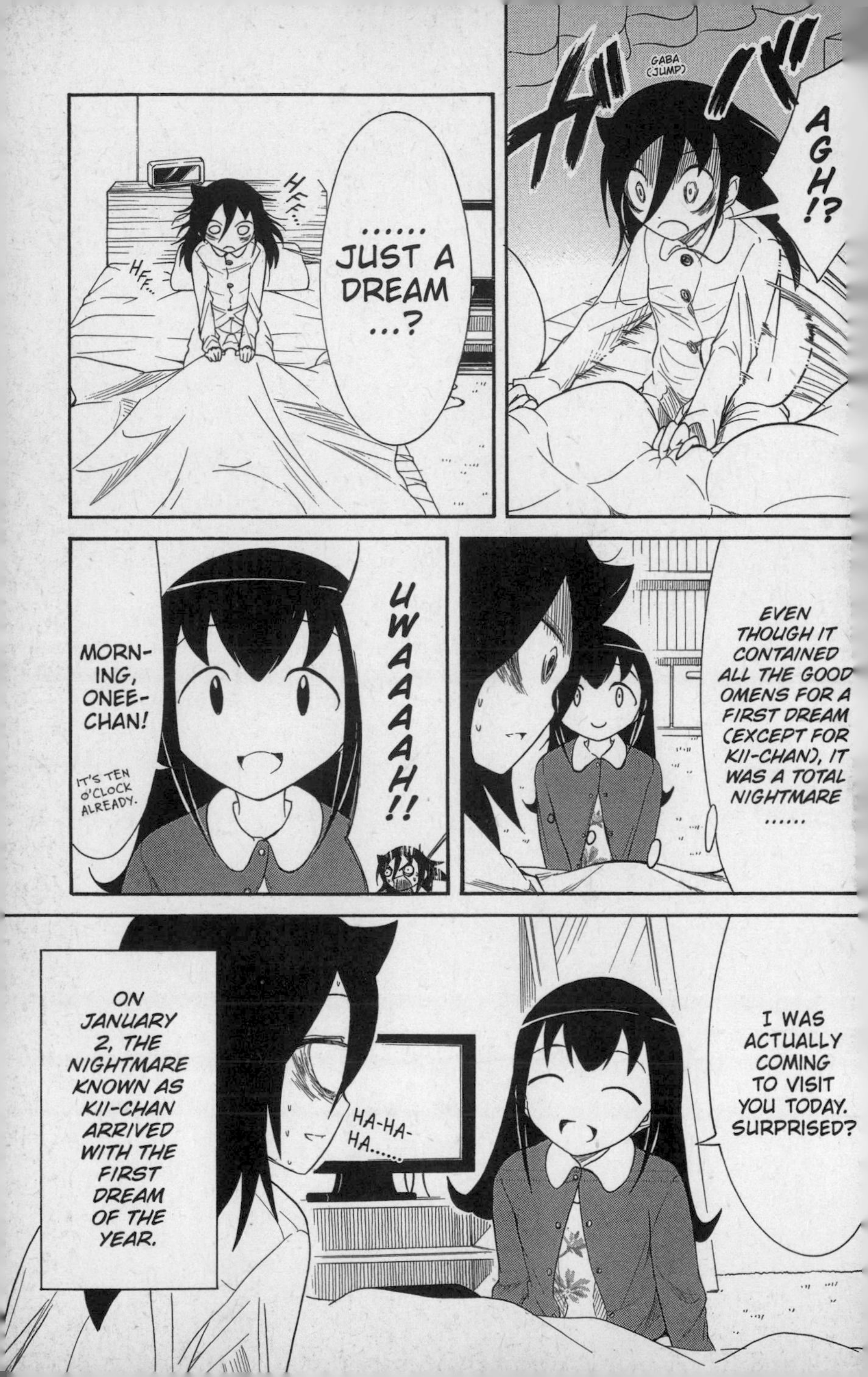
GABA (JUMP)
AGH!?
HFF...
HFF...
...... JUST A DREAM ...?
EVEN THOUGH IT CONTAINED ALL THE GOOD OMENS FOR A FIRST DREAM (EXCEPT FOR KII-CHAN), IT WAS A TOTAL NIGHTMARE ......
UWAAAAAH!!
MORNING, ONEE-CHAN!
IT'S TEN O'CLOCK ALREADY.
I WAS ACTUALLY COMING TO VISIT YOU TODAY. SURPRISED?
HA-HA-HA......
ON JANUARY 2, THE NIGHTMARE KNOWN AS KII-CHAN ARRIVED WITH THE FIRST DREAM OF THE YEAR.

No Matter How I Look at It, It's You Guys' Fault I'm Not Popular!

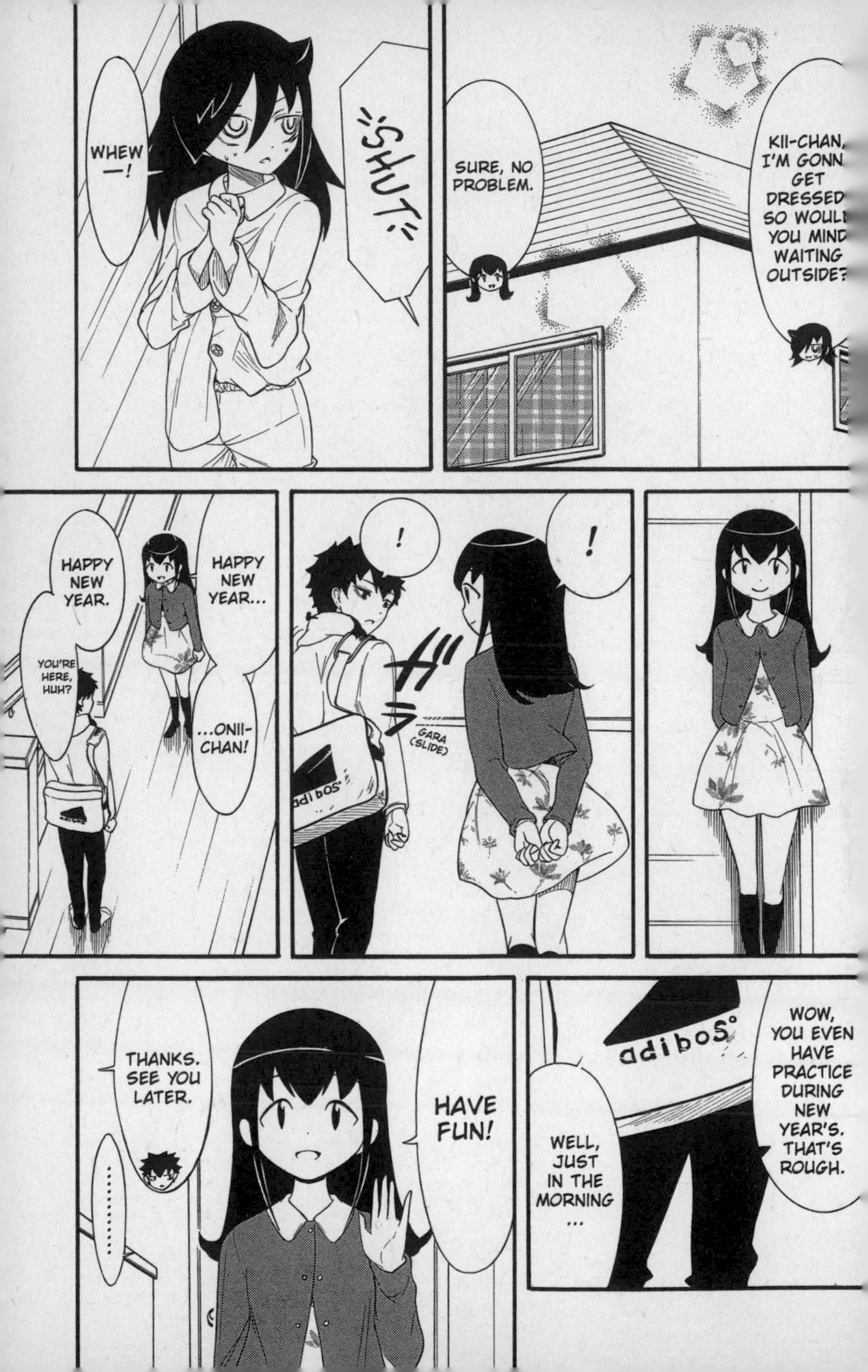
KII-CHAN, I'M GONN GET DRESSED SO WOUL YOU MIND WAITING OUTSIDE?
SURE, NO PROBLEM.
SHUT
WHEW—!
!
!
ガラ
GARA (SLIDE)
adiboS
HAPPY NEW YEAR...
...ONII-CHAN!
HAPPY NEW YEAR.
YOU'RE HERE, HUH?
adiboS
WOW, YOU EVEN HAVE PRACTICE DURING NEW YEAR'S. THAT'S ROUGH.
WELL, JUST IN THE MORNING...
HAVE FUN!
THANKS. SEE YOU LATER.
......

FAIL 104: I'M NOT POPULAR, SO KII-CHAN IS NOT NORMAL.

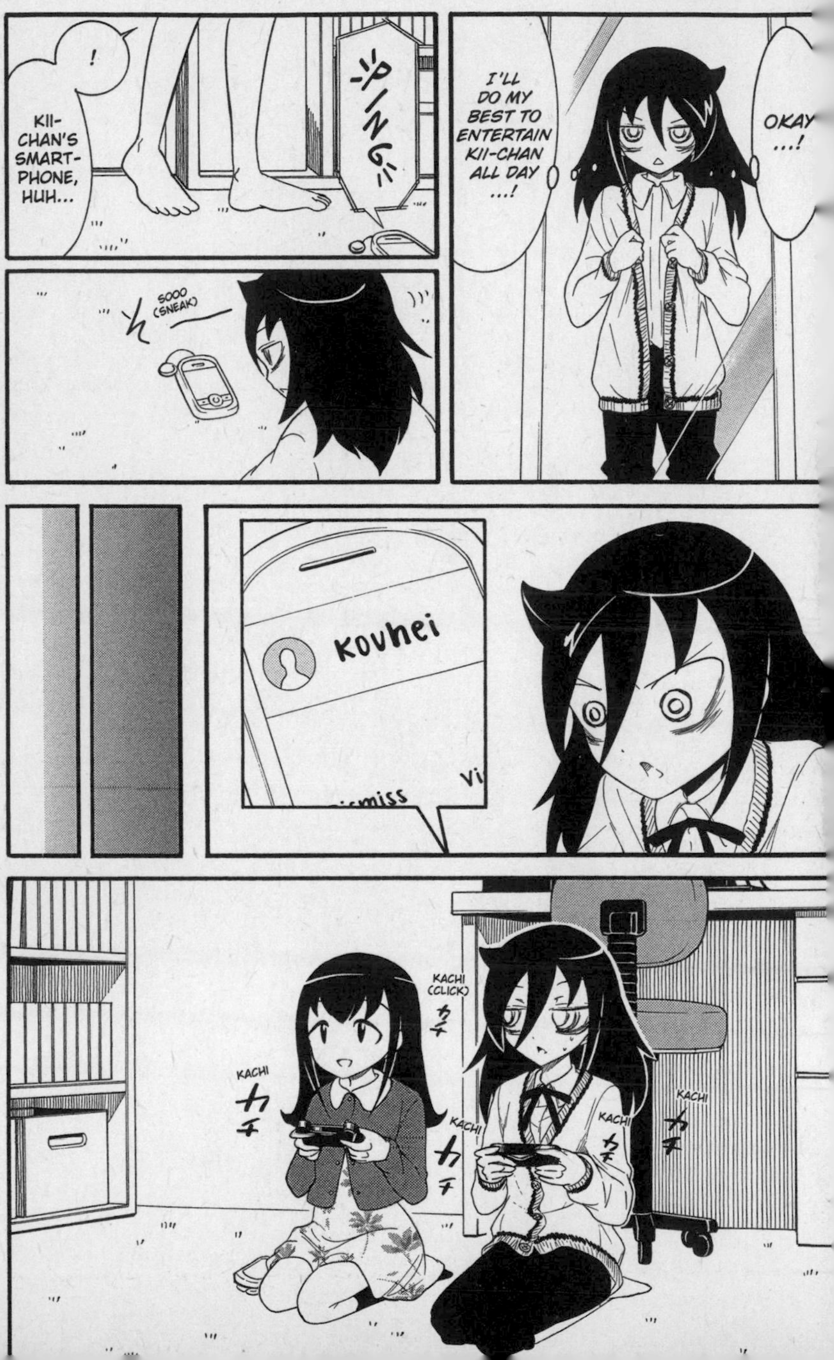
OKAY ...!
I'LL DO MY BEST TO ENTERTAIN KII-CHAN ALL DAY ...!
PING
!
KII-CHAN'S SMARTPHONE, HUH...
SOOO (SNEAK)
Kouhei
KACHI (CLICK)
KACHI
KACHI
KACHI
KACHI

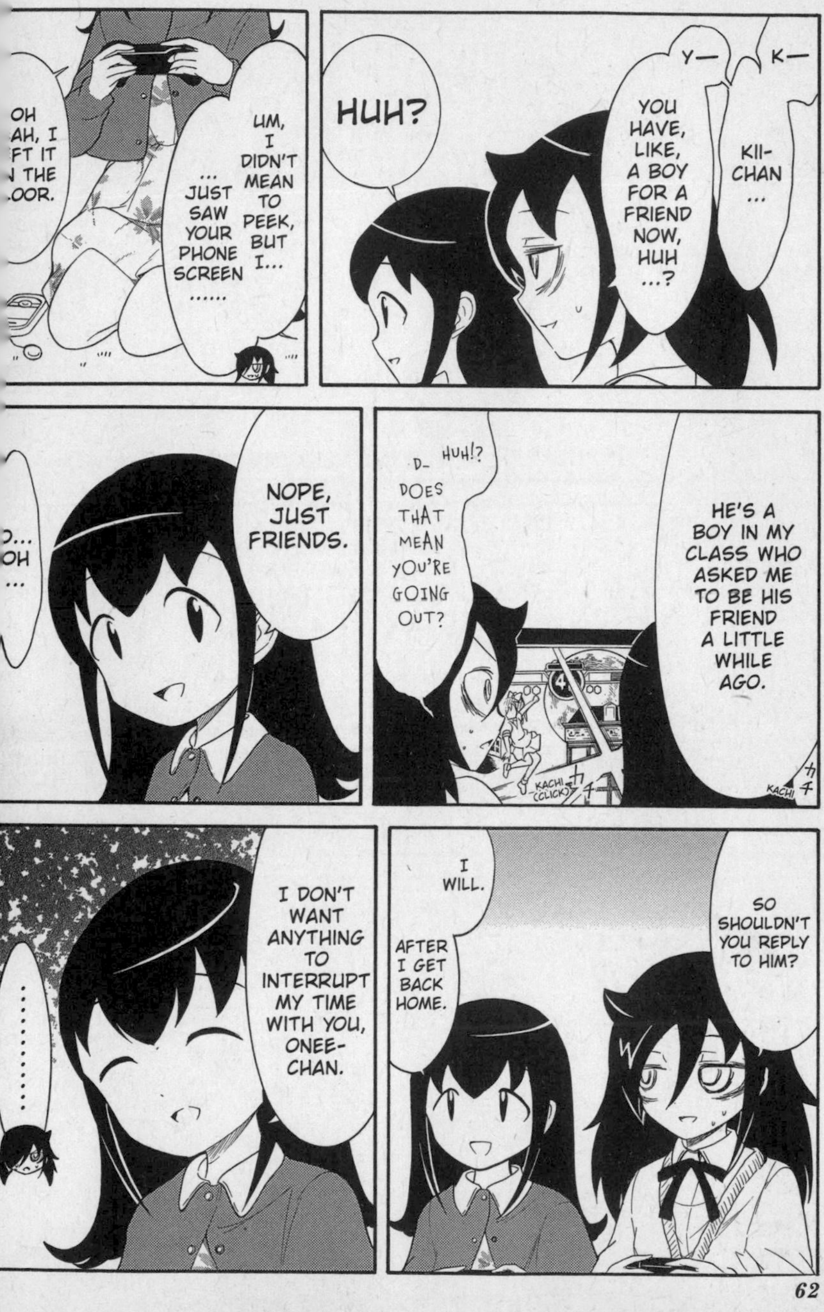
Y— K—
KII-CHAN ...
YOU HAVE, LIKE, A BOY FOR A FRIEND NOW, HUH ...?
HUH?
UM, I DIDN'T MEAN TO PEEK, BUT I...
... JUST SAW YOUR PHONE SCREEN ......
OH
AH, I
FT IT
N THE
OOR.
HE'S A BOY IN MY CLASS WHO ASKED ME TO BE HIS FRIEND A LITTLE WHILE AGO.
KACHI
HUH!?
D-DOES THAT MEAN YOU'RE GOING OUT?
KACHI (CLICK)
NOPE, JUST FRIENDS.
O... OH ...
SO SHOULDN'T YOU REPLY TO HIM?
I WILL.
AFTER I GET BACK HOME.
I DON'T WANT ANYTHING TO INTERRUPT MY TIME WITH YOU, ONEE-CHAN.
....

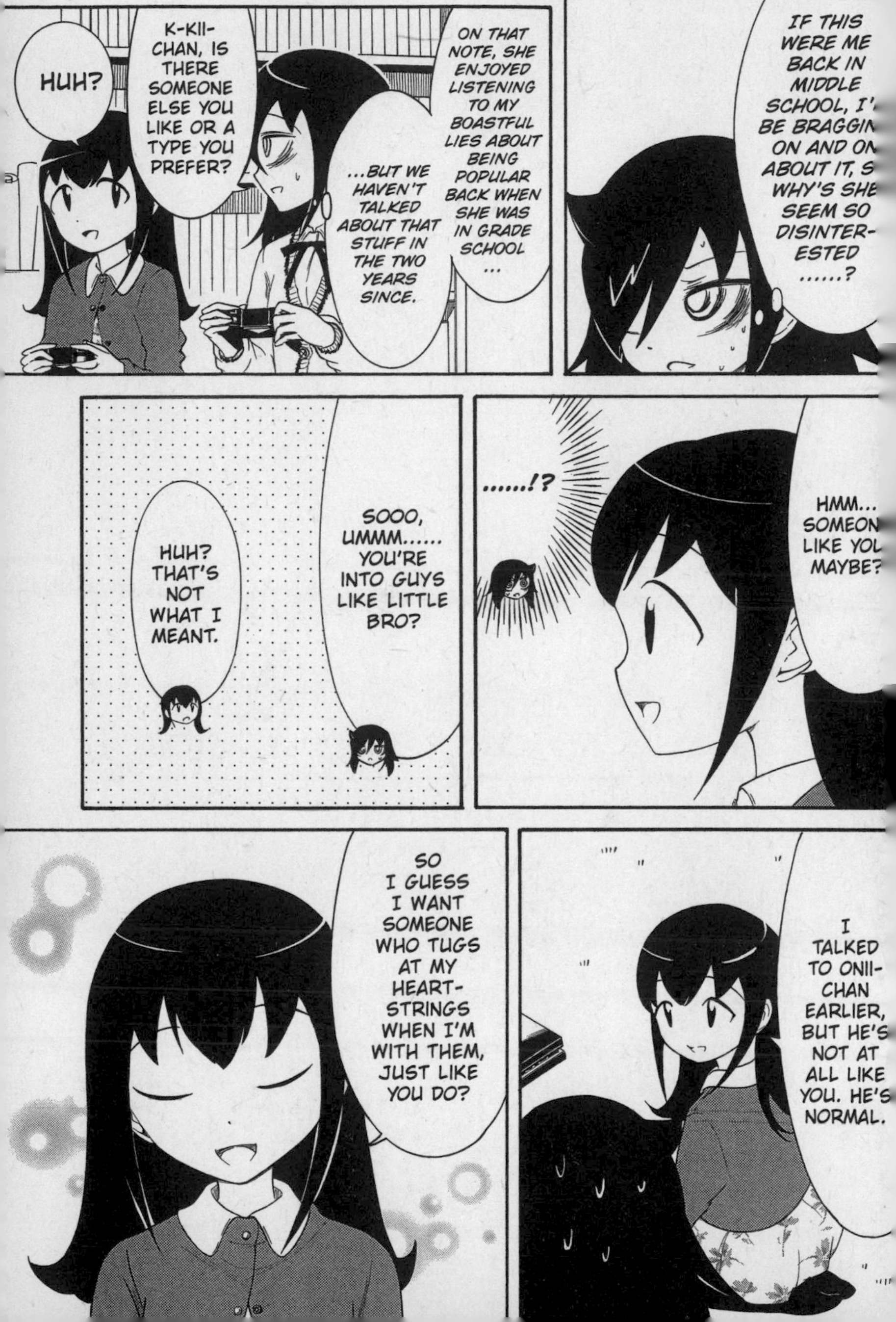
IF THIS WERE ME BACK IN MIDDLE SCHOOL, I'D BE BRAGGIN ON AND ON ABOUT IT, S WHY'S SHE SEEM SO DISINTER-ESTED ......?
ON THAT NOTE, SHE ENJOYED LISTENING TO MY BOASTFUL LIES ABOUT BEING POPULAR BACK WHEN SHE WAS IN GRADE SCHOOL ...
...BUT WE HAVEN'T TALKED ABOUT THAT STUFF IN THE TWO YEARS SINCE.
K-KII-CHAN, IS THERE SOMEONE ELSE YOU LIKE OR A TYPE YOU PREFER?
HUH?
HMM... SOMEON LIKE YOU MAYBE?
......!?
SOOO, UMMM...... YOU'RE INTO GUYS LIKE LITTLE BRO?
HUH? THAT'S NOT WHAT I MEANT.
I TALKED TO ONII-CHAN EARLIER, BUT HE'S NOT AT ALL LIKE YOU. HE'S NORMAL.
SO I GUESS I WANT SOMEONE WHO TUGS AT MY HEART-STRINGS WHEN I'M WITH THEM, JUST LIKE YOU DO?

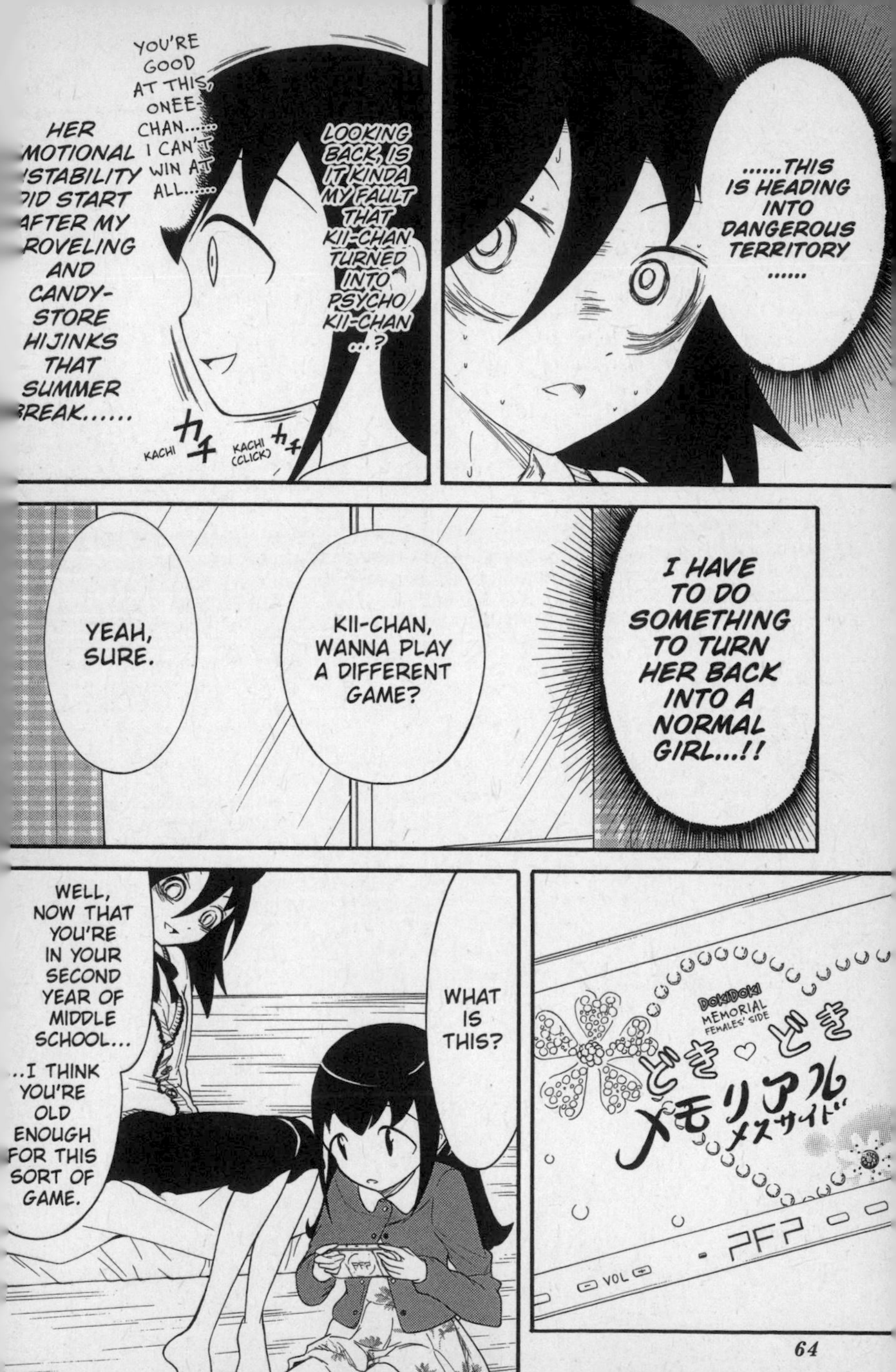
......THIS IS HEADING INTO DANGEROUS TERRITORY ......
LOOKING BACK, IS IT KINDA MY FAULT THAT KII-CHAN TURNED INTO PSYCHO KII-CHAN ...?
YOU'RE GOOD AT THIS, ONEE-CHAN...... I CAN'T WIN AT ALL......
HER MOTIONAL STABILITY DID START AFTER MY ROVELING AND CANDY-STORE HIJINKS THAT SUMMER BREAK......
カチ KACHI (CLICK)
カチ KACHI
I HAVE TO DO SOMETHING TO TURN HER BACK INTO A NORMAL GIRL...!!
KII-CHAN, WANNA PLAY A DIFFERENT GAME?
YEAH, SURE.
どき♡どき メモリアル メスサイド
DOKIDOKI MEMORIAL FEMALES' SIDE
PFP
VOL
WHAT IS THIS?
WELL, NOW THAT YOU'RE IN YOUR SECOND YEAR OF MIDDLE SCHOOL...
...I THINK YOU'RE OLD ENOUGH FOR THIS SORT OF GAME.

SEE, YOU SPEN[D] THREE YEA[RS] IN SCHOO[L] RAISING YO[UR] STATS IN STUFF LIK[E] ACADEMIC[S], STRENGT[H] AND CHAR[M]...

...AND GOING ON DATES WITH GUYS WHO APPEAR IN THE GAME.

HMM ......

Stress	10	Money	100
Academics	20	Arts	40
Athletics	20	Endurance	40
Fashion	20	Charm	40

Year 1, April 21 (Tues.)

AND IF IT DRAWS KII-CHAN TO THE GEEK SIDE TOO, SHE'LL BE EASIER TO MANAGE LATER!

FOR NOW, WE'LL GO THROUGH THE GAME TO GET KII-CHAN INTERESTED IN GUYS AGAIN.

'KAY.

WELL[,] JUST [?] PLAY [IT] THROU[GH] AND AS[K] ME IF THERE[?] ANYTHI[NG] YOU DO[N'T] GET.

KII-CHAN, HIGH SCHOOL FIRST-YEAR

...IT'D BE THE GAME'S FAULT INSTEAD OF MINE, SO THINGS WOULD BE BETTER THAN NOW!

EVEN IF SHE ENDS UP LIKE ME AS A RESULT...

YEAH, OKAY.

YOUR STATS ARE ALL ABOVE AVERAGE. WHY NOT TRY DATING SOMEONE NOW?

IT'S ALREADY BEEN HALF A YEAR IN THE GAME...

RAISING THE PARAMETERS FIRS[T] HUH...... AVERAGIN[G] EVERYTHIN[G] OUT...... SHE'S TH[E] BALANCED TYPE......

PIRON (CHIME)

ピロン ピロン

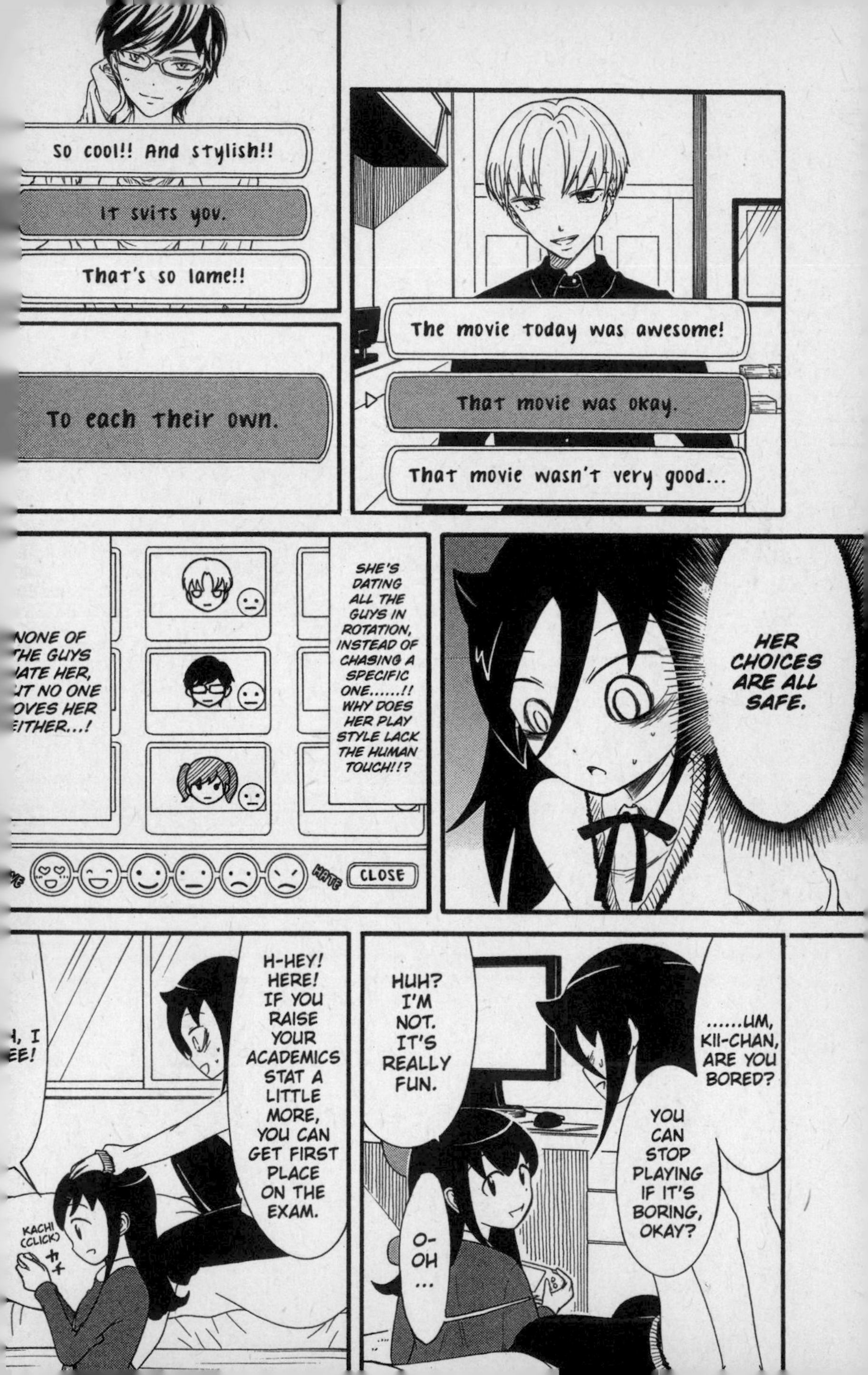
The movie today was awesome!
That movie was okay.
That movie wasn't very good...
So cool!! And stylish!!
It suits you.
That's so lame!!
To each their own.
HER CHOICES ARE ALL SAFE.
SHE'S DATING ALL THE GUYS IN ROTATION, INSTEAD OF CHASING A SPECIFIC ONE......!! WHY DOES HER PLAY STYLE LACK THE HUMAN TOUCH!!?
NONE OF THE GUYS ATE HER, UT NO ONE OVES HER EITHER...!
HATE
CLOSE
......UM, KII-CHAN, ARE YOU BORED?
YOU CAN STOP PLAYING IF IT'S BORING, OKAY?
HUH? I'M NOT. IT'S REALLY FUN.
O-OH...
H-HEY! HERE! IF YOU RAISE YOUR ACADEMICS STAT A LITTLE MORE, YOU CAN GET FIRST PLACE ON THE EXAM.
KACHI (CLICK)

THEN I'LL BE FINE NOT DOING ANYTHING ELSE.

HUH......?

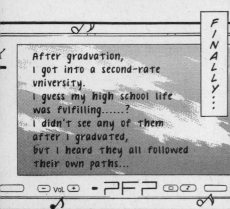

FINALLY...

After graduation, I got into a second-rate university.
I guess my high school life was fulfilling......?
I didn't see any of them after I graduated, but I heard they all followed their own paths...

VOL. ⊖ ⊕ ♪PFP ⊡ ⋯⃝

I BEAT THE GAME, ONEE-CHAN

Y-YEAH. BUT THE GAME'S S'POSED TO BE ABOUT DATING, NOT GRADUATING HIGH SCHOOL.

I WAS HOPING THE GAME WOULD LET ME GET A GLIMPSE INSIDE KII-CHAN, BUT...

...ALL I CAN SEE IS DARK-NESS...

WHAT WOULD BE A GOOD ROMANCE GAME TO HOOK HER?

OH, ONII-CHAN'S BACK.

SLIDE

SHUT

HEY, KII-CHAN. YOU LOVE DOGS, RIGHT?

YUP! I LIKE ANIMALS IN GENERAL.

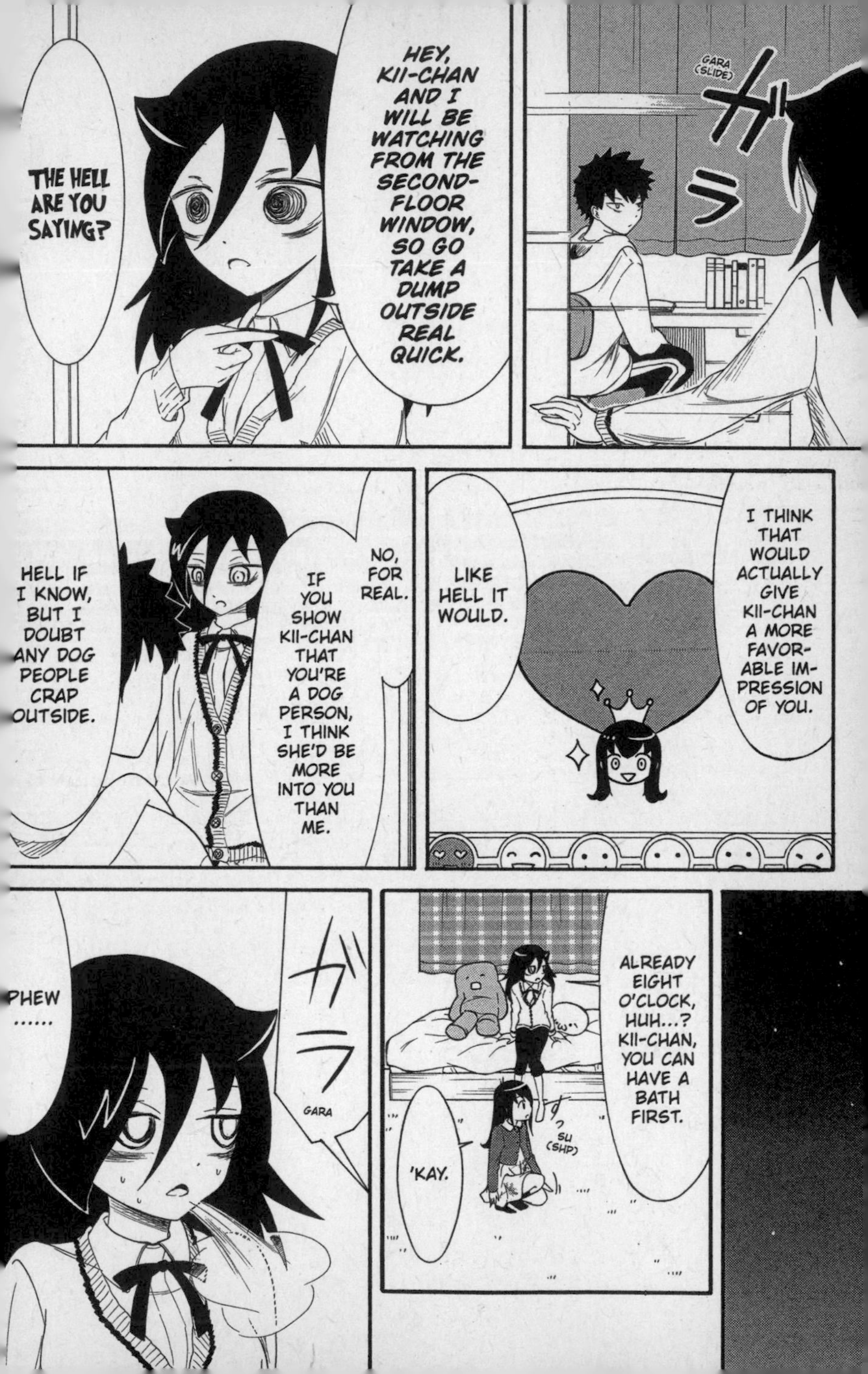
ガラ
GARA (SLIDE)
HEY, KII-CHAN AND I WILL BE WATCHING FROM THE SECOND-FLOOR WINDOW, SO GO TAKE A DUMP OUTSIDE REAL QUICK.
THE HELL ARE YOU SAYING?
I THINK THAT WOULD ACTUALLY GIVE KII-CHAN A MORE FAVOR-ABLE IM-PRESSION OF YOU.
LIKE HELL IT WOULD.
NO, FOR REAL.
IF YOU SHOW KII-CHAN THAT YOU'RE A DOG PERSON, I THINK SHE'D BE MORE INTO YOU THAN ME.
HELL IF I KNOW, BUT I DOUBT ANY DOG PEOPLE CRAP OUTSIDE.
ALREADY EIGHT O'CLOCK, HUH...? KII-CHAN, YOU CAN HAVE A BATH FIRST.
SU (SHP)
'KAY.
ガラ
GARA
PHEW ......

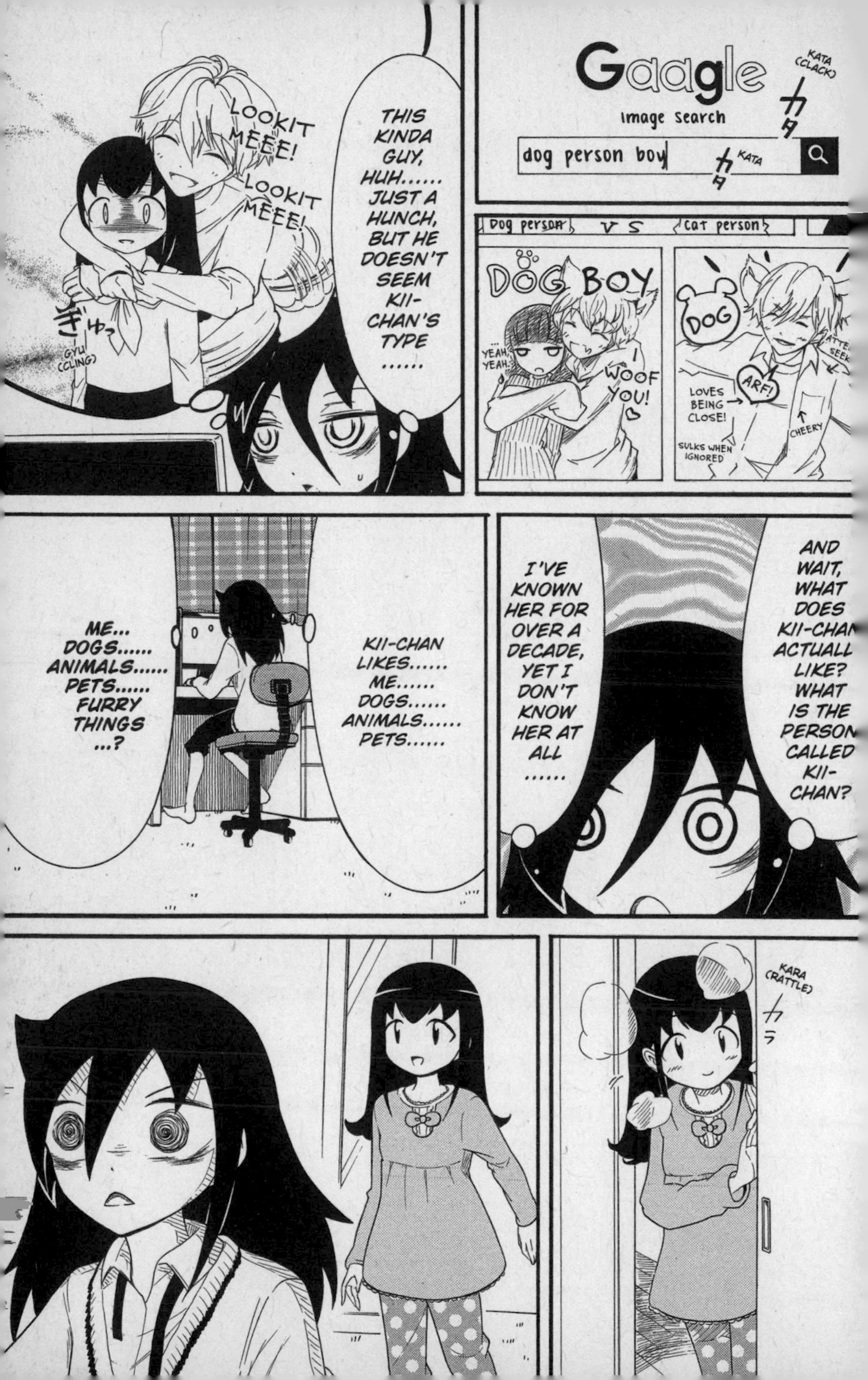

Gaagle
image search
dog person boy
KATA (CLACK)
KATA
Dog person VS cat person
ARF!
DOG
LOVES BEING CLOSE!
CHEERY
SULKS WHEN IGNORED
DOG BOY
... YEAH, YEAH.
I WOOF YOU!
THIS KINDA GUY, HUH...... JUST A HUNCH, BUT HE DOESN'T SEEM KII-CHAN'S TYPE ......
LOOKIT MEEE!
LOOKIT MEEE!
GYU (CLING)
AND WAIT, WHAT DOES KII-CHAN ACTUALLY LIKE? WHAT IS THE PERSON CALLED KII-CHAN?
I'VE KNOWN HER FOR OVER A DECADE, YET I DON'T KNOW HER AT ALL ......
KII-CHAN LIKES...... ME...... DOGS...... ANIMALS...... PETS......
ME... DOGS...... ANIMALS...... PETS...... FURRY THINGS ...?
KARA (RATTLE)

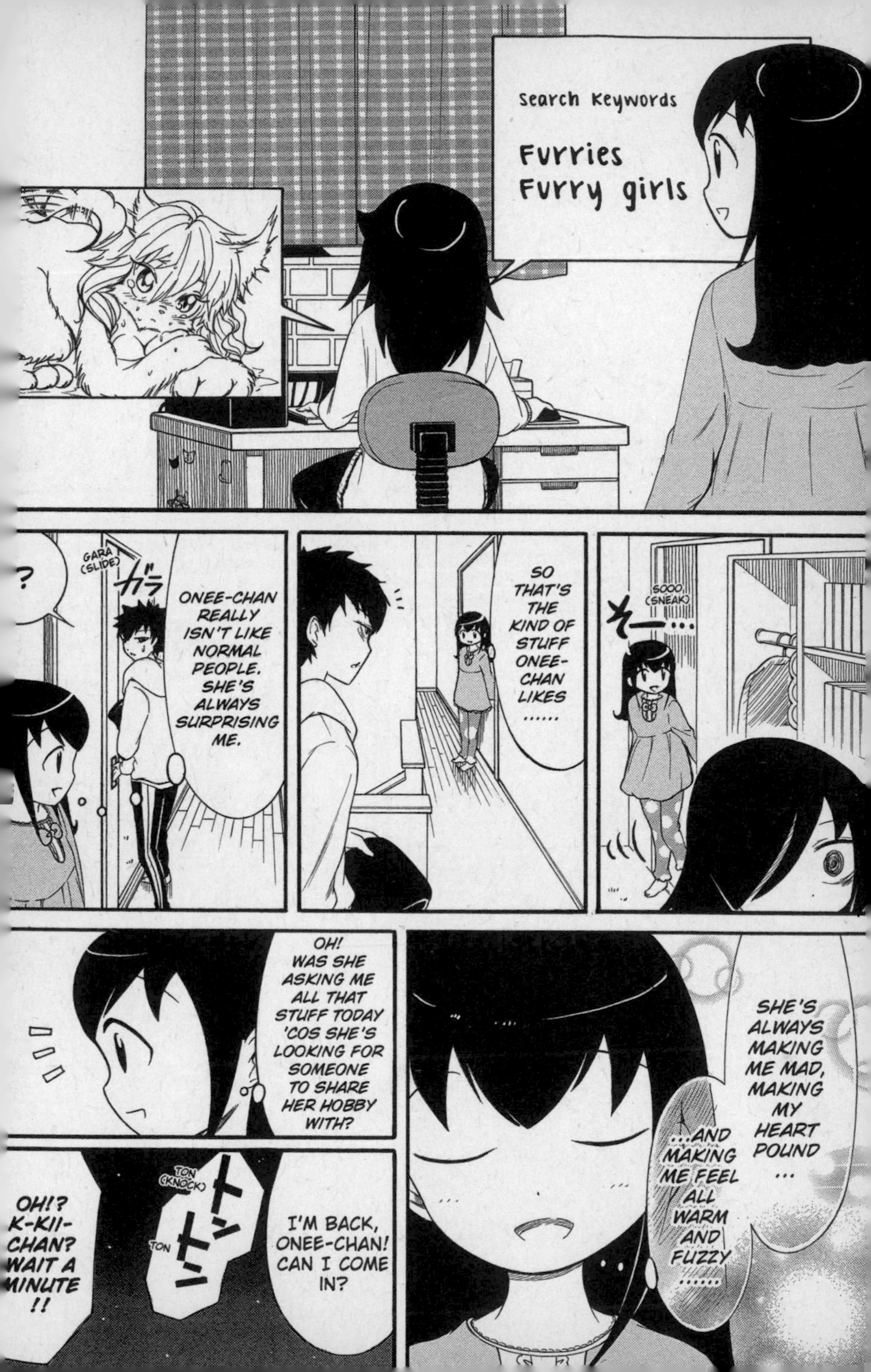
Search Keywords
Furries
Furry girls
SOOO (SNEAK)
そー…
SO THAT'S THE KIND OF STUFF ONEE-CHAN LIKES ......
?
GARA (SLIDE)
ガラ
ONEE-CHAN REALLY ISN'T LIKE NORMAL PEOPLE. SHE'S ALWAYS SURPRISING ME.
SHE'S ALWAYS MAKING ME MAD, MAKING MY HEART POUND ...
...AND MAKING ME FEEL ALL WARM AND FUZZY ......
OH! WAS SHE ASKING ME ALL THAT STUFF TODAY 'COS SHE'S LOOKING FOR SOMEONE TO SHARE HER HOBBY WITH?
TON (KNOCK)
トン
TON
トン
I'M BACK, ONEE-CHAN! CAN I COME IN?
OH!? K-KII-CHAN? WAIT A MINUTE !!

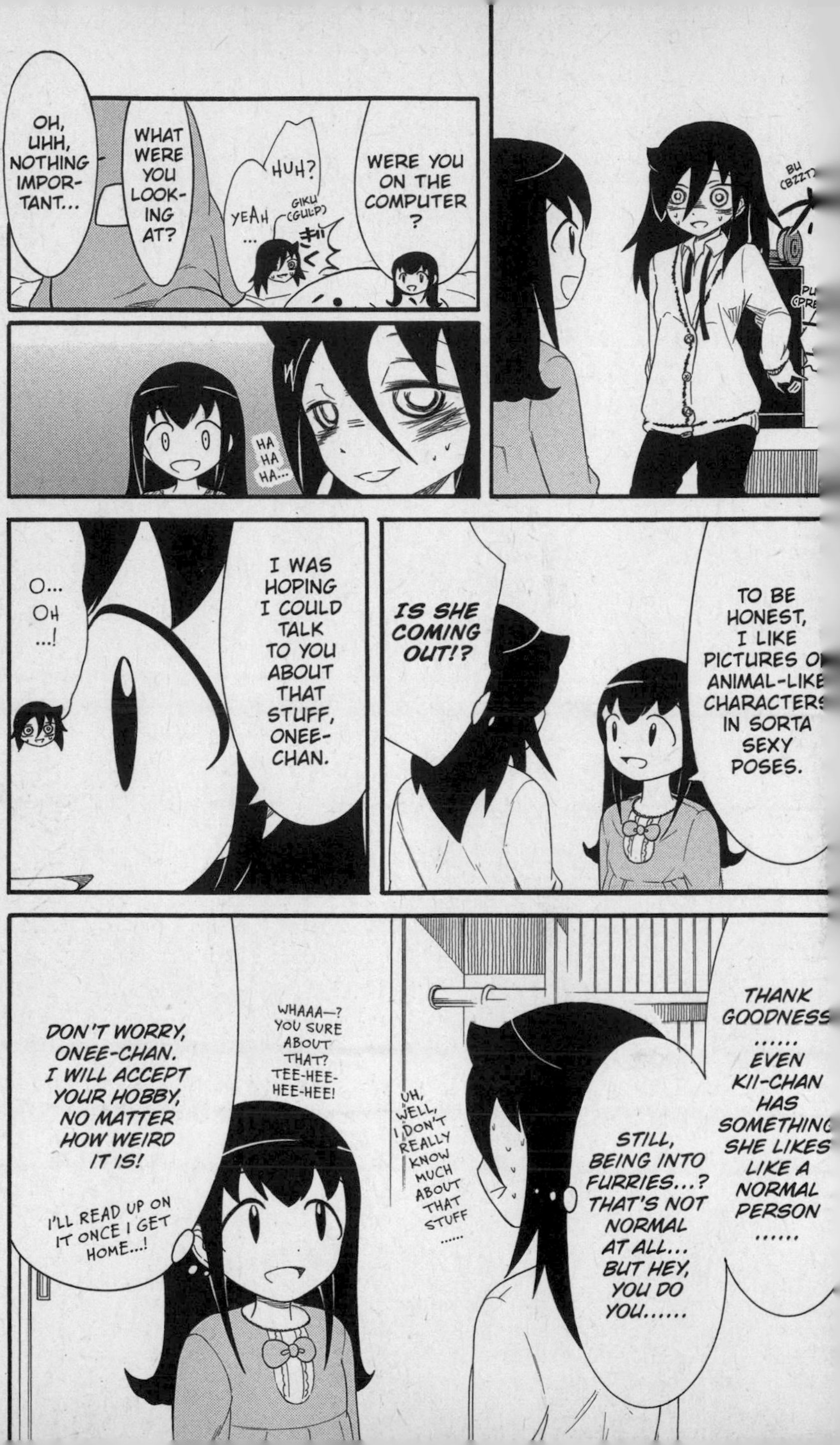
BU (BZZT)
WERE YOU ON THE COMPUTER?
HUH?
GIKU (GULP)
YEAH ...
WHAT WERE YOU LOOKING AT?
OH, UHH, NOTHING IMPORTANT...
HA HA HA...
TO BE HONEST, I LIKE PICTURES OF ANIMAL-LIKE CHARACTERS IN SORTA SEXY POSES.
IS SHE COMING OUT!?
I WAS HOPING I COULD TALK TO YOU ABOUT THAT STUFF, ONEE-CHAN.
O... OH ...!
THANK GOODNESS ...... EVEN KII-CHAN HAS SOMETHING SHE LIKES LIKE A NORMAL PERSON ......
STILL, BEING INTO FURRIES...? THAT'S NOT NORMAL AT ALL... BUT HEY, YOU DO YOU......
UH, WELL, I DON'T REALLY KNOW MUCH ABOUT THAT STUFF ......
WHAAA—? YOU SURE ABOUT THAT? TEE-HEE-HEE-HEE!
DON'T WORRY, ONEE-CHAN. I WILL ACCEPT YOUR HOBBY, NO MATTER HOW WEIRD IT IS!
I'LL READ UP ON IT ONCE I GET HOME...!

No Matter How I Look at It, It's You Guys' Fault I'm Not Popular!

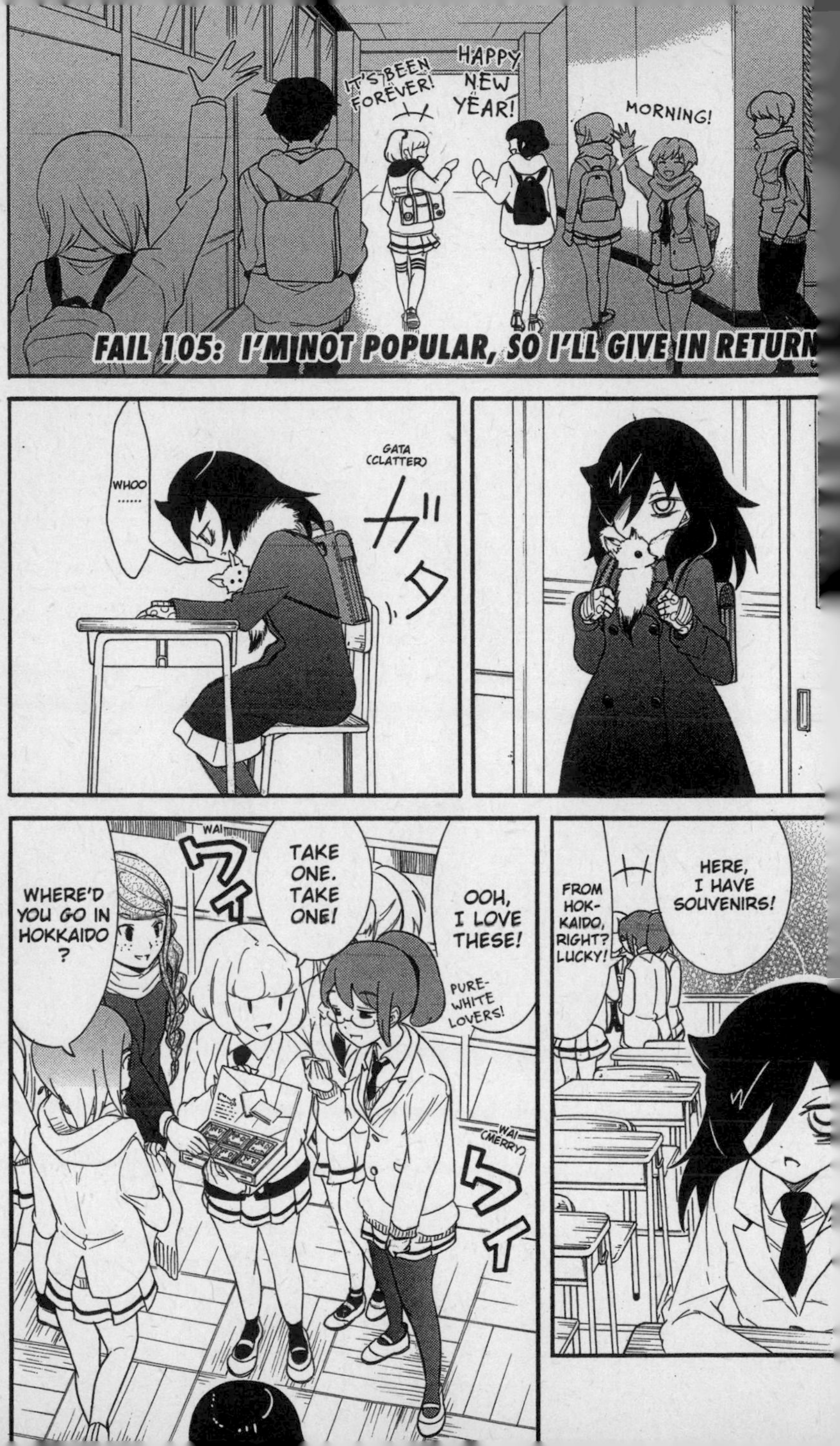
MORNING!
HAPPY NEW YEAR!
IT'S BEEN FOREVER!
FAIL 105: I'M NOT POPULAR, SO I'LL GIVE IN RETURN
GATA (CLATTER)
ガタ
WHOO ......
HERE, I HAVE SOUVENIRS!
FROM HOK-KAIDO, RIGHT? LUCKY!
OOH, I LOVE THESE!
PURE-WHITE LOVERS!
WAI (MERRY)
ワイ
TAKE ONE. TAKE ONE!
WAI
ワイ
WHERE'D YOU GO IN HOKKAIDO?

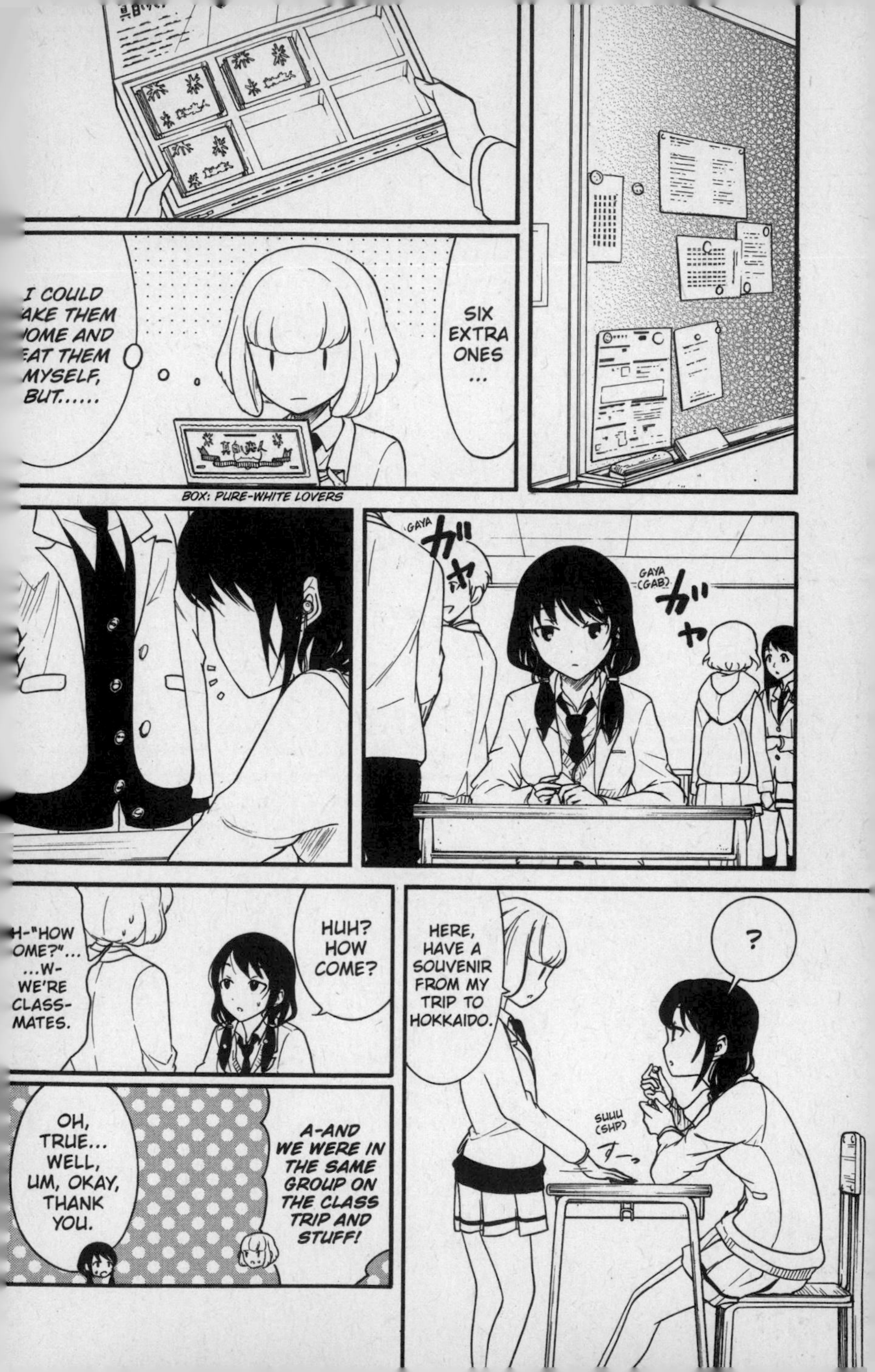
SIX EXTRA ONES ...
I COULD AKE THEM OME AND EAT THEM MYSELF, BUT......
BOX: PURE-WHITE LOVERS
GAYA
GAYA (GAB)
?
HERE, HAVE A SOUVENIR FROM MY TRIP TO HOKKAIDO.
SUUU (SHP)
HUH? HOW COME?
H-"HOW OME?"... ...W-WE'RE CLASS-MATES.
A-AND WE WERE IN THE SAME GROUP ON THE CLASS TRIP AND STUFF!
OH, TRUE... WELL, UM, OKAY, THANK YOU.

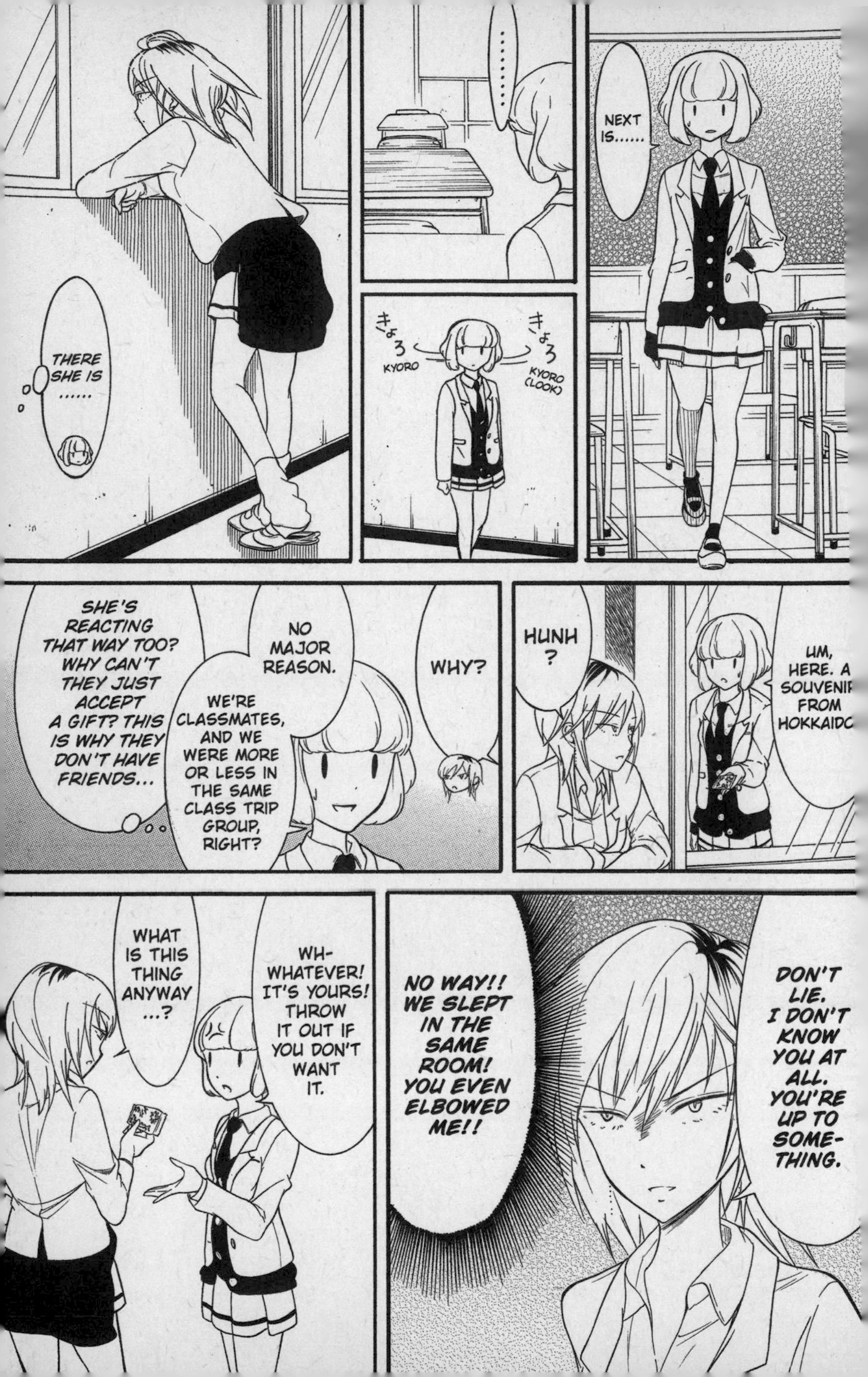
NEXT IS......
......
きょろ KYORO (LOOK)
きょろ KYORO
THERE SHE IS ......
UM, HERE. A SOUVENIR FROM HOKKAIDO
HUNH ?
WHY?
NO MAJOR REASON.
WE'RE CLASSMATES, AND WE WERE MORE OR LESS IN THE SAME CLASS TRIP GROUP, RIGHT?
SHE'S REACTING THAT WAY TOO? WHY CAN'T THEY JUST ACCEPT A GIFT? THIS IS WHY THEY DON'T HAVE FRIENDS...
DON'T LIE. I DON'T KNOW YOU AT ALL. YOU'RE UP TO SOME-THING.
NO WAY!! WE SLEPT IN THE SAME ROOM! YOU EVEN ELBOWED ME!!
WHAT IS THIS THING ANYWAY ...?
WH- WHATEVER! IT'S YOURS! THROW IT OUT IF YOU DON'T WANT IT.

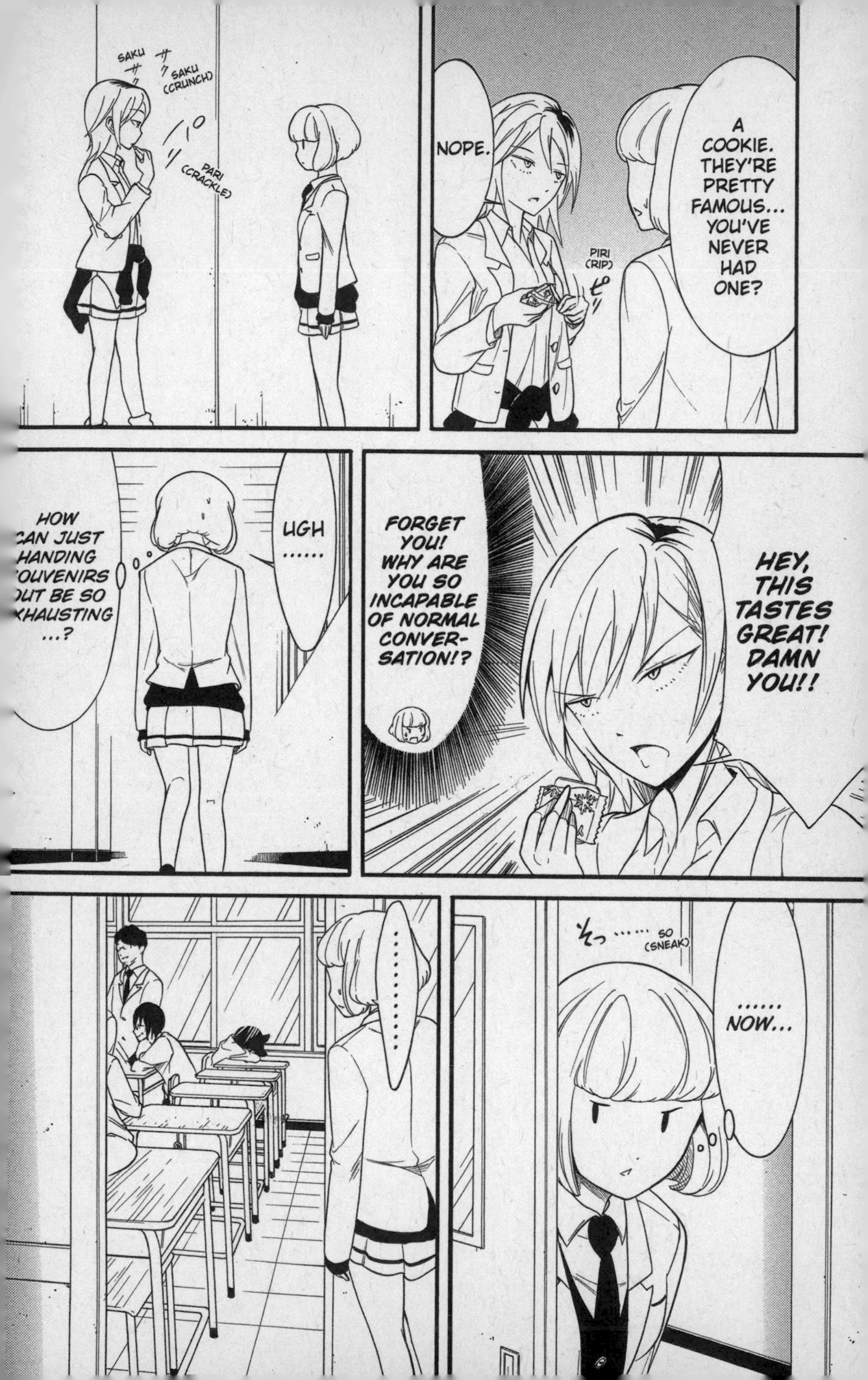
A COOKIE. THEY'RE PRETTY FAMOUS... YOU'VE NEVER HAD ONE?
NOPE.
PIRI (RIP)
SAKU
SAKU (CRUNCH)
PARI (CRACKLE)
HEY, THIS TASTES GREAT! DAMN YOU!!
FORGET YOU! WHY ARE YOU SO INCAPABLE OF NORMAL CONVER-SATION!?
UGH ......
HOW CAN JUST HANDING OUVENIRS UT BE SO XHAUSTING ...?
...... SO (SNEAK)
...... NOW...
......

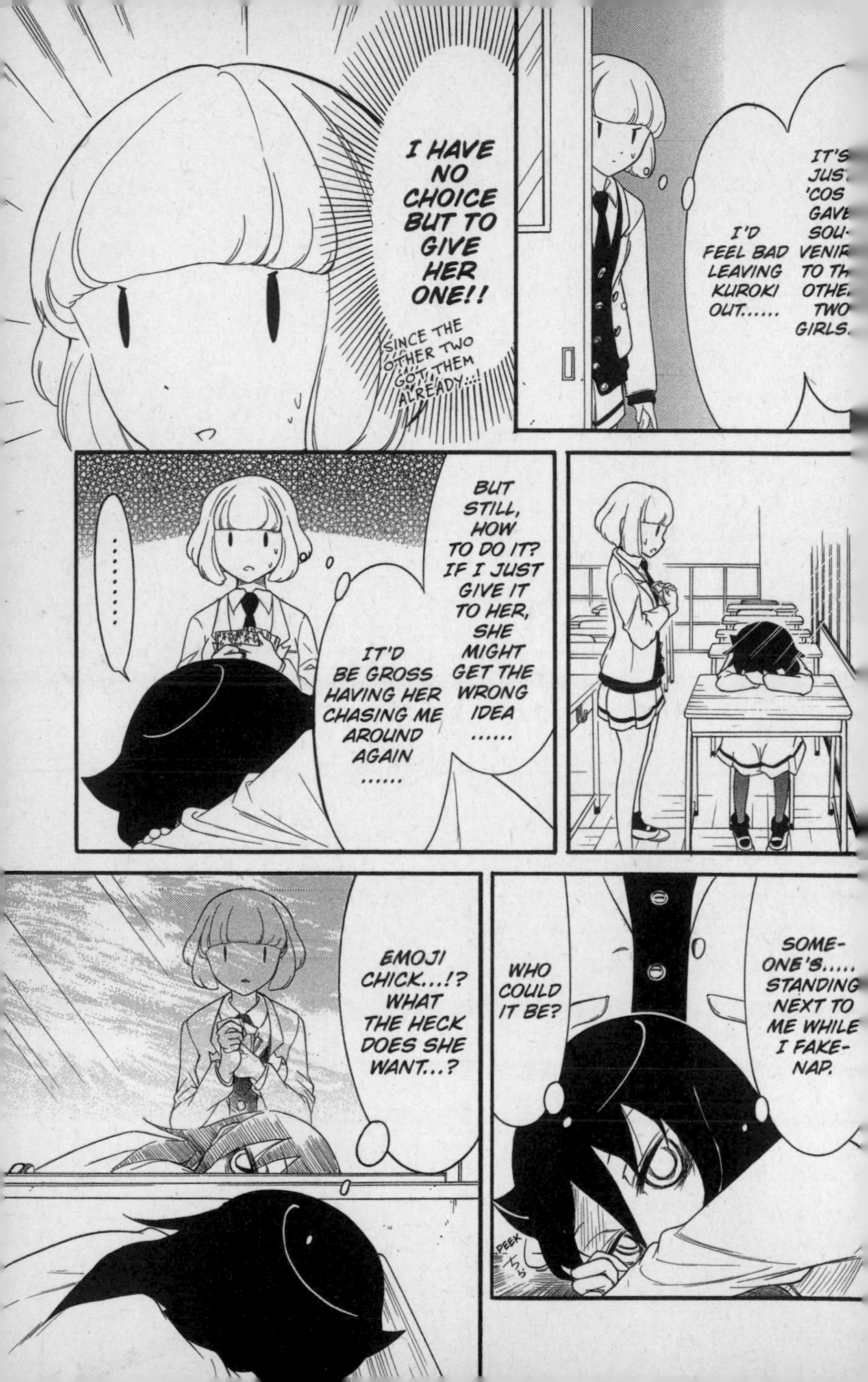
IT'S JUS 'COS GAVE SOU- VENIR TO TH OTHE TWO GIRLS.
I'D FEEL BAD LEAVING KUROKI OUT......
I HAVE NO CHOICE BUT TO GIVE HER ONE!!
SINCE THE OTHER TWO GOT THEM ALREADY...!
BUT STILL, HOW TO DO IT? IF I JUST GIVE IT TO HER, SHE MIGHT GET THE WRONG IDEA......
IT'D BE GROSS HAVING HER CHASING ME AROUND AGAIN......
......
SOME-ONE'S..... STANDING NEXT TO ME WHILE I FAKE-NAP.
WHO COULD IT BE?
PEEK
EMOJI CHICK...!? WHAT THE HECK DOES SHE WANT...?

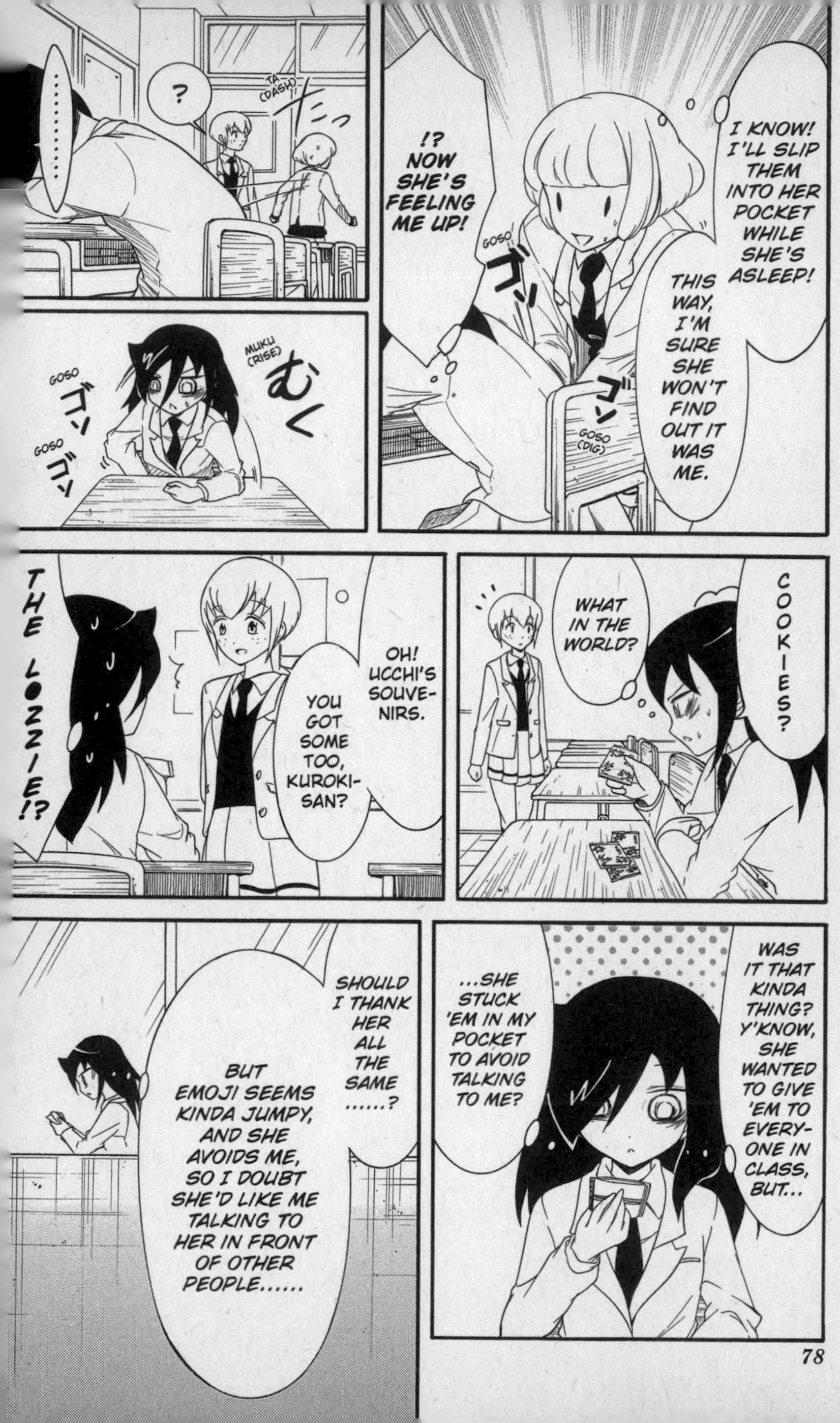
I KNOW! I'LL SLIP THEM INTO HER POCKET WHILE SHE'S ASLEEP!
THIS WAY, I'M SURE SHE WON'T FIND OUT IT WAS ME.
GOSO
!? NOW SHE'S FEELING ME UP!
GOSO (DIG)
?
TA (DASH)
......
MUKU (RISE)
GOSO
GOSO
COOKIES?
WHAT IN THE WORLD?
OH! UCCHI'S SOUVENIRS.
YOU GOT SOME TOO, KUROKI-SAN?
THE LOZZIE!?
WAS IT THAT KINDA THING? Y'KNOW, SHE WANTED TO GIVE 'EM TO EVERYONE IN CLASS, BUT...
...SHE STUCK 'EM IN MY POCKET TO AVOID TALKING TO ME?
SHOULD I THANK HER ALL THE SAME ......?
BUT EMOJI SEEMS KINDA JUMPY, AND SHE AVOIDS ME, SO I DOUBT SHE'D LIKE ME TALKING TO HER IN FRONT OF OTHER PEOPLE......

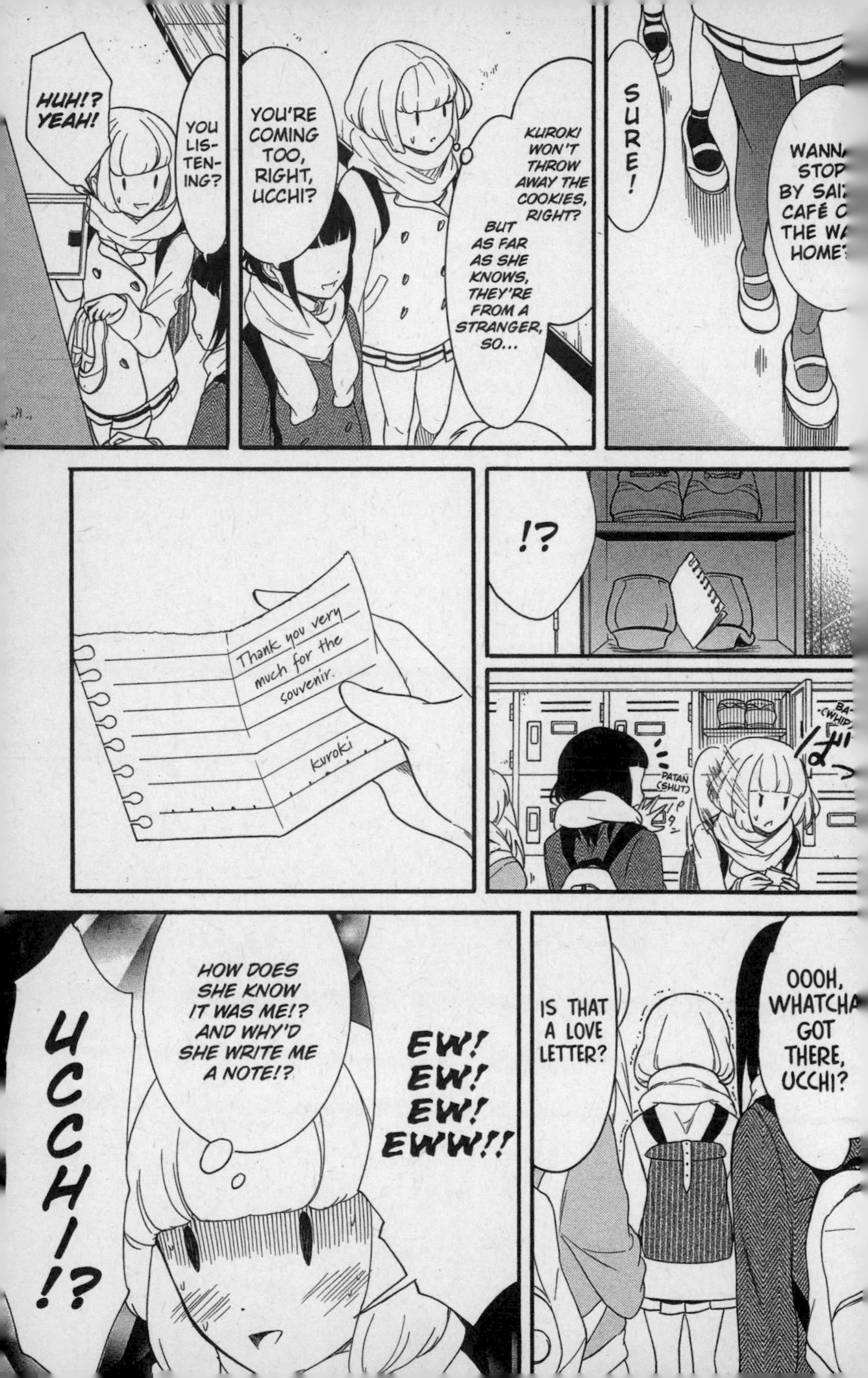
WANNA STOP BY SAI CAFÉ O THE WA HOME?
SURE!
KUROKI WON'T THROW AWAY THE COOKIES, RIGHT?
BUT AS FAR AS SHE KNOWS, THEY'RE FROM A STRANGER, SO...
YOU'RE COMING TOO, RIGHT, UCCHI?
YOU LISTENING?
HUH!? YEAH!
!?
BA- (WHIP)
PATAN (SHUT)
Thank you very much for the souvenir.
kuroki
OOOH, WHATCHA GOT THERE, UCCHI?
IS THAT A LOVE LETTER?
HOW DOES SHE KNOW IT WAS ME!? AND WHY'D SHE WRITE ME A NOTE!?
EW! EW! EW! EWW!!
UCCHI!?

No Matter How I Look at It, It's You Guys' Fault I'm Not Popular!

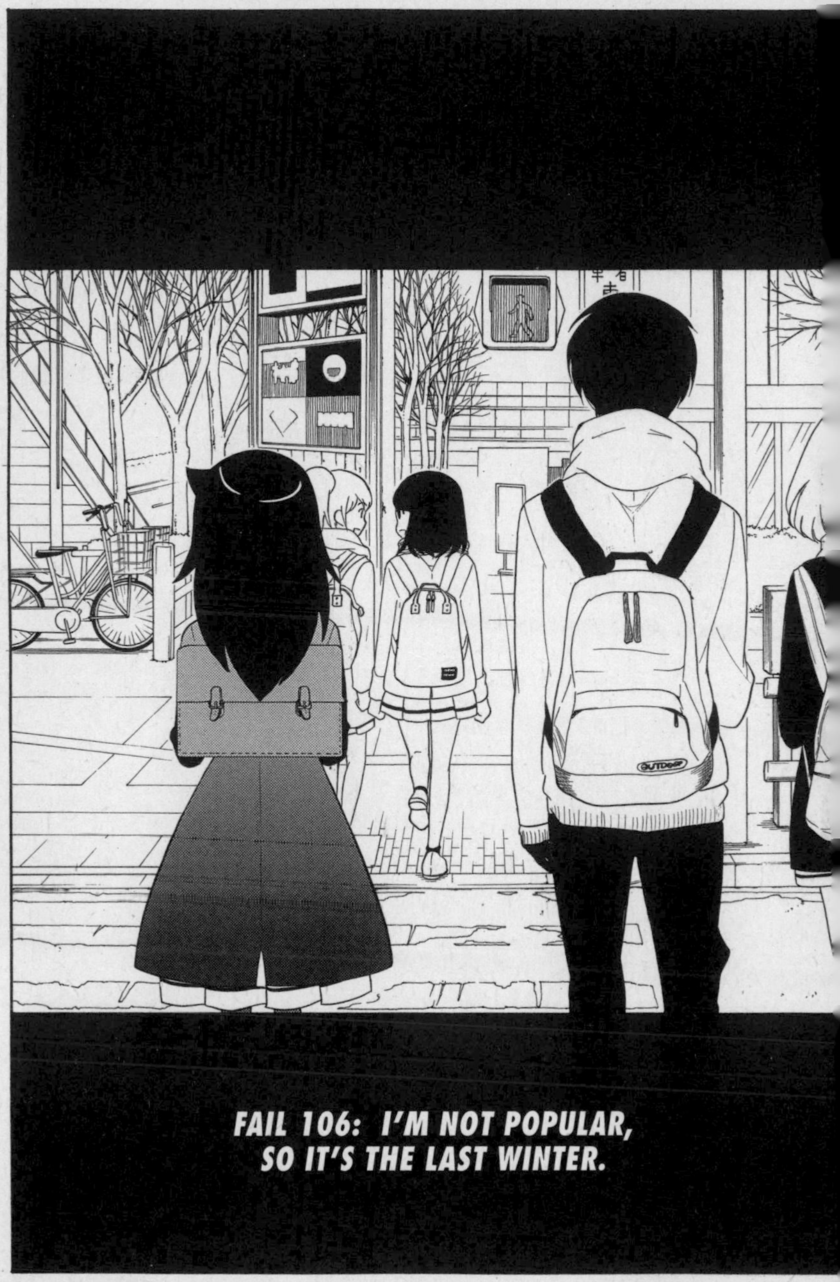
FAIL 106: I'M NOT POPULAR, SO IT'S THE LAST WINTER.

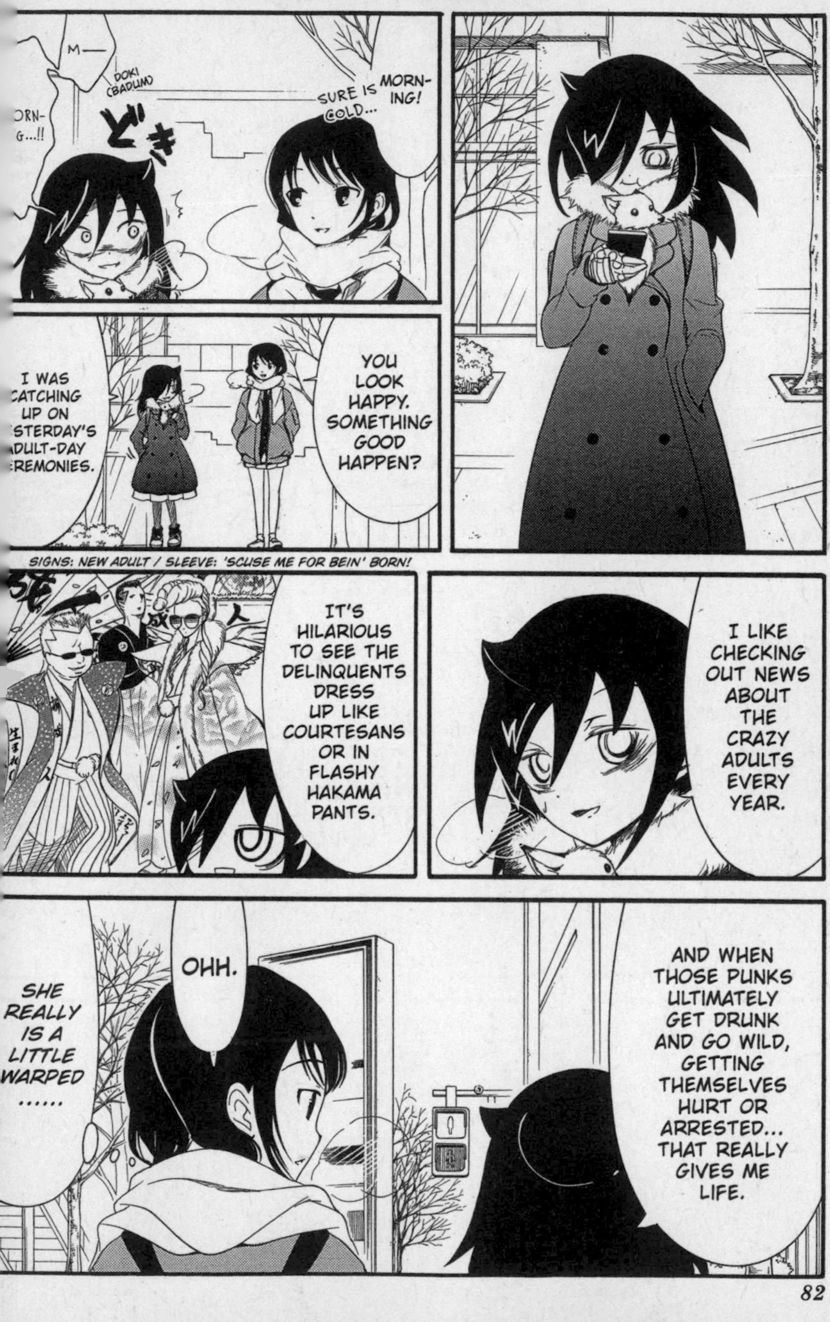
MORN-ING!
SURE IS COLD...
DOKI (BADUM)
M—
ORN-G...!!
YOU LOOK HAPPY. SOMETHING GOOD HAPPEN?
I WAS CATCHING UP ON STERDAY'S ADULT-DAY EREMONIES.
SIGNS: NEW ADULT / SLEEVE: 'SCUSE ME FOR BEIN' BORN!
I LIKE CHECKING OUT NEWS ABOUT THE CRAZY ADULTS EVERY YEAR.
IT'S HILARIOUS TO SEE THE DELINQUENTS DRESS UP LIKE COURTESANS OR IN FLASHY HAKAMA PANTS.
AND WHEN THOSE PUNKS ULTIMATELY GET DRUNK AND GO WILD, GETTING THEMSELVES HURT OR ARRESTED... THAT REALLY GIVES ME LIFE.
OHH.
SHE REALLY IS A LITTLE WARPED ......

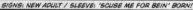

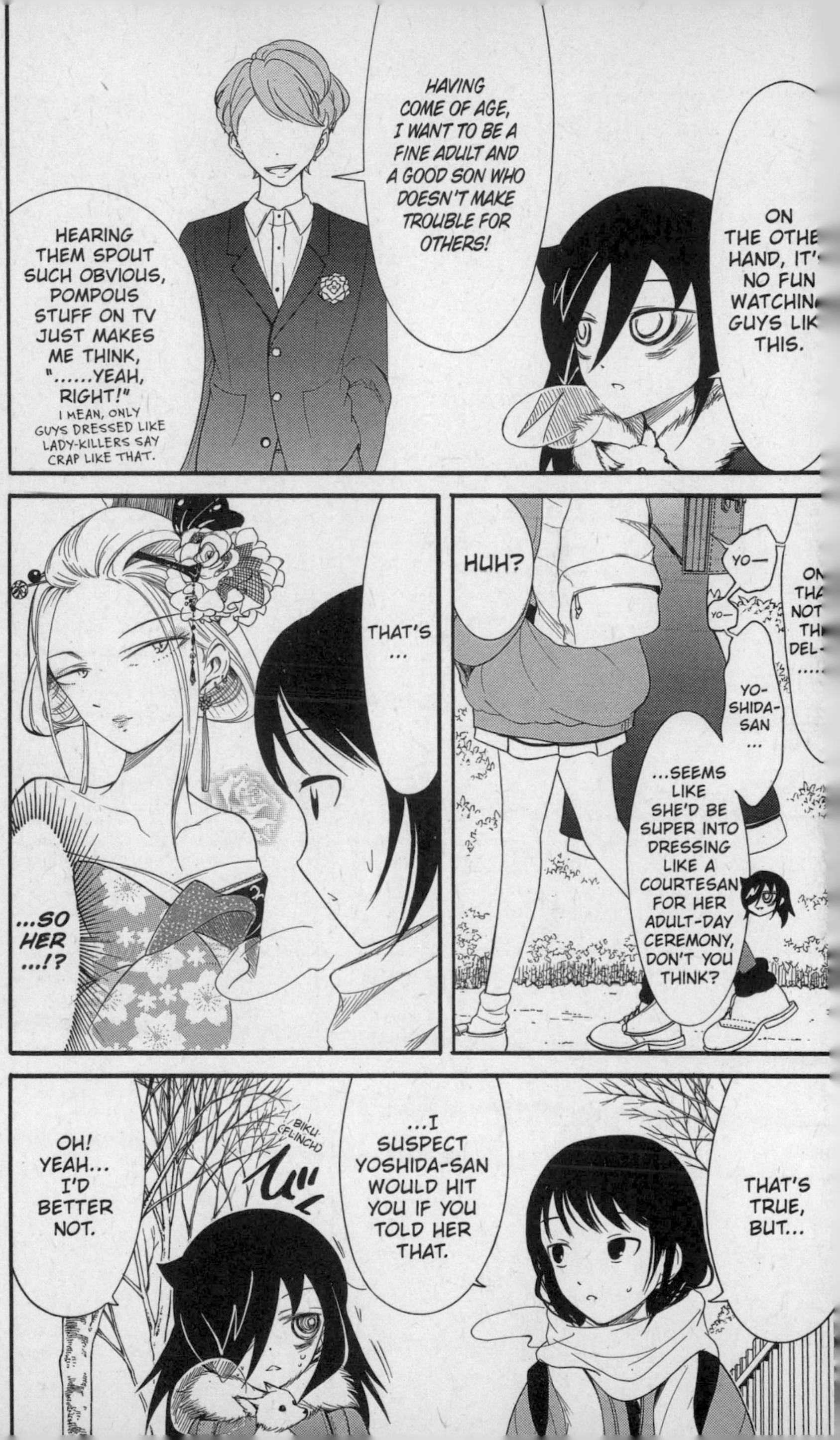
ON THE OTHE HAND, IT'S NO FUN WATCHIN GUYS LIK THIS.
HAVING COME OF AGE, I WANT TO BE A FINE ADULT AND A GOOD SON WHO DOESN'T MAKE TROUBLE FOR OTHERS!
HEARING THEM SPOUT SUCH OBVIOUS, POMPOUS STUFF ON TV JUST MAKES ME THINK, "......YEAH, RIGHT!"
I MEAN, ONLY GUYS DRESSED LIKE LADY-KILLERS SAY CRAP LIKE THAT.
ON THA NOT TH DEL-....
YO—
YO—
HUH?
YO-SHIDA-SAN...
...SEEMS LIKE SHE'D BE SUPER INTO DRESSING LIKE A COURTESAN FOR HER ADULT-DAY CEREMONY, DON'T YOU THINK?
THAT'S...
...SO HER ...!?
THAT'S TRUE, BUT...
...I SUSPECT YOSHIDA-SAN WOULD HIT YOU IF YOU TOLD HER THAT.
BIKU (FLINCH)
OH! YEAH... I'D BETTER NOT.

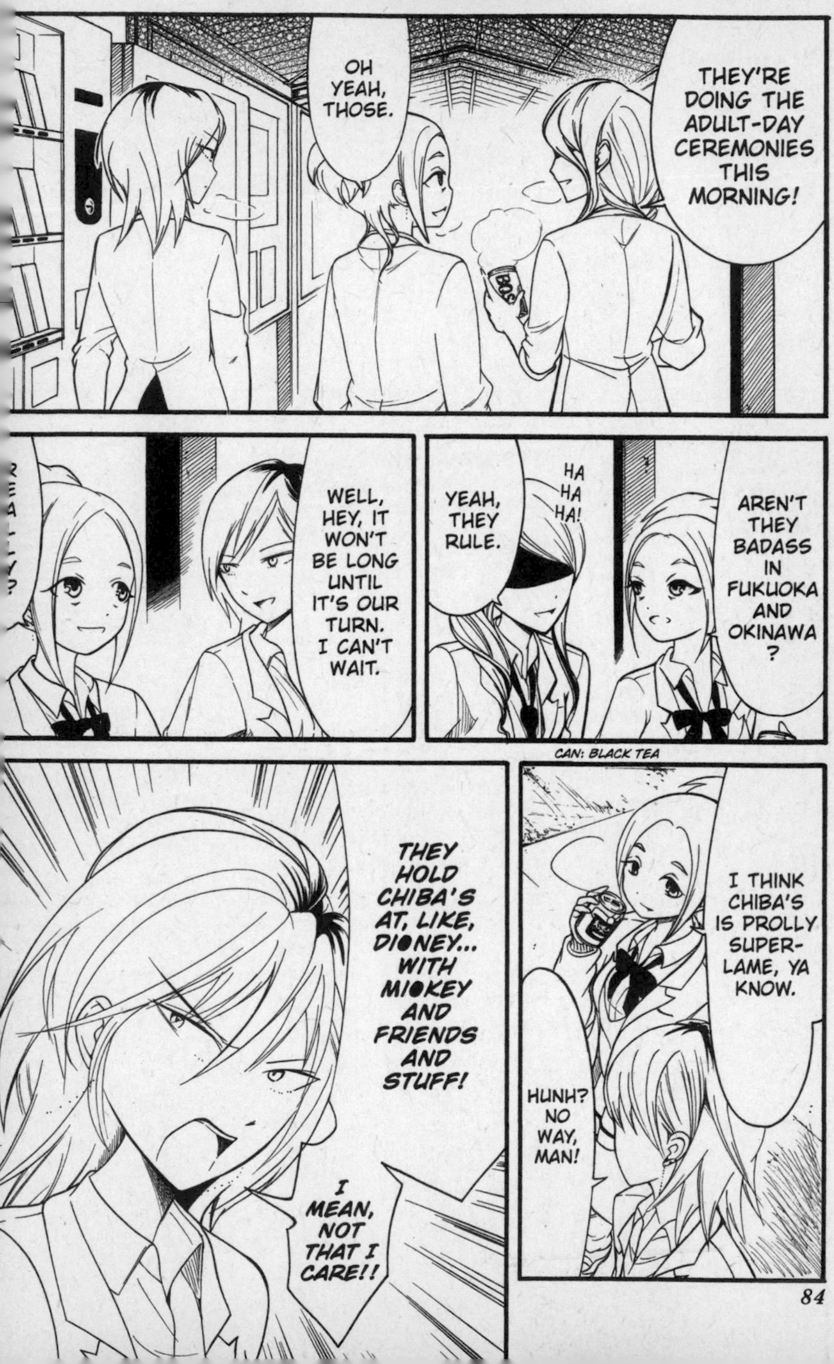
THEY'RE DOING THE ADULT-DAY CEREMONIES THIS MORNING!
OH YEAH, THOSE.
AREN'T THEY BADASS IN FUKUOKA AND OKINAWA?
HA HA HA!
YEAH, THEY RULE.
WELL, HEY, IT WON'T BE LONG UNTIL IT'S OUR TURN. I CAN'T WAIT.
CAN: BLACK TEA
I THINK CHIBA'S IS PROLLY SUPER-LAME, YA KNOW.
HUNH? NO WAY, MAN!
THEY HOLD CHIBA'S AT, LIKE, DIONEY... WITH MIOKEY AND FRIENDS AND STUFF!
I MEAN, NOT THAT I CARE!!

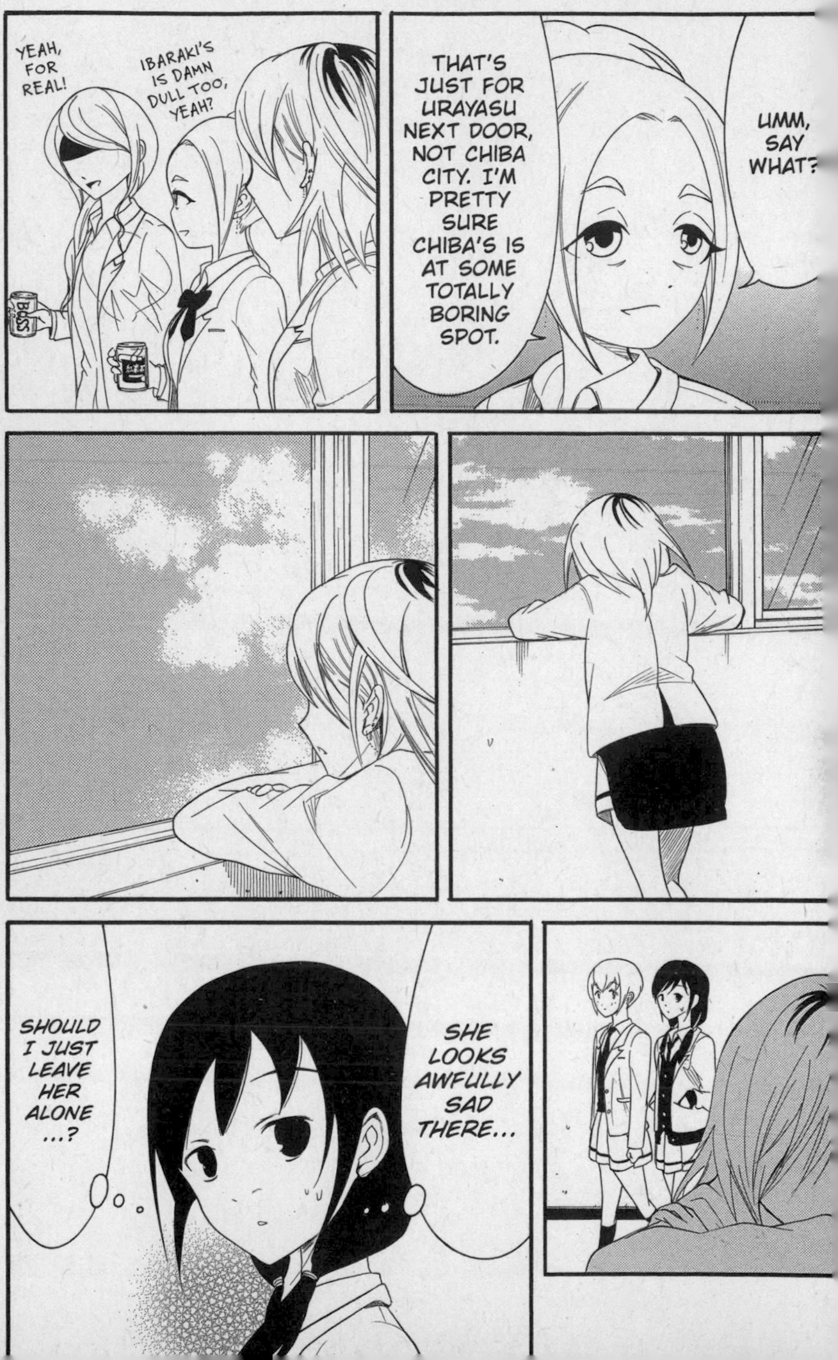
UMM, SAY WHAT?
THAT'S JUST FOR URAYASU NEXT DOOR, NOT CHIBA CITY. I'M PRETTY SURE CHIBA'S IS AT SOME TOTALLY BORING SPOT.
IBARAKI'S IS DAMN DULL TOO, YEAH?
YEAH, FOR REAL!
BOSS
SHE LOOKS AWFULLY SAD THERE...
SHOULD I JUST LEAVE HER ALONE ...?

CLEAR AT A GLANCE

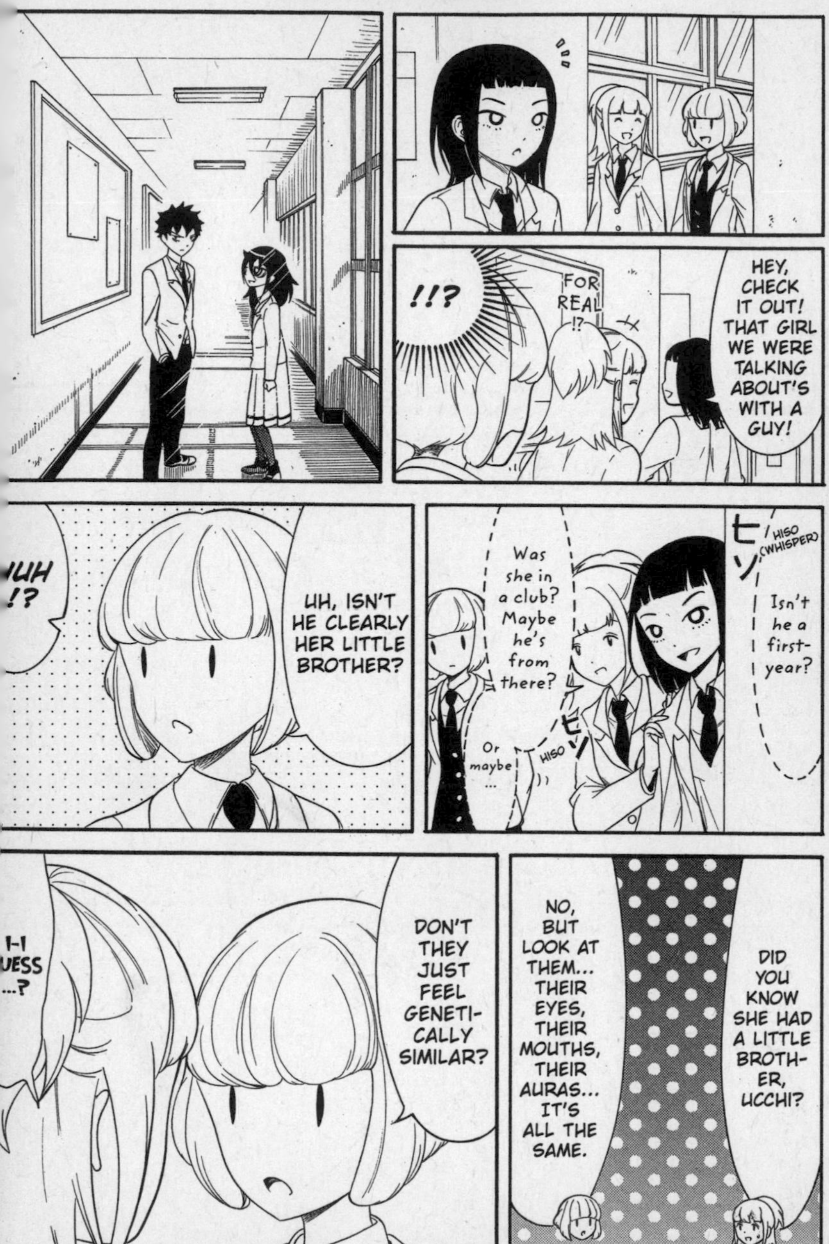

HEY, CHECK IT OUT! THAT GIRL WE WERE TALKING ABOUT'S WITH A GUY!
FOR REAL !?
!!?
ヒソ HISO (WHISPER)
Isn't he a first-year?
Was she in a club? Maybe he's from there?
ヒソ HISO
Or maybe ...
UH, ISN'T HE CLEARLY HER LITTLE BROTHER?
UH !?
DID YOU KNOW SHE HAD A LITTLE BROTHER, UCCHI?
NO, BUT LOOK AT THEM... THEIR EYES, THEIR MOUTHS, THEIR AURAS... IT'S ALL THE SAME.
DON'T THEY JUST FEEL GENETICALLY SIMILAR?
I-I UESS ...?

GREETINGS

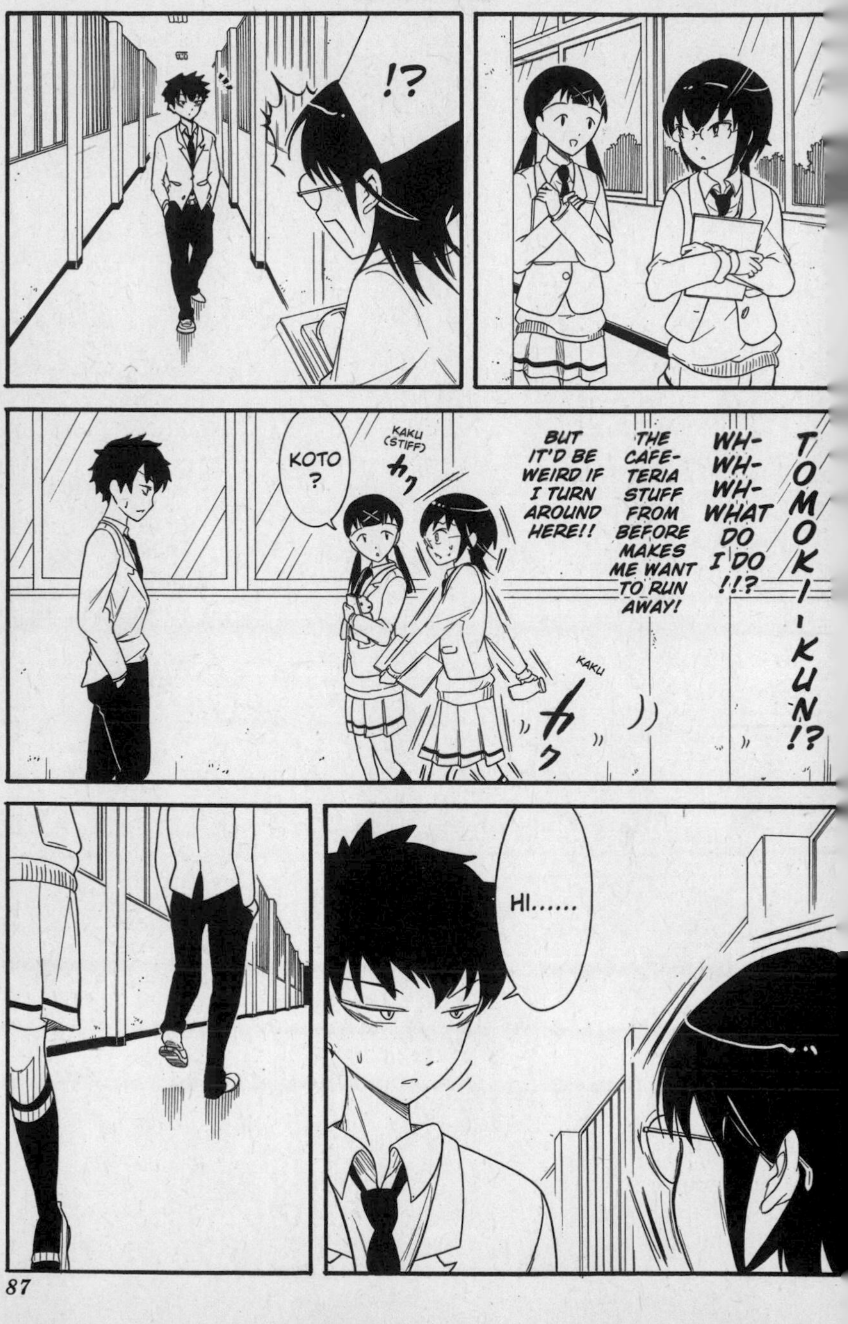
!?
TOMOKI-KUN!?
WH-WH-WH-WHAT DO I DO!!?
THE CAFETERIA STUFF FROM BEFORE MAKES ME WANT TO RUN AWAY!
BUT IT'D BE WEIRD IF I TURN AROUND HERE!!
KAKU (STIFF)
KOTO?
KAKU
HI......

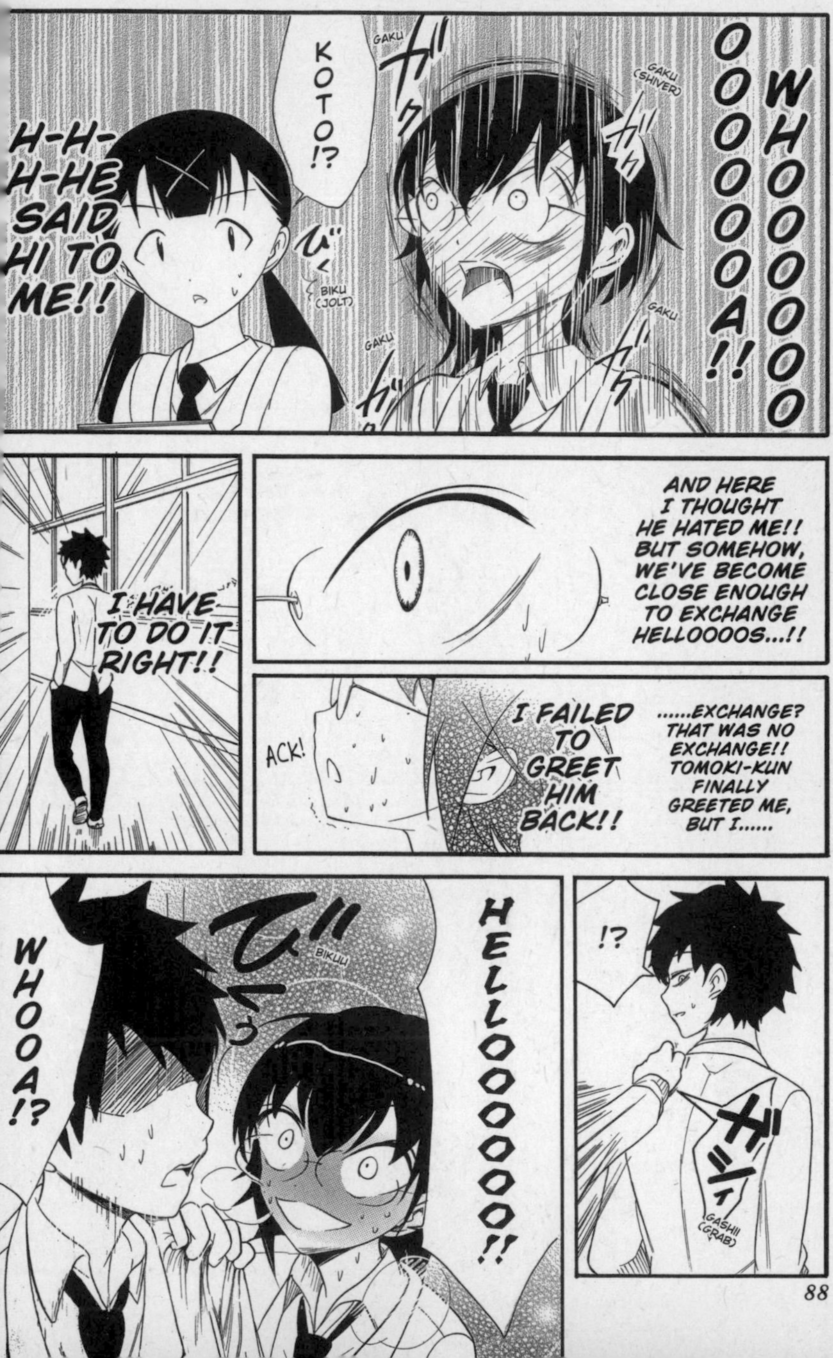
WHOOOOOOOOOOOOA!!
GAKU (SHIVER)
GAKU
KOTO!?
H-H-H-HE SAID HI TO ME!!
BIKU (JOLT)
GAKU
GAKU
AND HERE I THOUGHT HE HATED ME!! BUT SOMEHOW, WE'VE BECOME CLOSE ENOUGH TO EXCHANGE HELLOOOOS...!!
......EXCHANGE? THAT WAS NO EXCHANGE!! TOMOKI-KUN FINALLY GREETED ME, BUT I......
I FAILED TO GREET HIM BACK!!
ACK!
I HAVE TO DO IT RIGHT!!
!?
GASHII (GRAB)
HELLOOOOOOOO!!
BIKUU
WHOOOA!?

A DEEP BREATH

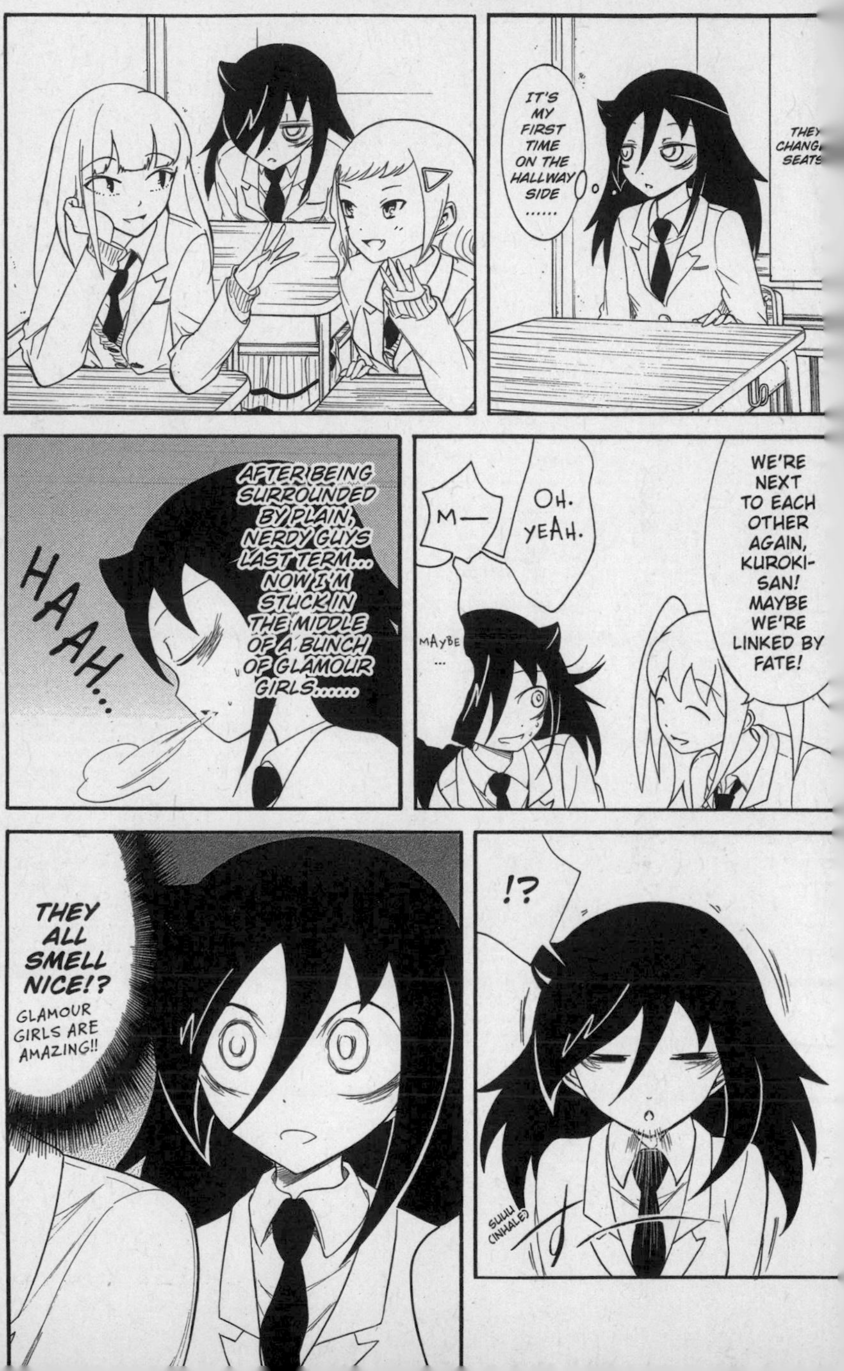
THEY CHANG SEATS
IT'S MY FIRST TIME ON THE HALLWAY SIDE ......
WE'RE NEXT TO EACH OTHER AGAIN, KUROKI-SAN! MAYBE WE'RE LINKED BY FATE!
OH. YEAH.
M—
MAYBE ...
AFTER BEING SURROUNDED BY PLAIN, NERDY GUYS LAST TERM... NOW I'M STUCK IN THE MIDDLE OF A BUNCH OF GLAMOUR GIRLS......
HAAAH...
!?
SUUU (INHALE)
THEY ALL SMELL NICE!?
GLAMOUR GIRLS ARE AMAZING!!

INEXCUSABLE

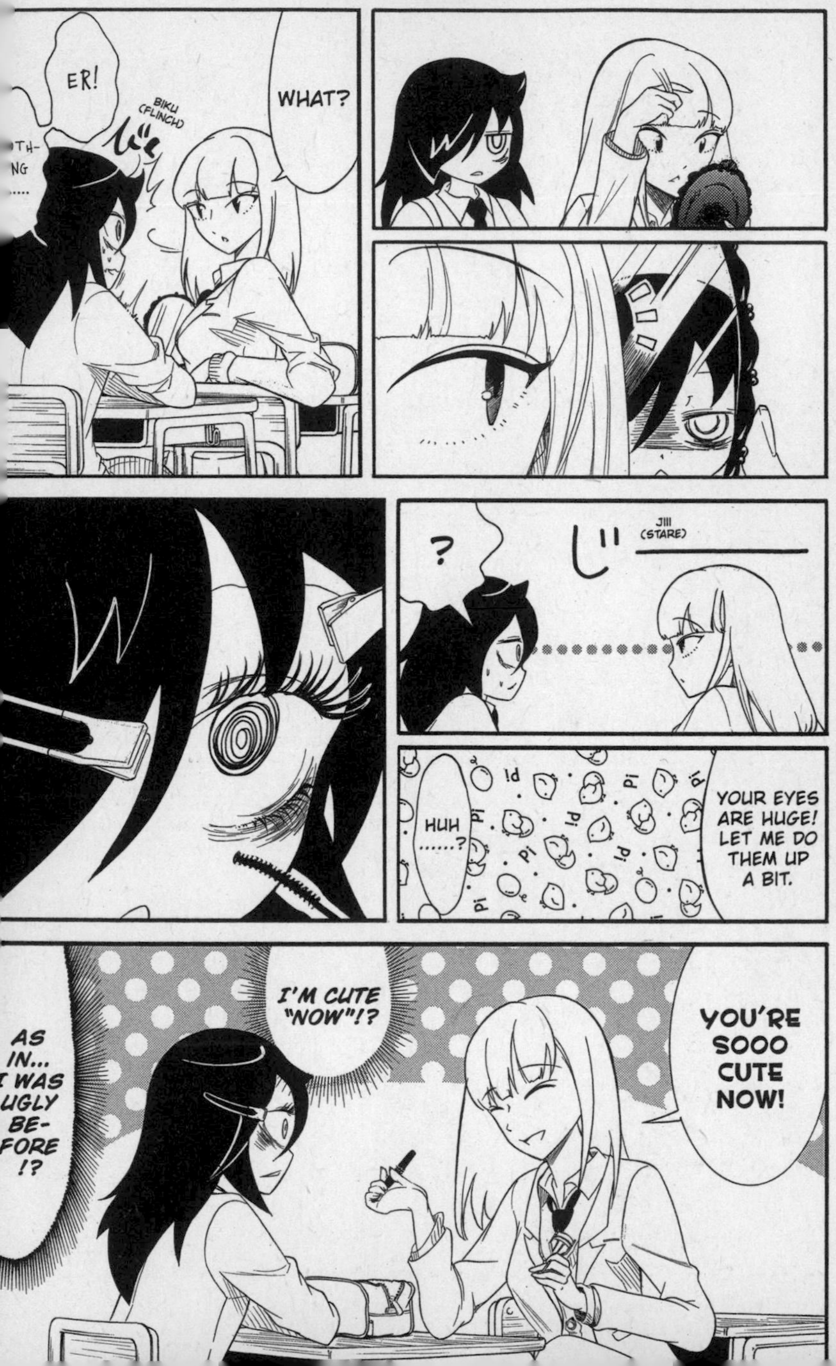
WHAT?
BIKU (FLINCH)
ER!
JIII (STARE)
?
YOUR EYES ARE HUGE! LET ME DO THEM UP A BIT.
Pi
HUH ......?
YOU'RE SOOO CUTE NOW!
I'M CUTE "NOW"!?
AS IN... I WAS UGLY BEFORE!?

A SURPRISE ATTACK

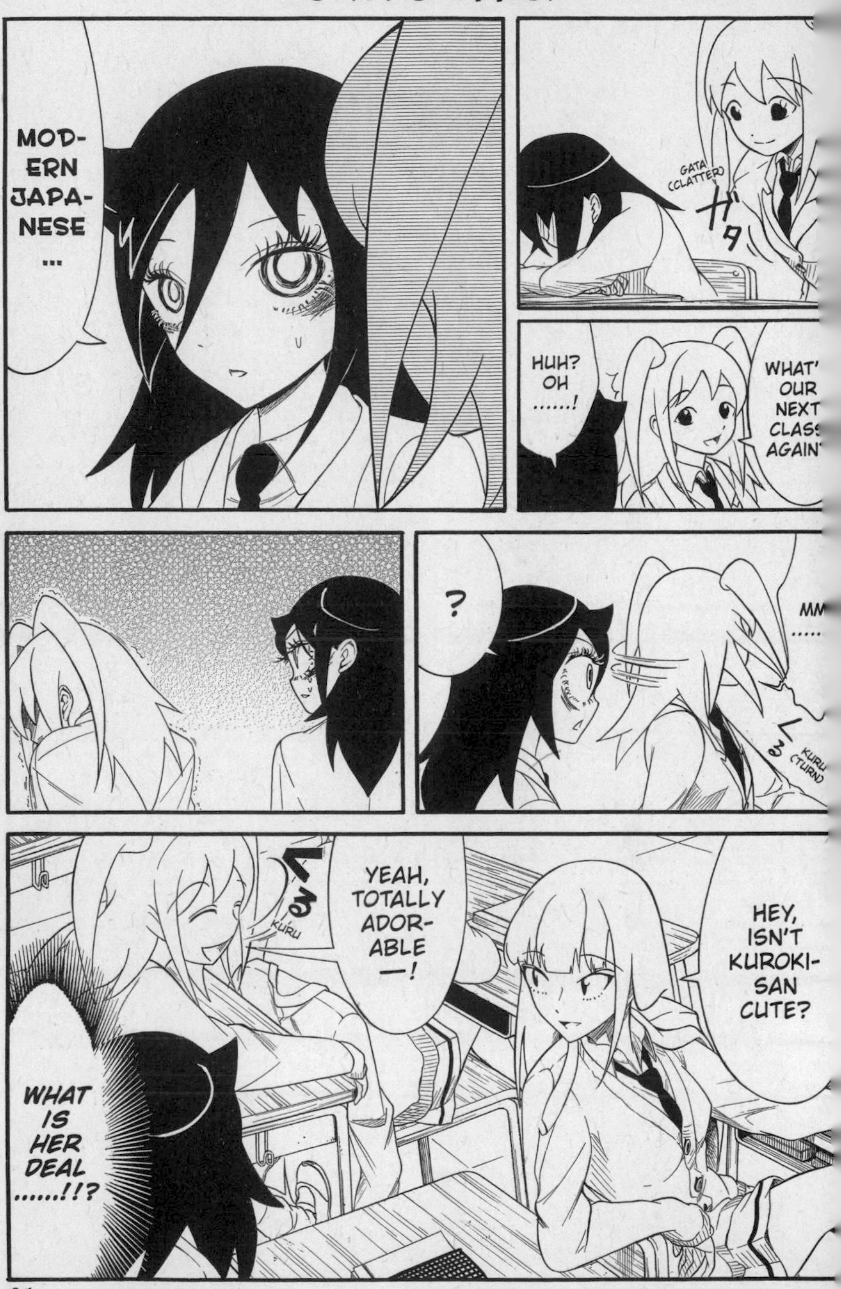
GATA (CLATTER)
WHAT' OUR NEXT CLASS AGAIN'
HUH? OH ......!
MOD-ERN JAPA-NESE ...
MM .....
?
KURU (TURN)
HEY, ISN'T KUROKI-SAN CUTE?
YEAH, TOTALLY ADOR-ABLE —!
KURU
WHAT IS HER DEAL ......!!?

THE LAST THIRD TERM

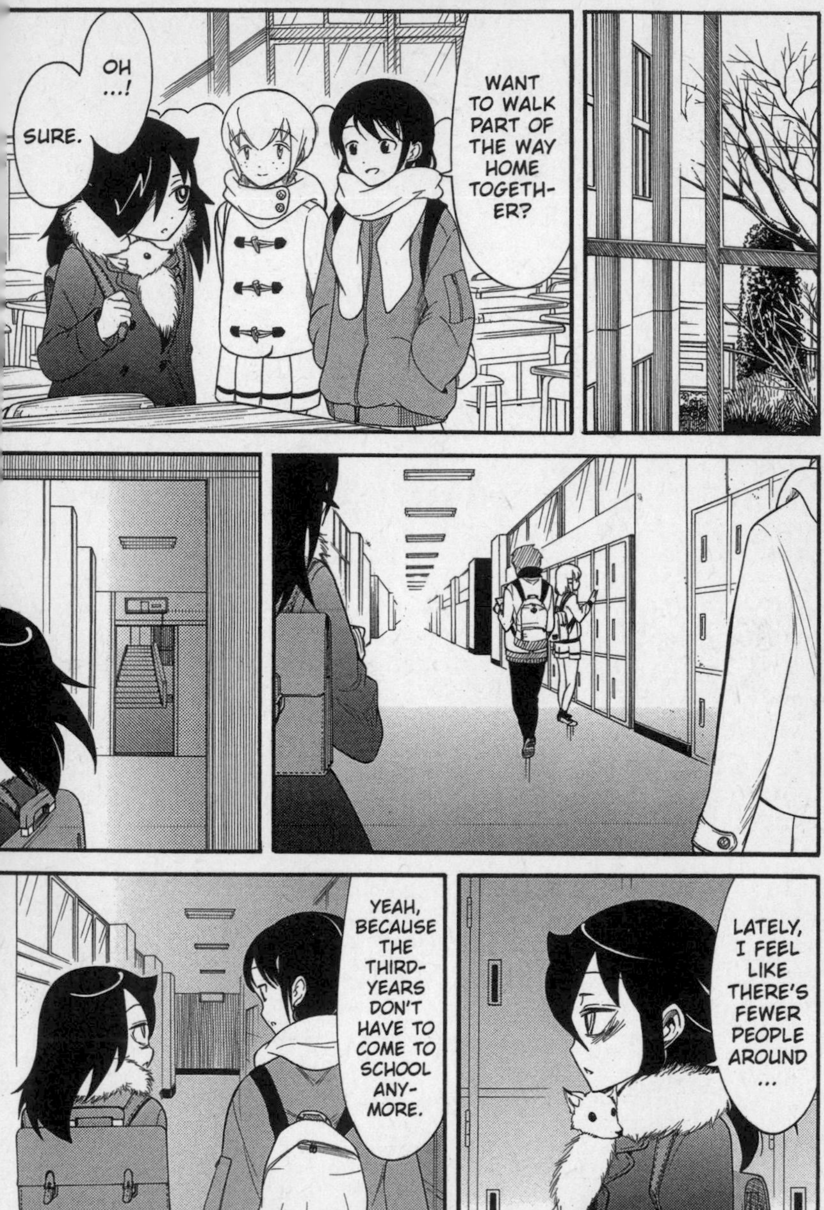
WANT TO WALK PART OF THE WAY HOME TOGETHER?
OH ...! SURE.
LATELY, I FEEL LIKE THERE'S FEWER PEOPLE AROUND ...
YEAH, BECAUSE THE THIRD-YEARS DON'T HAVE TO COME TO SCHOOL ANYMORE.

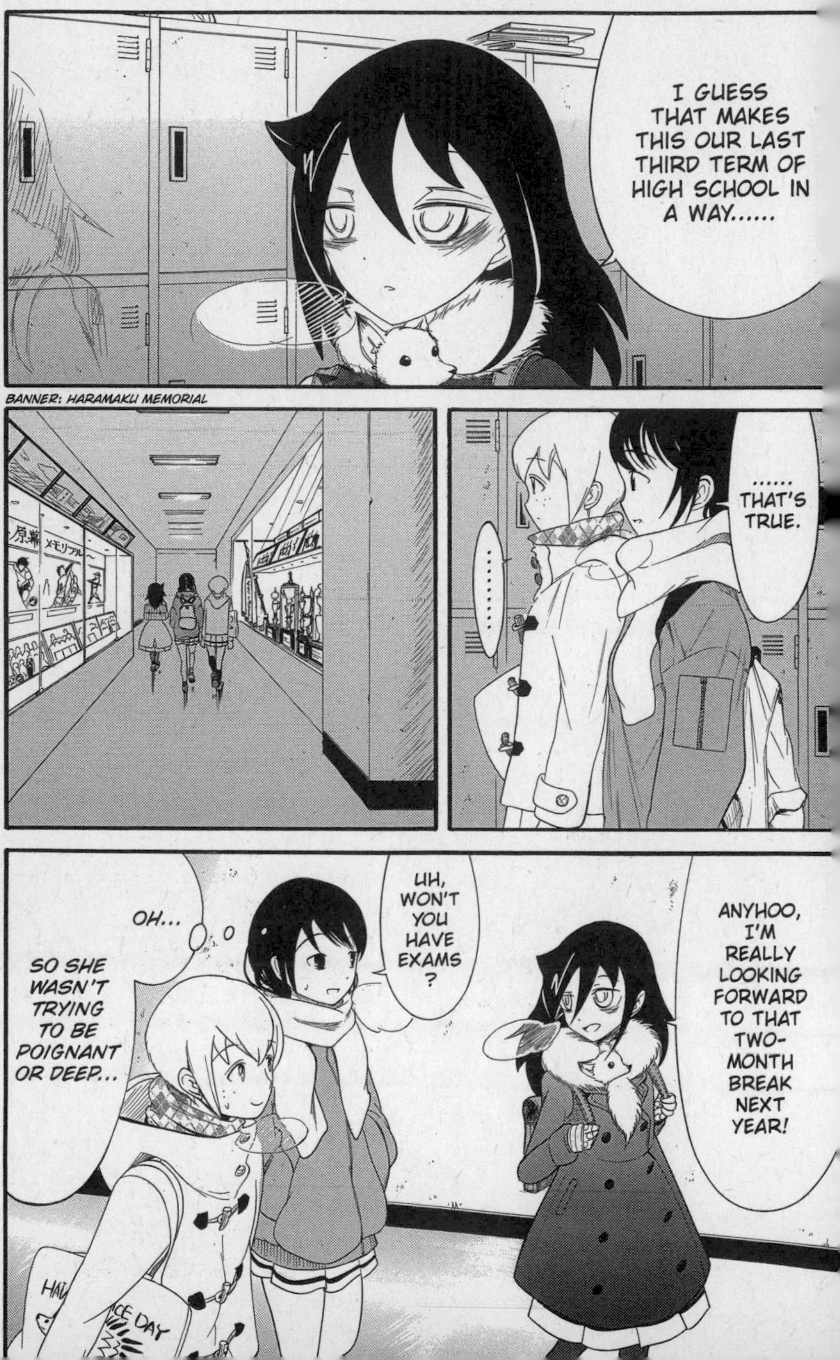
I GUESS THAT MAKES THIS OUR LAST THIRD TERM OF HIGH SCHOOL IN A WAY......
...... THAT'S TRUE.
......
ANYHOO, I'M REALLY LOOKING FORWARD TO THAT TWO-MONTH BREAK NEXT YEAR!
UH, WON'T YOU HAVE EXAMS?
OH...
SO SHE WASN'T TRYING TO BE POIGNANT OR DEEP...

BANNER: HARAMAKU MEMORIAL

No Matter How I Look at It, It's You Guys' Fault I'm Not Popular!

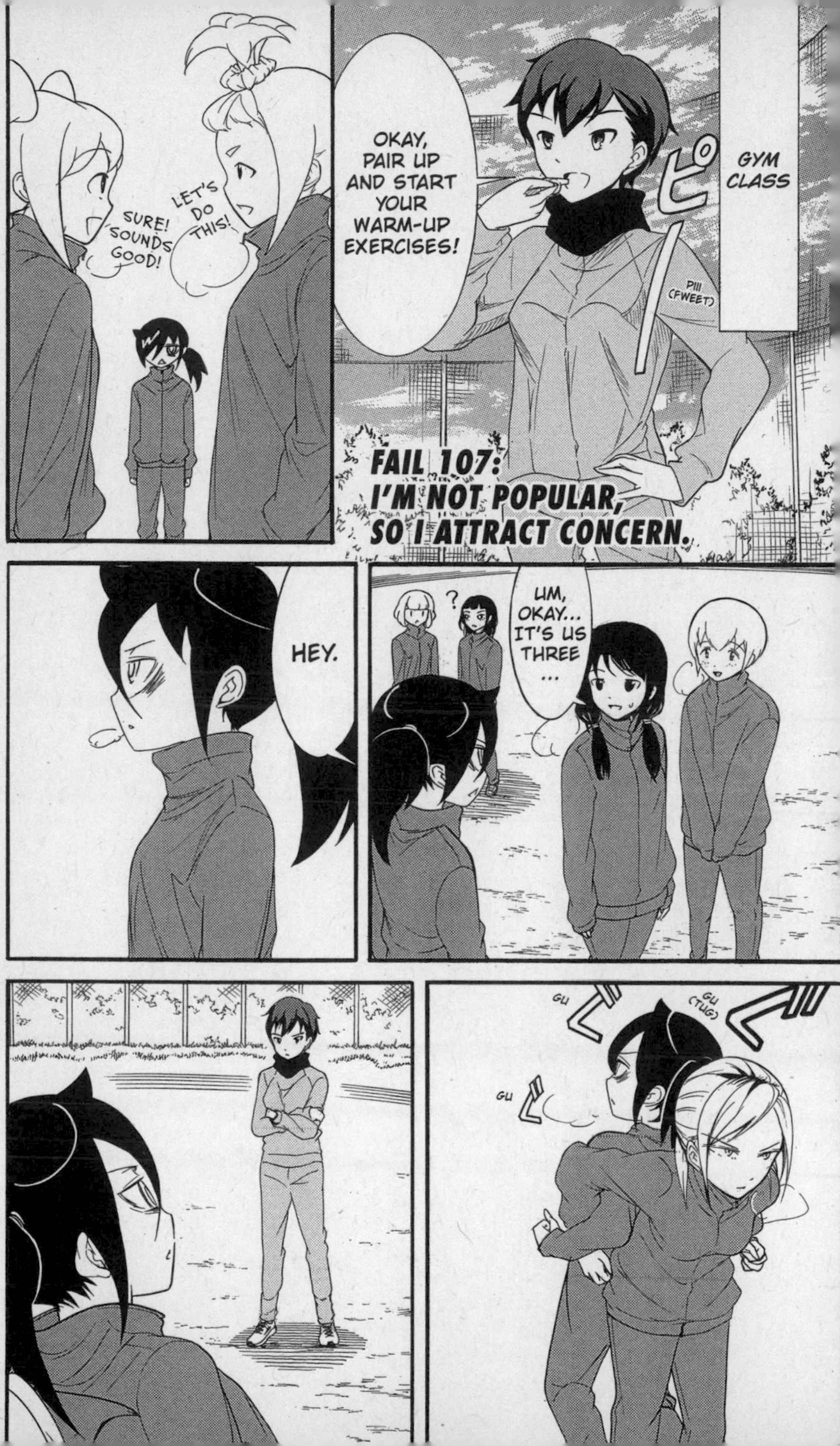
GYM CLASS
PIII (FWEET)
OKAY, PAIR UP AND START YOUR WARM-UP EXERCISES!
FAIL 107: I'M NOT POPULAR, SO I ATTRACT CONCERN.
LET'S DO THIS!
SURE! SOUNDS GOOD!
UM, OKAY... IT'S US THREE ...
?
HEY.
GU (TUG)
GU
GU

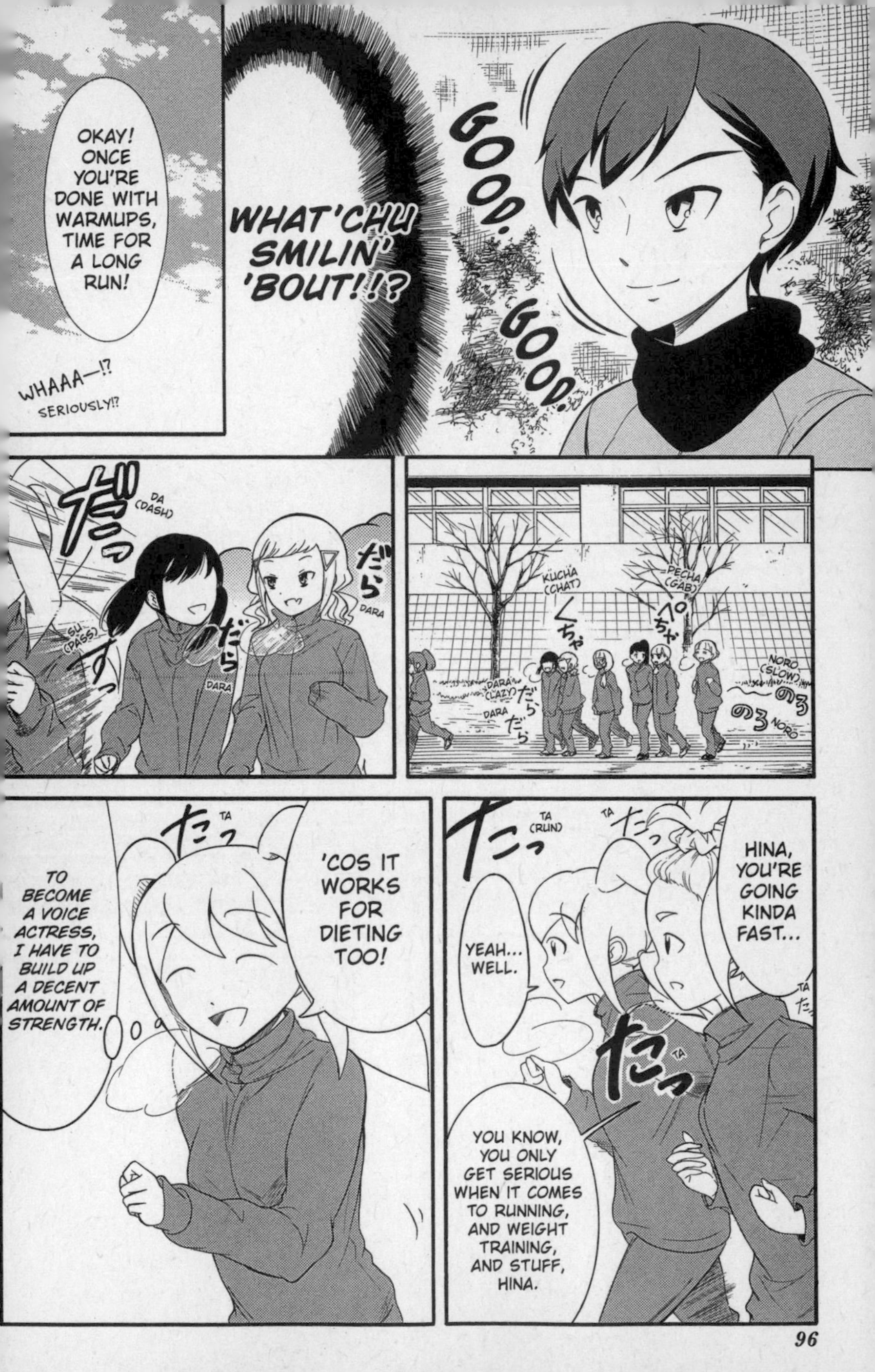

GOOD. GOOD.
WHAT'CHU SMILIN' 'BOUT!!?
OKAY! ONCE YOU'RE DONE WITH WARMUPS, TIME FOR A LONG RUN!
WHAAA—!?
SERIOUSLY!?
ぺちゃ
PECHA (GAB)
くちゃ
KUCHA (CHAT)
のろのろ
NORO (SLOW)
NORO
だらだら
DARA (LAZY)
DARA
だらっ
DARA
DA (DASH)
だっ
だら
DARA
すっ
SU (PASS)
DARA
HINA, YOU'RE GOING KINDA FAST...
たっ
TA (RUN)
たっ
TA
YEAH... WELL.
たっ
TA
TA
YOU KNOW, YOU ONLY GET SERIOUS WHEN IT COMES TO RUNNING, AND WEIGHT TRAINING, AND STUFF, HINA.
たっ
TA
'COS IT WORKS FOR DIETING TOO!
TO BECOME A VOICE ACTRESS, I HAVE TO BUILD UP A DECENT AMOUNT OF STRENGTH.

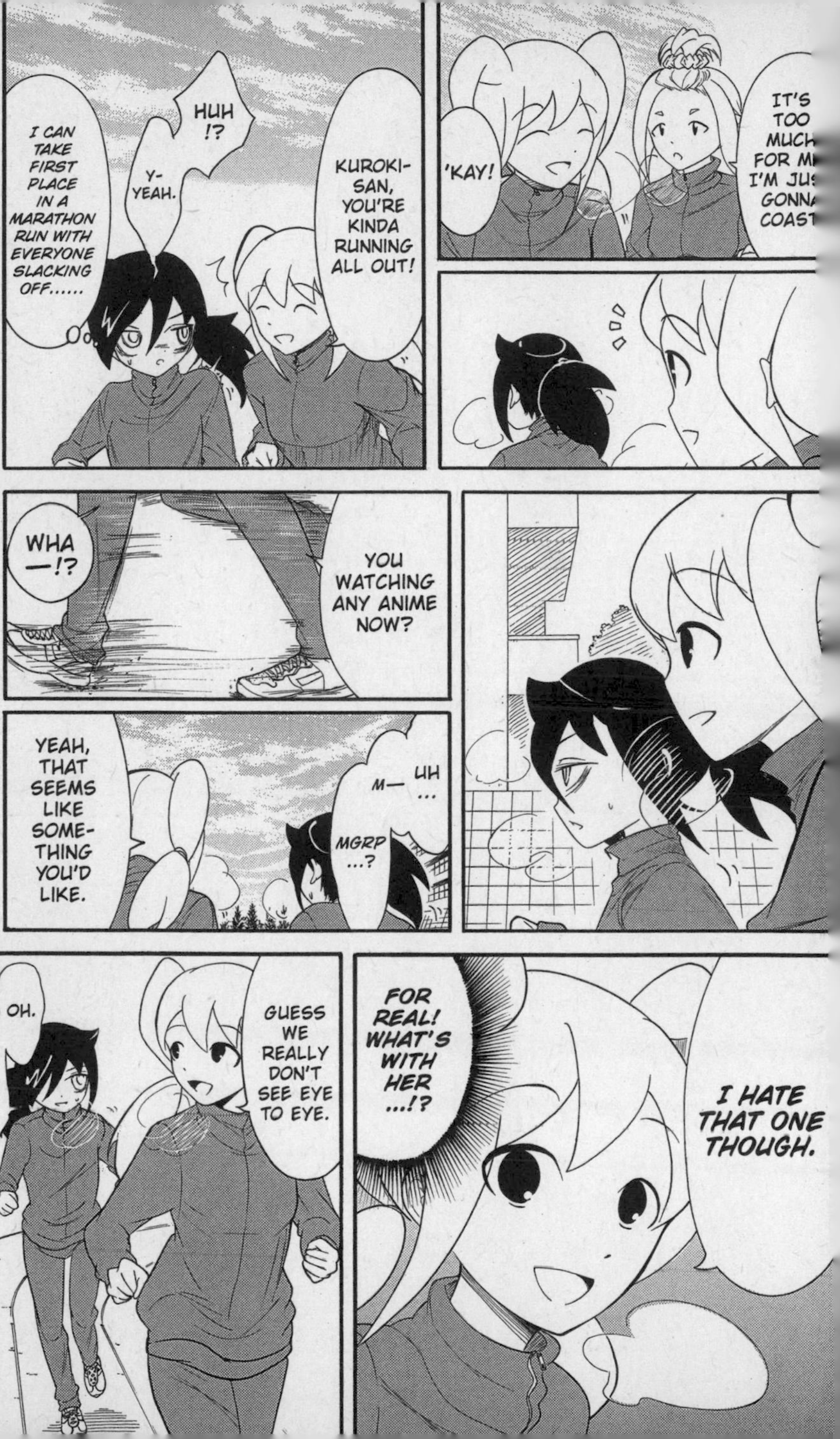
IT'S TOO MUCH FOR M I'M JUS GONNA COAST
'KAY!
KUROKI-SAN, YOU'RE KINDA RUNNING ALL OUT!
HUH !?
Y-YEAH.
I CAN TAKE FIRST PLACE IN A MARATHON RUN WITH EVERYONE SLACKING OFF......
YOU WATCHING ANY ANIME NOW?
WHA—!?
UH ...
M—
MGRP ...?
YEAH, THAT SEEMS LIKE SOME-THING YOU'D LIKE.
I HATE THAT ONE THOUGH.
FOR REAL! WHAT'S WITH HER ...!?
GUESS WE REALLY DON'T SEE EYE TO EYE.
OH.
YEP.

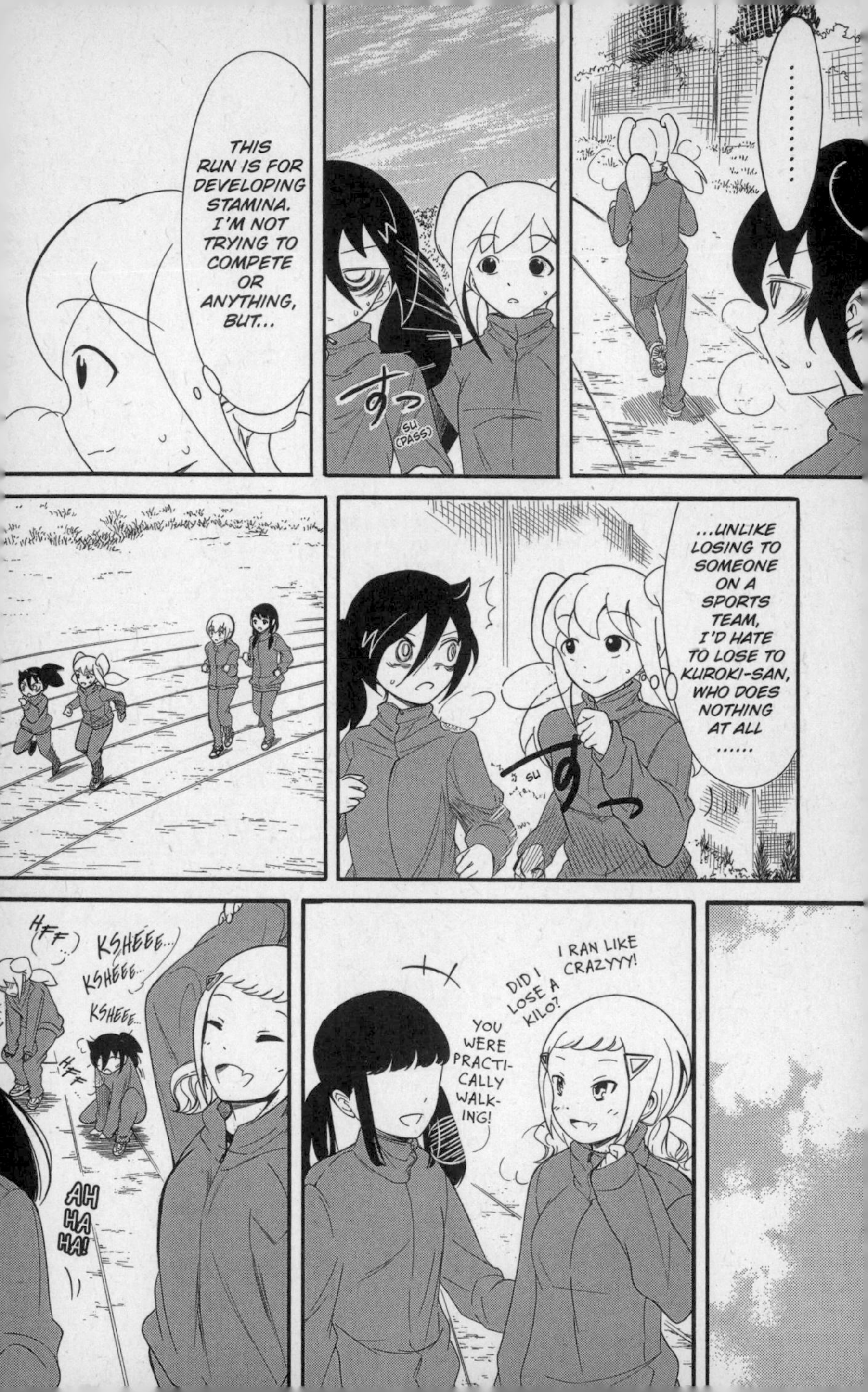
……
すっ
SU (PASS)
THIS RUN IS FOR DEVELOPING STAMINA. I'M NOT TRYING TO COMPETE OR ANYTHING, BUT…
…UNLIKE LOSING TO SOMEONE ON A SPORTS TEAM, I'D HATE TO LOSE TO KUROKI-SAN, WHO DOES NOTHING AT ALL ……
すっ
SU
I RAN LIKE CRAZYYY!
DID I LOSE A KILO?
YOU WERE PRACTI-CALLY WALK-ING!
AH HA HA!
HFF…
KSHEEE…
KSHEEE…
KSHEEE…
HFF

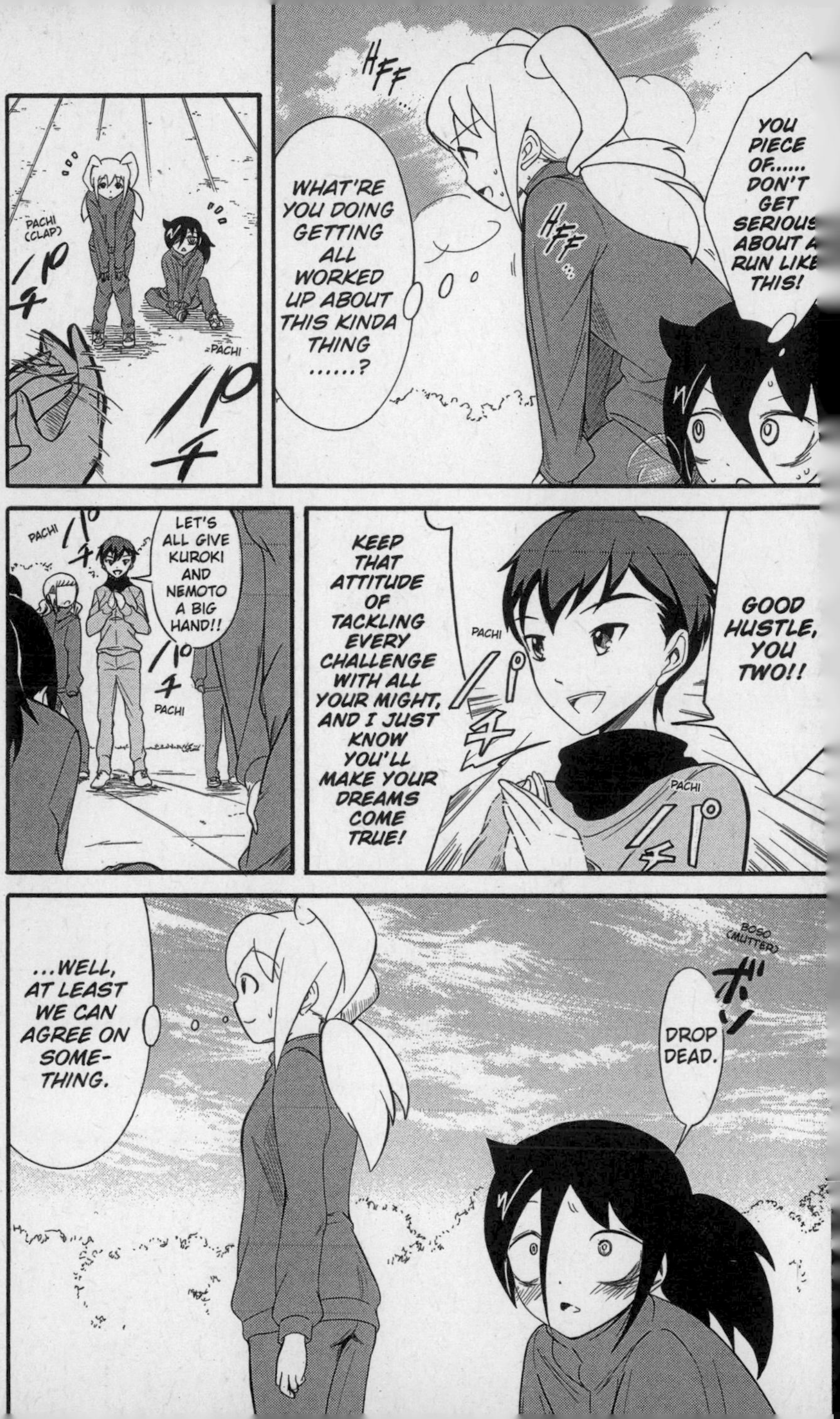
HFF...
YOU PIECE OF..... DON'T GET SERIOUS ABOUT A RUN LIKE THIS!
WHAT'RE YOU DOING GETTING ALL WORKED UP ABOUT THIS KINDA THING ......?
HFF...
PACHI (CLAP)
PACHI
GOOD HUSTLE, YOU TWO!!
KEEP THAT ATTITUDE OF TACKLING EVERY CHALLENGE WITH ALL YOUR MIGHT, AND I JUST KNOW YOU'LL MAKE YOUR DREAMS COME TRUE!
PACHI
PACHI
PACHI
LET'S ALL GIVE KUROKI AND NEMOTO A BIG HAND!!
PACHI
BOSO (MUTTER)
DROP DEAD.
...WELL, AT LEAST WE CAN AGREE ON SOME-THING.

NoMatter How I Look at It, It's You Guys' Fault I'm Not Popular!

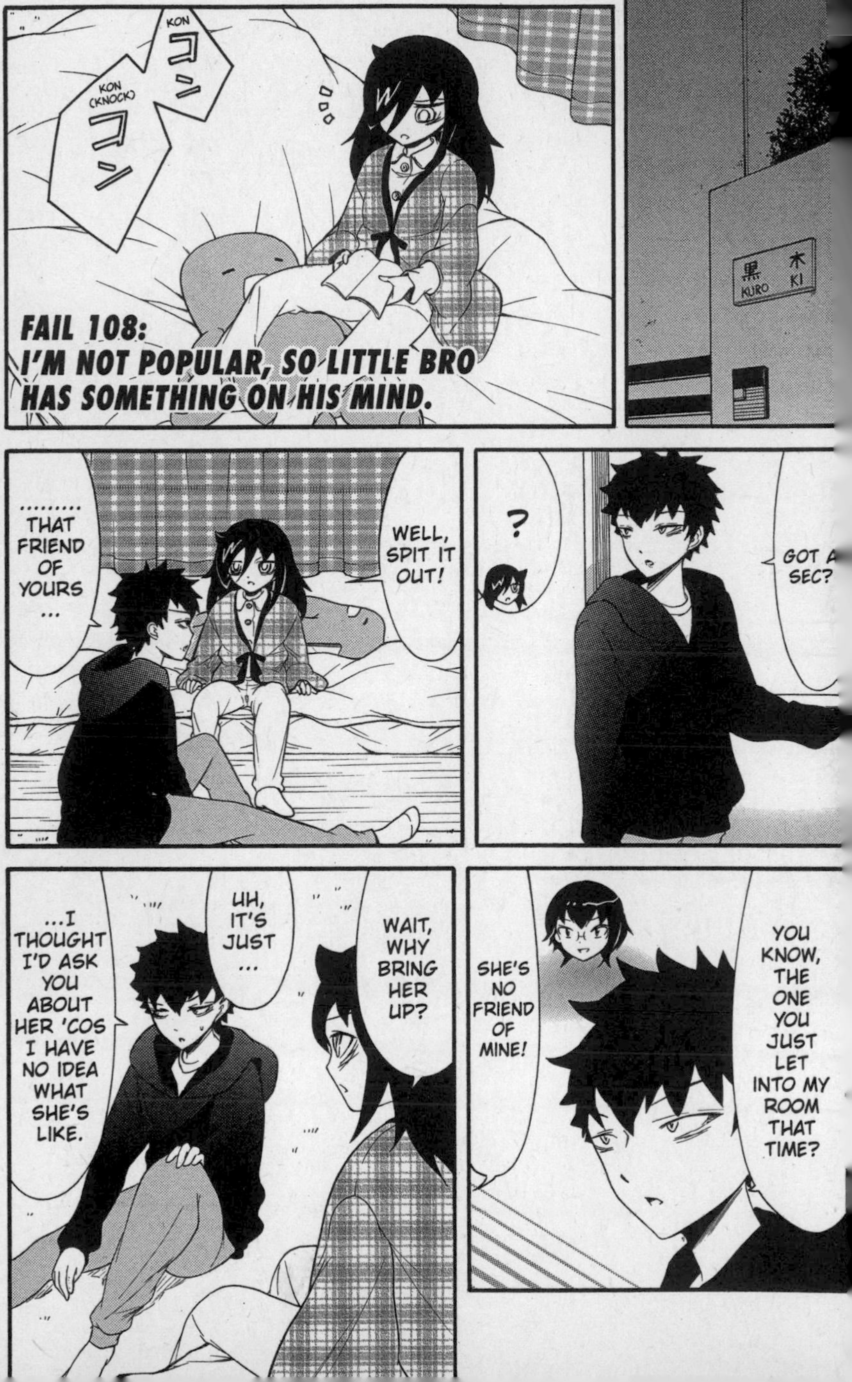
黒 木
KURO KI
KON
コン
KON (KNOCK)
コン
FAIL 108:
I'M NOT POPULAR, SO LITTLE BRO HAS SOMETHING ON HIS MIND.
GOT A SEC?
?
WELL, SPIT IT OUT!
.... THAT FRIEND OF YOURS ...
YOU KNOW, THE ONE YOU JUST LET INTO MY ROOM THAT TIME?
SHE'S NO FRIEND OF MINE!
WAIT, WHY BRING HER UP?
UH, IT'S JUST ...
...I THOUGHT I'D ASK YOU ABOUT HER 'COS I HAVE NO IDEA WHAT SHE'S LIKE.

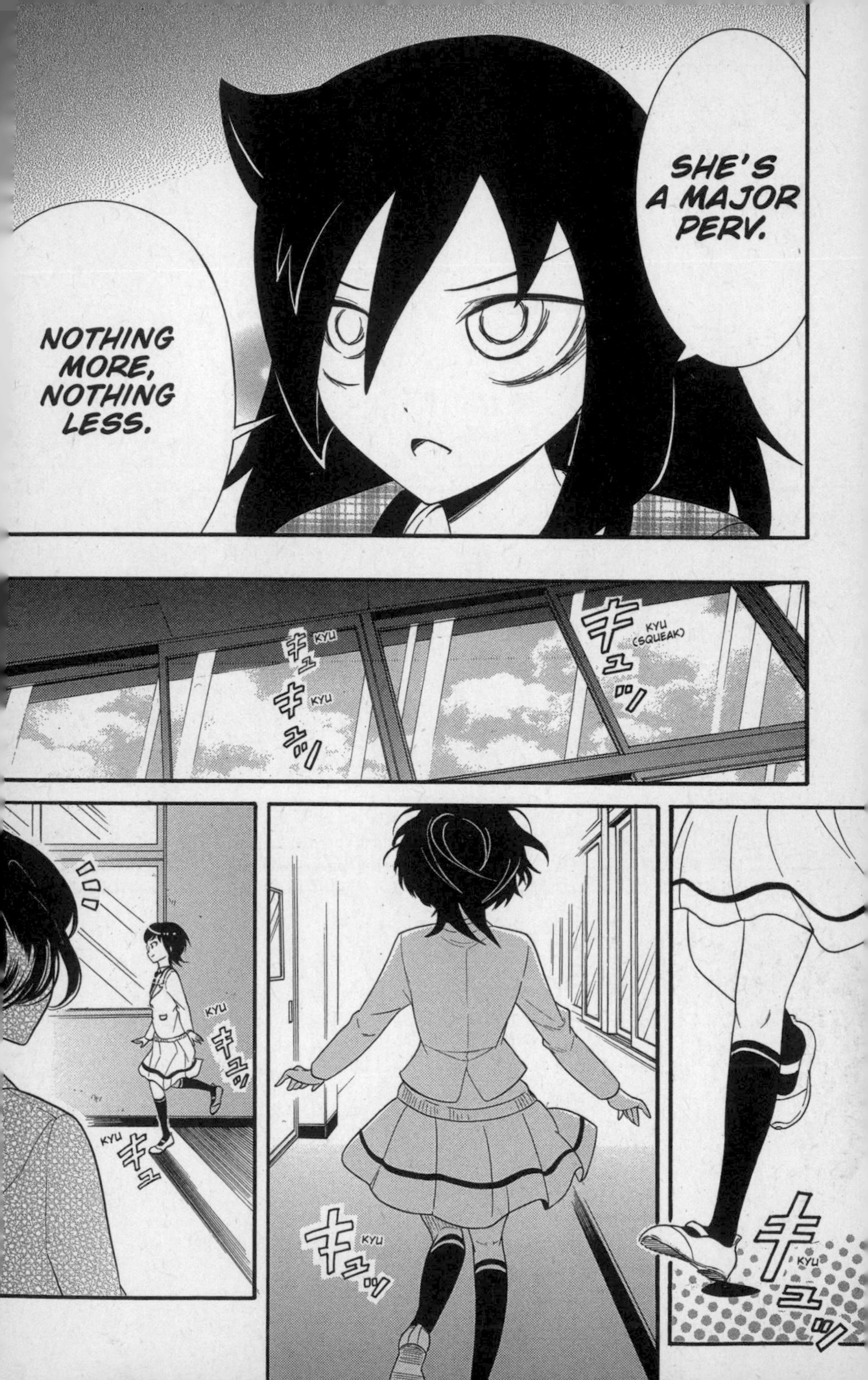
SHE'S A MAJOR PERV.
NOTHING MORE, NOTHING LESS.
キュッ
KYU (SQUEAK)
キュ
KYU
キュッ
KYU
キュッ
KYU
キュッ
KYU
キュッ
KYU
キュ
KYU

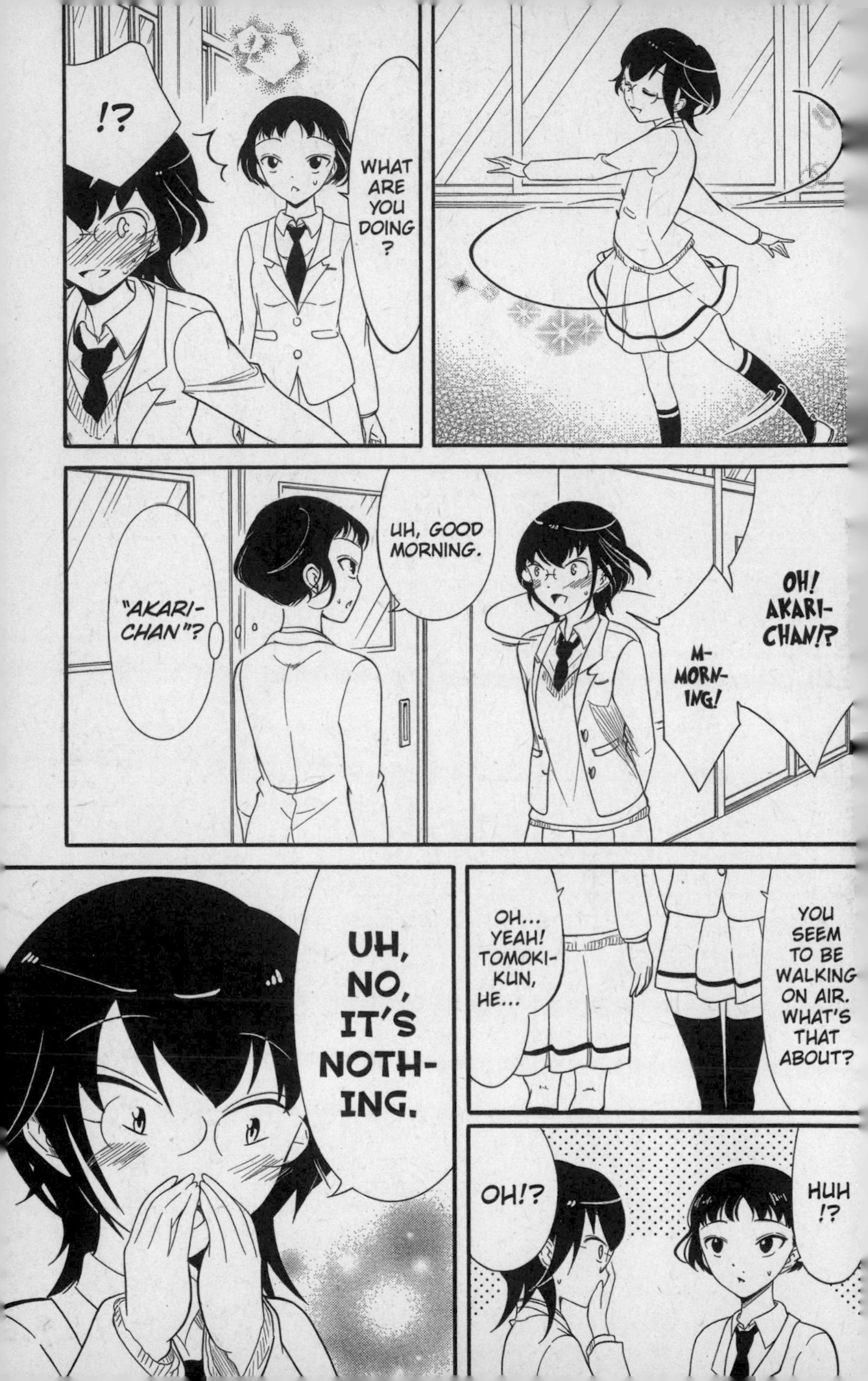
WHAT ARE YOU DOING?
!?
OH! AKARI-CHAN!?
M-MORNING!
UH, GOOD MORNING.
"AKARI-CHAN"?
YOU SEEM TO BE WALKING ON AIR. WHAT'S THAT ABOUT?
OH... YEAH! TOMOKI-KUN, HE...
HUH!?
OH!?
UH, NO, IT'S NOTHING.

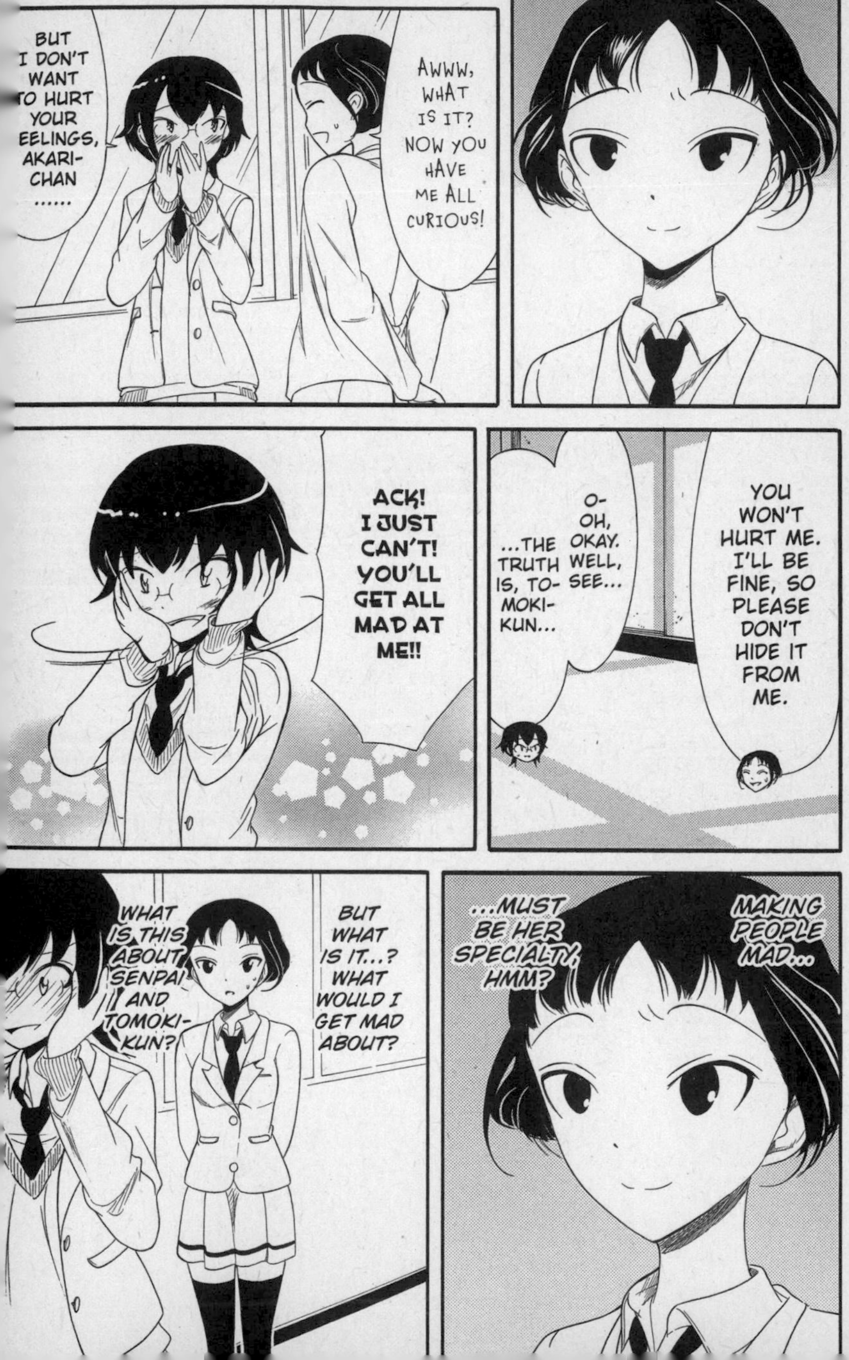
AWWW, WHAT IS IT? NOW YOU HAVE ME ALL CURIOUS!
BUT I DON'T WANT TO HURT YOUR EELINGS, AKARI-CHAN ......
YOU WON'T HURT ME. I'LL BE FINE, SO PLEASE DON'T HIDE IT FROM ME.
O-OH, OKAY. WELL, SEE...
...THE TRUTH IS, TO-MOKI-KUN...
ACK! I JUST CAN'T! YOU'LL GET ALL MAD AT ME!!
MAKING PEOPLE MAD...
...MUST BE HER SPECIALTY, HMM?
BUT WHAT IS IT...? WHAT WOULD I GET MAD ABOUT?
WHAT IS THIS ABOUT SENPAI AND TOMOKI-KUN?

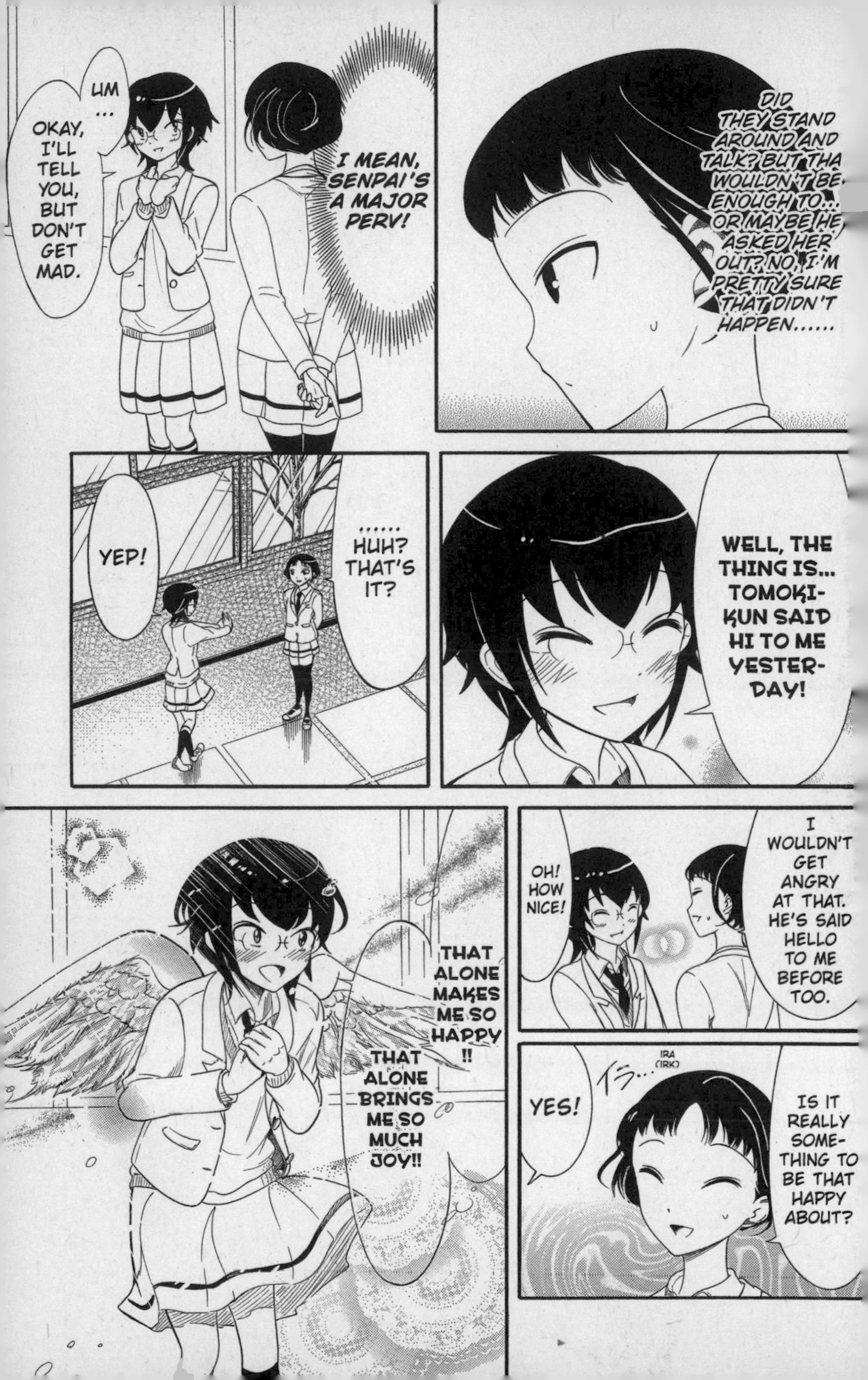
DID THEY STAND AROUND AND TALK? BUT THA WOULDN'T BE ENOUGH TO... OR MAYBE HE ASKED HER OUT? NO, I'M PRETTY SURE THAT DIDN'T HAPPEN......
UM ... OKAY, I'LL TELL YOU, BUT DON'T GET MAD.
I MEAN, SENPAI'S A MAJOR PERV!
WELL, THE THING IS... TOMOKI-KUN SAID HI TO ME YESTER-DAY!
...... HUH? THAT'S IT?
YEP!
I WOULDN'T GET ANGRY AT THAT. HE'S SAID HELLO TO ME BEFORE TOO.
OH! HOW NICE!
IS IT REALLY SOME-THING TO BE THAT HAPPY ABOUT?
IRA (IRK)
YES!
THAT ALONE MAKES ME SO HAPPY!!
THAT ALONE BRINGS ME SO MUCH JOY!!

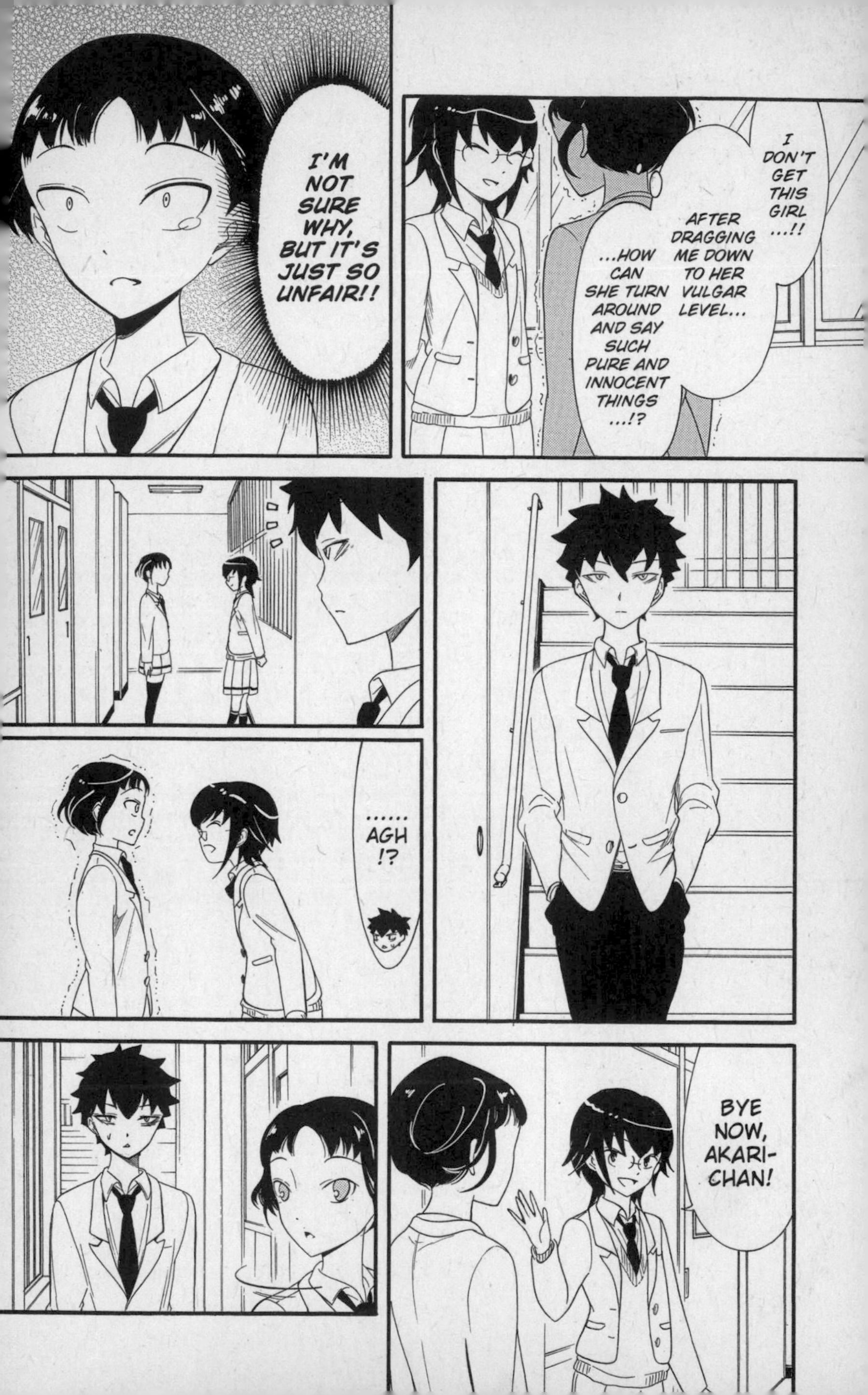
I DON'T GET THIS GIRL ...!!
AFTER DRAGGING ME DOWN TO HER VULGAR LEVEL...
...HOW CAN SHE TURN AROUND AND SAY SUCH PURE AND INNOCENT THINGS ...!?
I'M NOT SURE WHY, BUT IT'S JUST SO UNFAIR!!
...... AGH !?
BYE NOW, AKARI-CHAN!

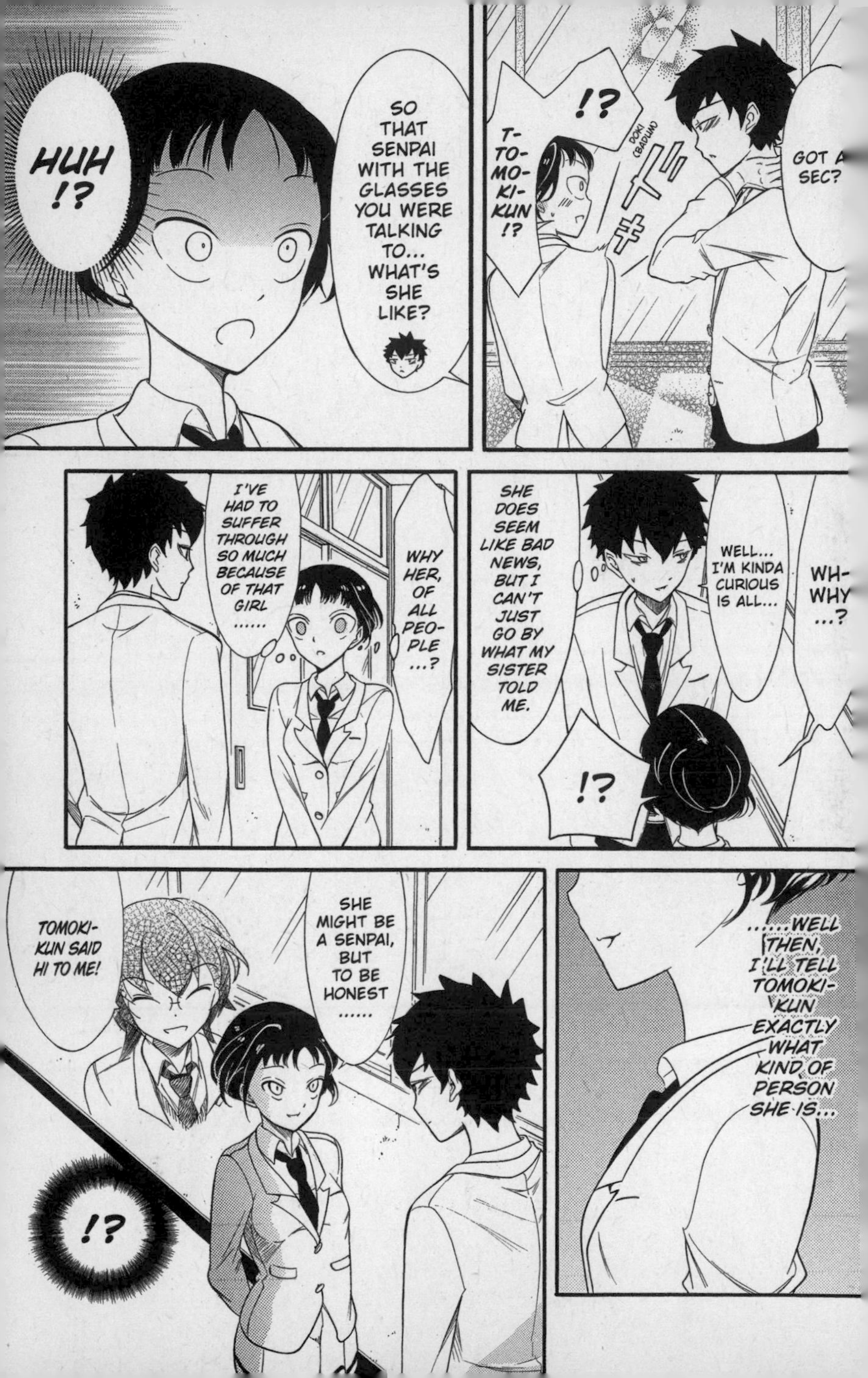
GOT A SEC?
!?
T-TOMOKI-KUN!?
DOKI (BADUM)
SO THAT SENPAI WITH THE GLASSES YOU WERE TALKING TO... WHAT'S SHE LIKE?
HUH!?
WH-WHY...?
WELL... I'M KINDA CURIOUS IS ALL...
!?
SHE DOES SEEM LIKE BAD NEWS, BUT I CAN'T JUST GO BY WHAT MY SISTER TOLD ME.
WHY HER, OF ALL PEOPLE...?
I'VE HAD TO SUFFER THROUGH SO MUCH BECAUSE OF THAT GIRL......
......WELL THEN, I'LL TELL TOMOKI-KUN EXACTLY WHAT KIND OF PERSON SHE IS...
SHE MIGHT BE A SENPAI, BUT TO BE HONEST......
TOMOKI-KUN SAID HI TO ME!
!?

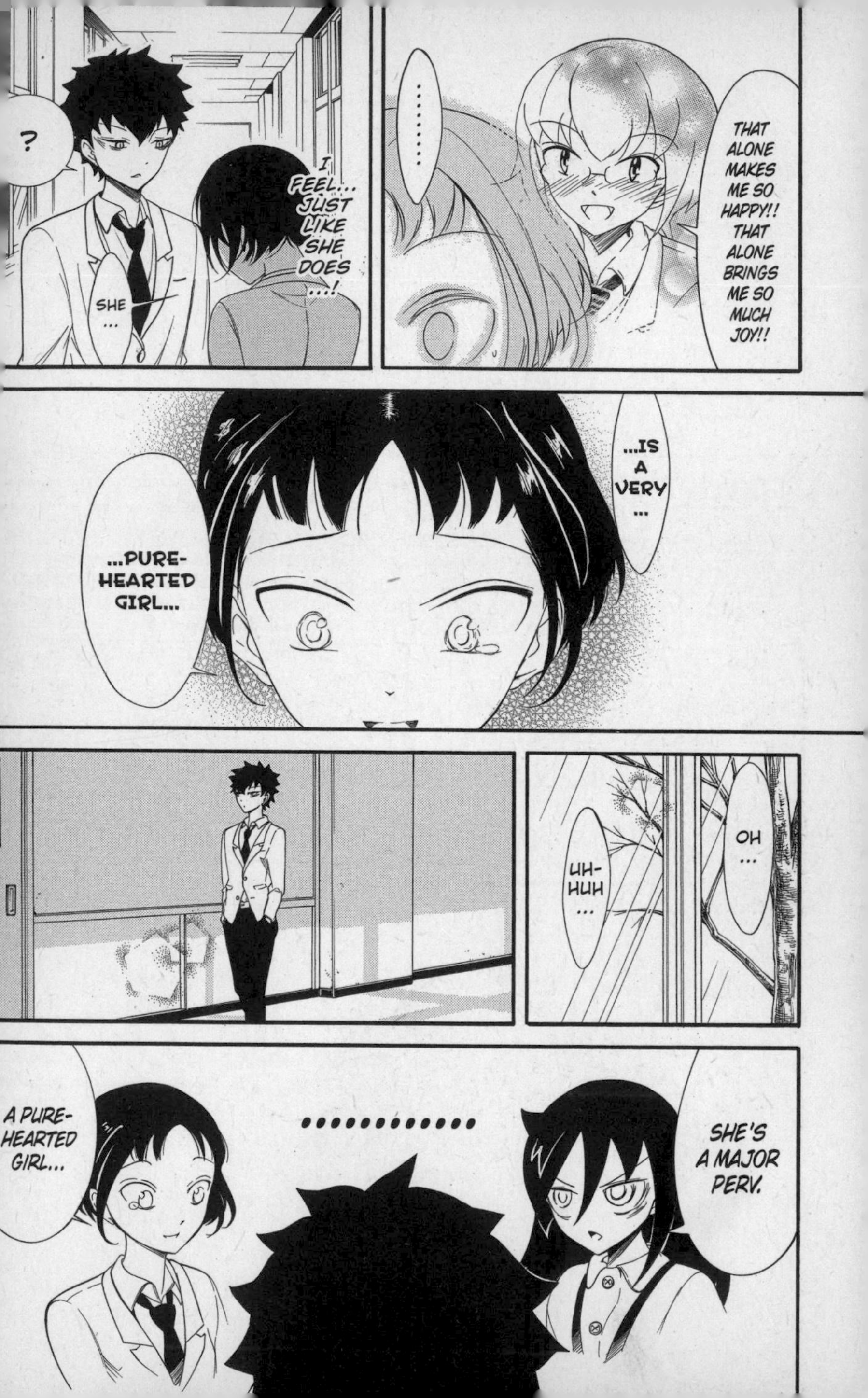
THAT ALONE MAKES ME SO HAPPY!! THAT ALONE BRINGS ME SO MUCH JOY!!
......
I FEEL... JUST LIKE SHE DOES...!
?
SHE ...
...IS A VERY ...
...PURE-HEARTED GIRL...
OH ...
UH-HUH ...
SHE'S A MAJOR PERV.
....
A PURE-HEARTED GIRL...

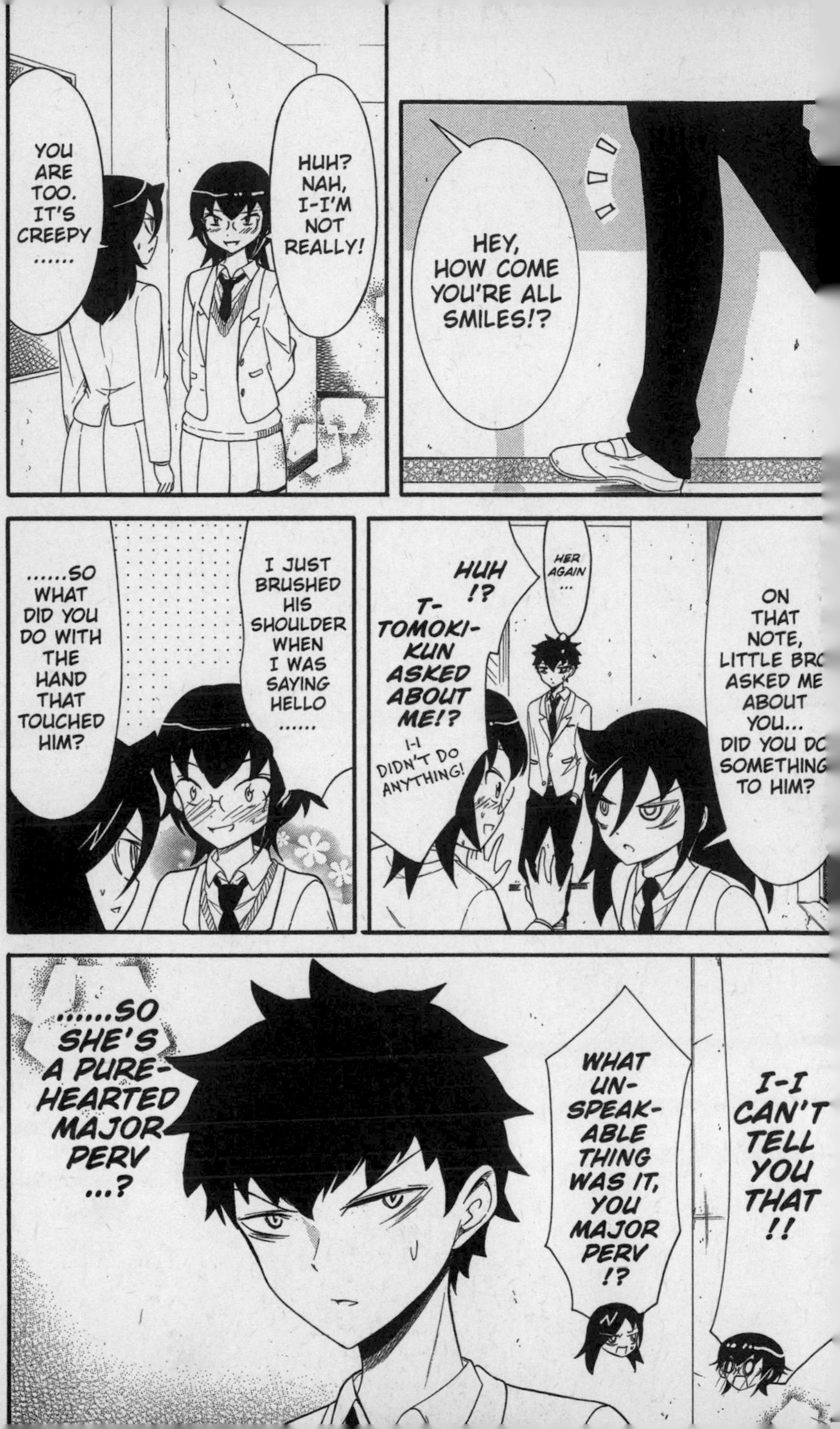
HEY, HOW COME YOU'RE ALL SMILES!?
HUH? NAH, I-I'M NOT REALLY!
YOU ARE TOO. IT'S CREEPY ......
ON THAT NOTE, LITTLE BRO ASKED ME ABOUT YOU... DID YOU DO SOMETHING TO HIM?
HER AGAIN ...
HUH!? T-TOMOKI-KUN ASKED ABOUT ME!?
I-I DIDN'T DO ANYTHING!
I JUST BRUSHED HIS SHOULDER WHEN I WAS SAYING HELLO ......
......SO WHAT DID YOU DO WITH THE HAND THAT TOUCHED HIM?
I-I CAN'T TELL YOU THAT!!
WHAT UN-SPEAK-ABLE THING WAS IT, YOU MAJOR PERV!?
......SO SHE'S A PURE-HEARTED MAJOR PERV...?

No Matter How I Look at It, It's You Guys' Fault I'm Not Popular!

FAIL 109: I'M NOT POPULAR, SO I'M AT SCHOOL ON A SNOWY DAY.

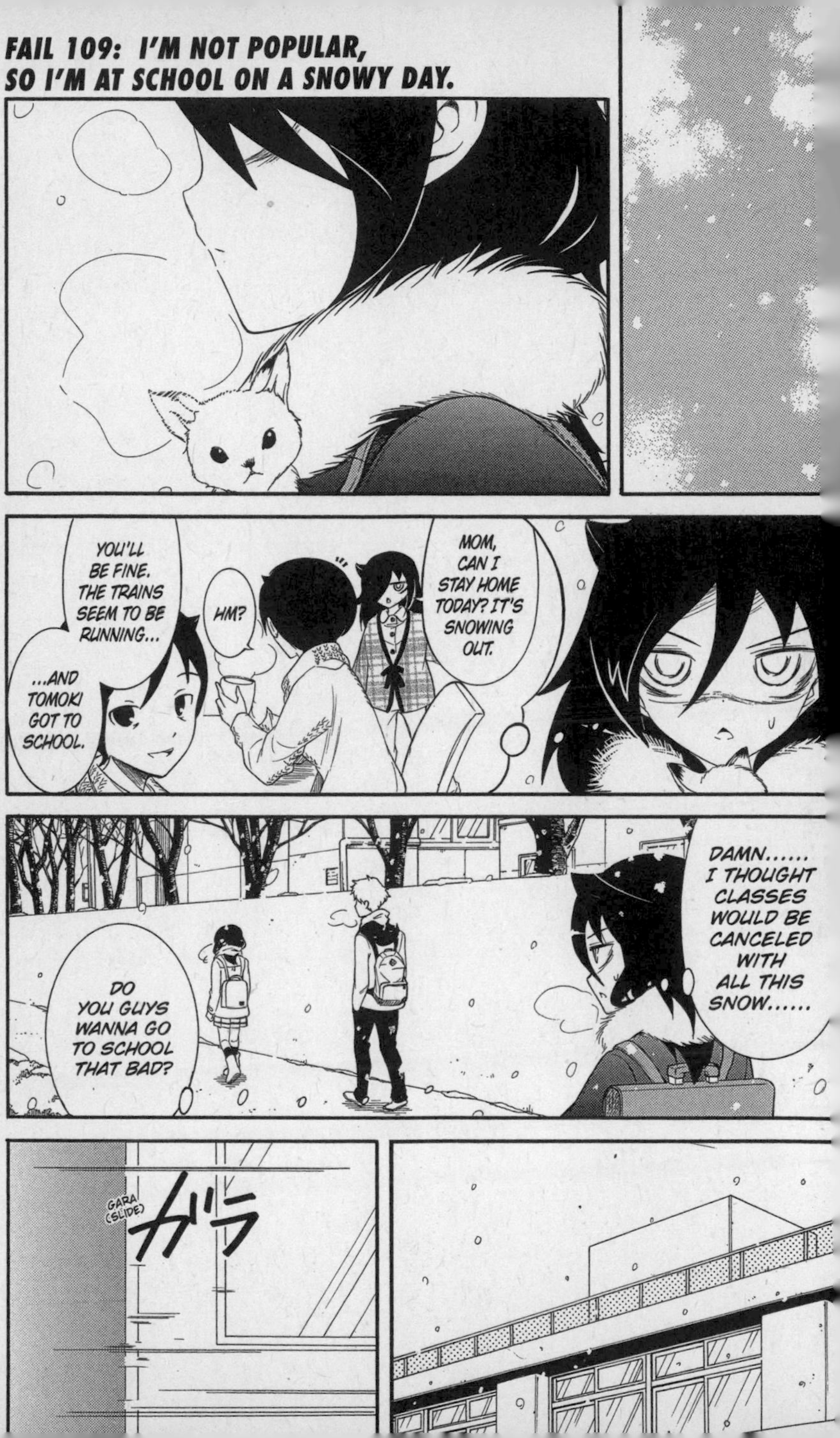
MOM, CAN I STAY HOME TODAY? IT'S SNOWING OUT.
HM?
YOU'LL BE FINE. THE TRAINS SEEM TO BE RUNNING...
...AND TOMOKI GOT TO SCHOOL.
DAMN...... I THOUGHT CLASSES WOULD BE CANCELED WITH ALL THIS SNOW......
DO YOU GUYS WANNA GO TO SCHOOL THAT BAD?
GARA (SLIDE)
ガラ

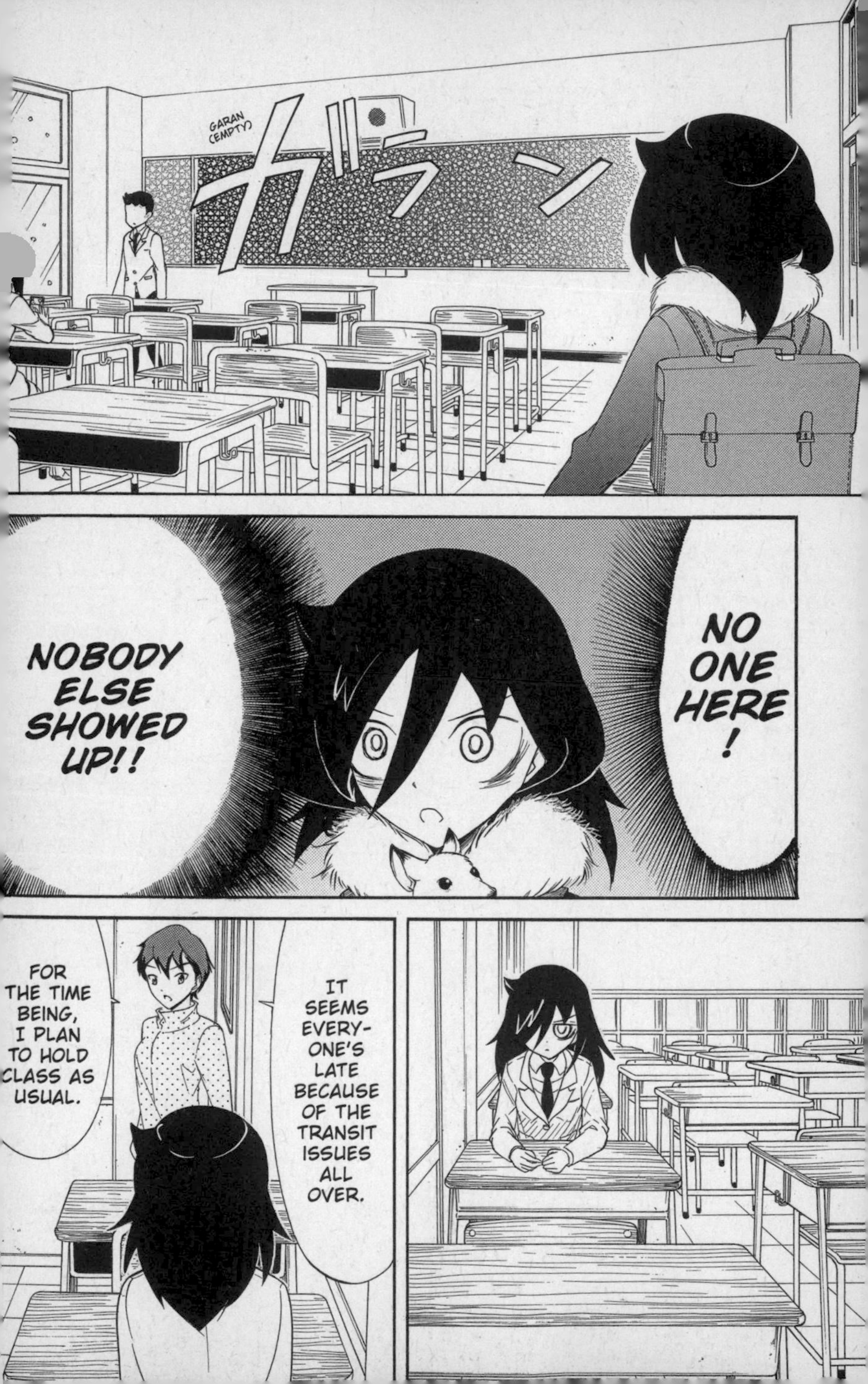
ガラーン
GARAN (EMPTY)
NO ONE HERE!
NOBODY ELSE SHOWED UP!!
IT SEEMS EVERYONE'S LATE BECAUSE OF THE TRANSIT ISSUES ALL OVER.
FOR THE TIME BEING, I PLAN TO HOLD CLASS AS USUAL.

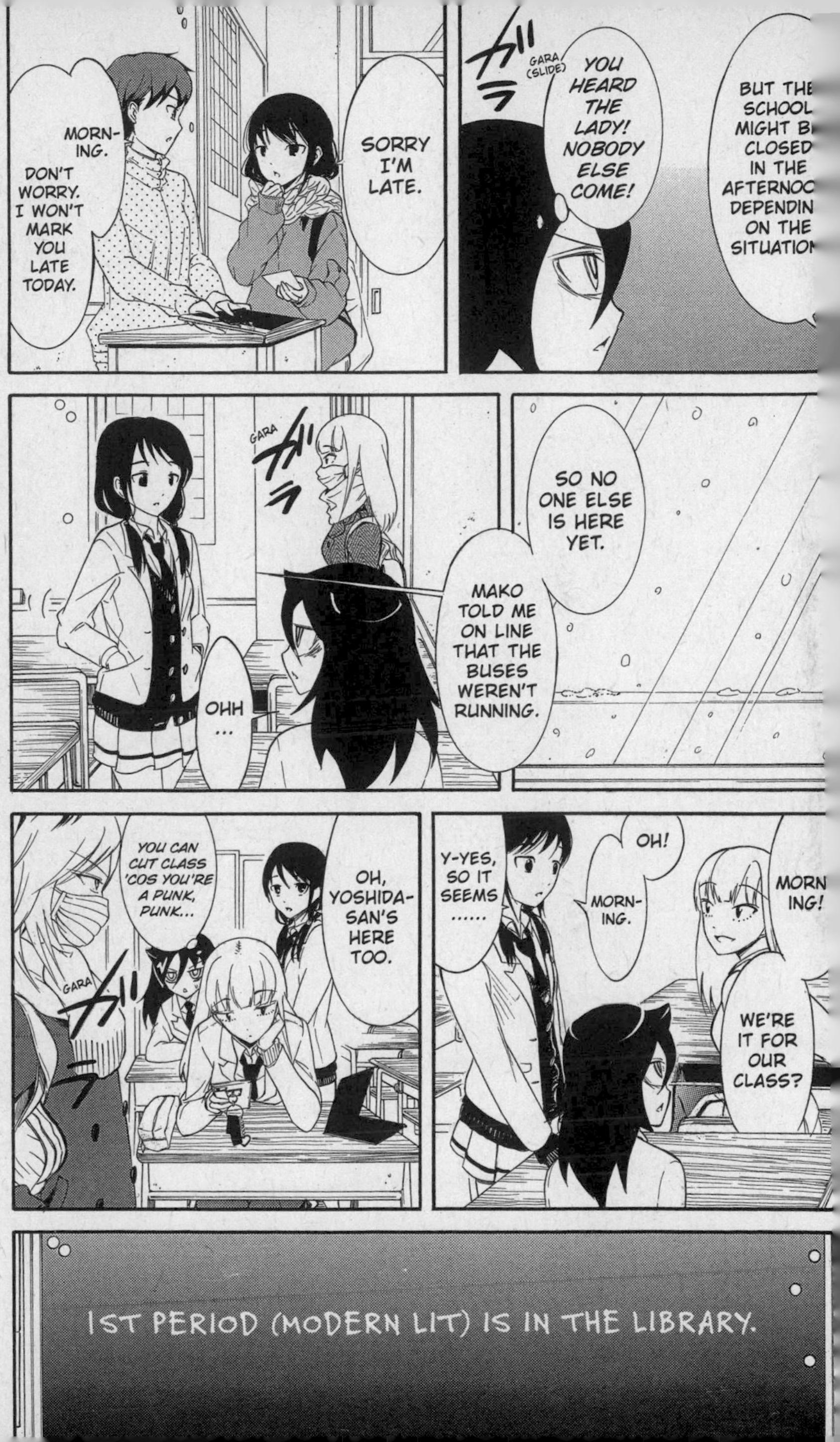
BUT THE SCHOOL MIGHT B CLOSED IN THE AFTERNOO DEPENDIN ON THE SITUATIO
YOU HEARD THE LADY! NOBODY ELSE COME!
GARA (SLIDE)
SORRY I'M LATE.
MORNING. DON'T WORRY. I WON'T MARK YOU LATE TODAY.
SO NO ONE ELSE IS HERE YET.
MAKO TOLD ME ON LINE THAT THE BUSES WEREN'T RUNNING.
GARA
OHH...
MORN ING!
WE'RE IT FOR OUR CLASS?
OH!
MORNING.
Y-YES, SO IT SEEMS......
OH, YOSHIDA-SAN'S HERE TOO.
YOU CAN CUT CLASS 'COS YOU'RE A PUNK, PUNK...
GARA
1ST PERIOD (MODERN LIT) IS IN THE LIBRARY.

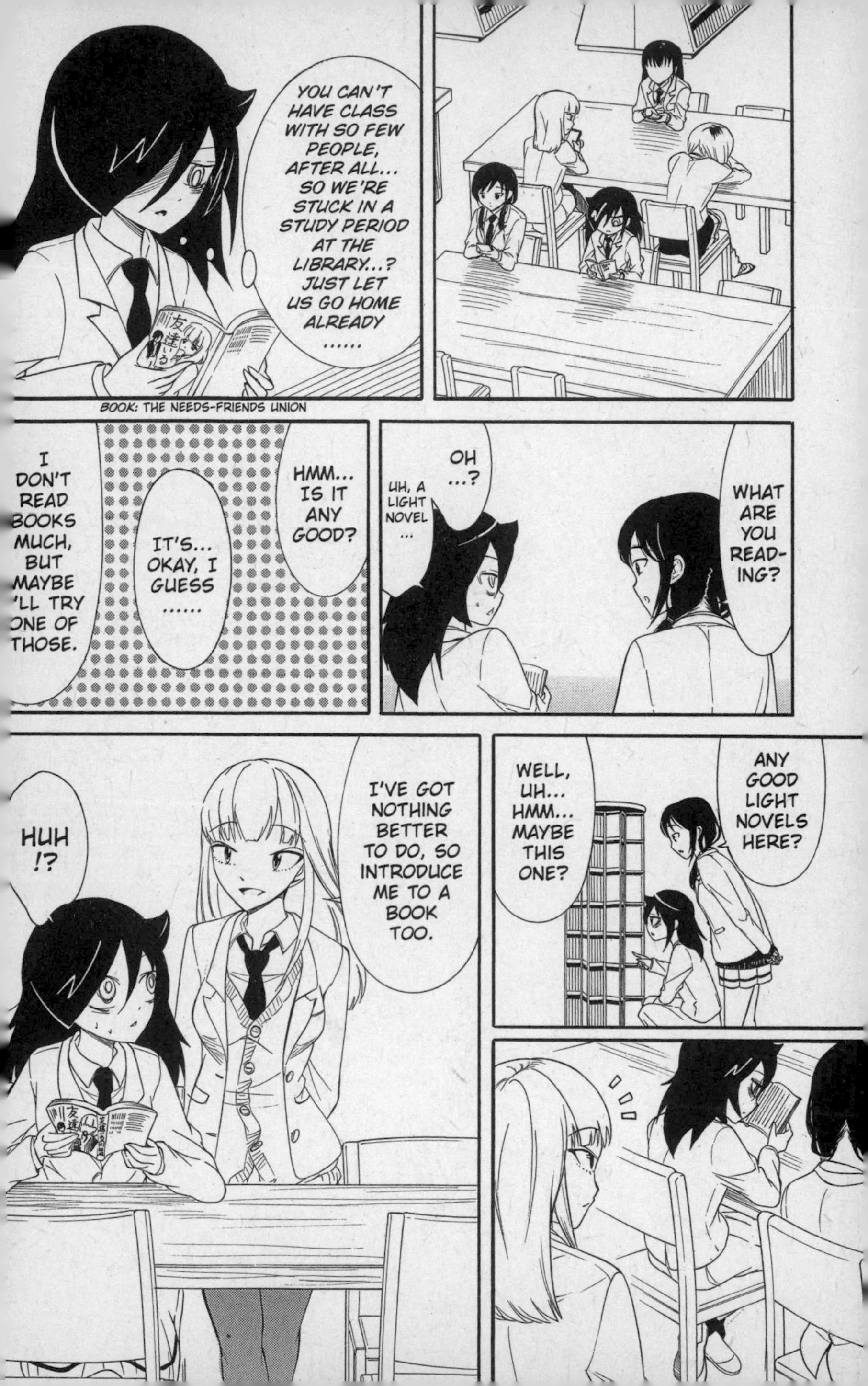
YOU CAN'T HAVE CLASS WITH SO FEW PEOPLE, AFTER ALL... SO WE'RE STUCK IN A STUDY PERIOD AT THE LIBRARY...? JUST LET US GO HOME ALREADY ......
BOOK: THE NEEDS-FRIENDS UNION
WHAT ARE YOU READ-ING?
OH ...?
UH, A LIGHT NOVEL ...
HMM... IS IT ANY GOOD?
IT'S... OKAY, I GUESS ......
I DON'T READ BOOKS MUCH, BUT MAYBE 'LL TRY ONE OF THOSE.
ANY GOOD LIGHT NOVELS HERE?
WELL, UH... HMM... MAYBE THIS ONE?
I'VE GOT NOTHING BETTER TO DO, SO INTRODUCE ME TO A BOOK TOO.
HUH !?

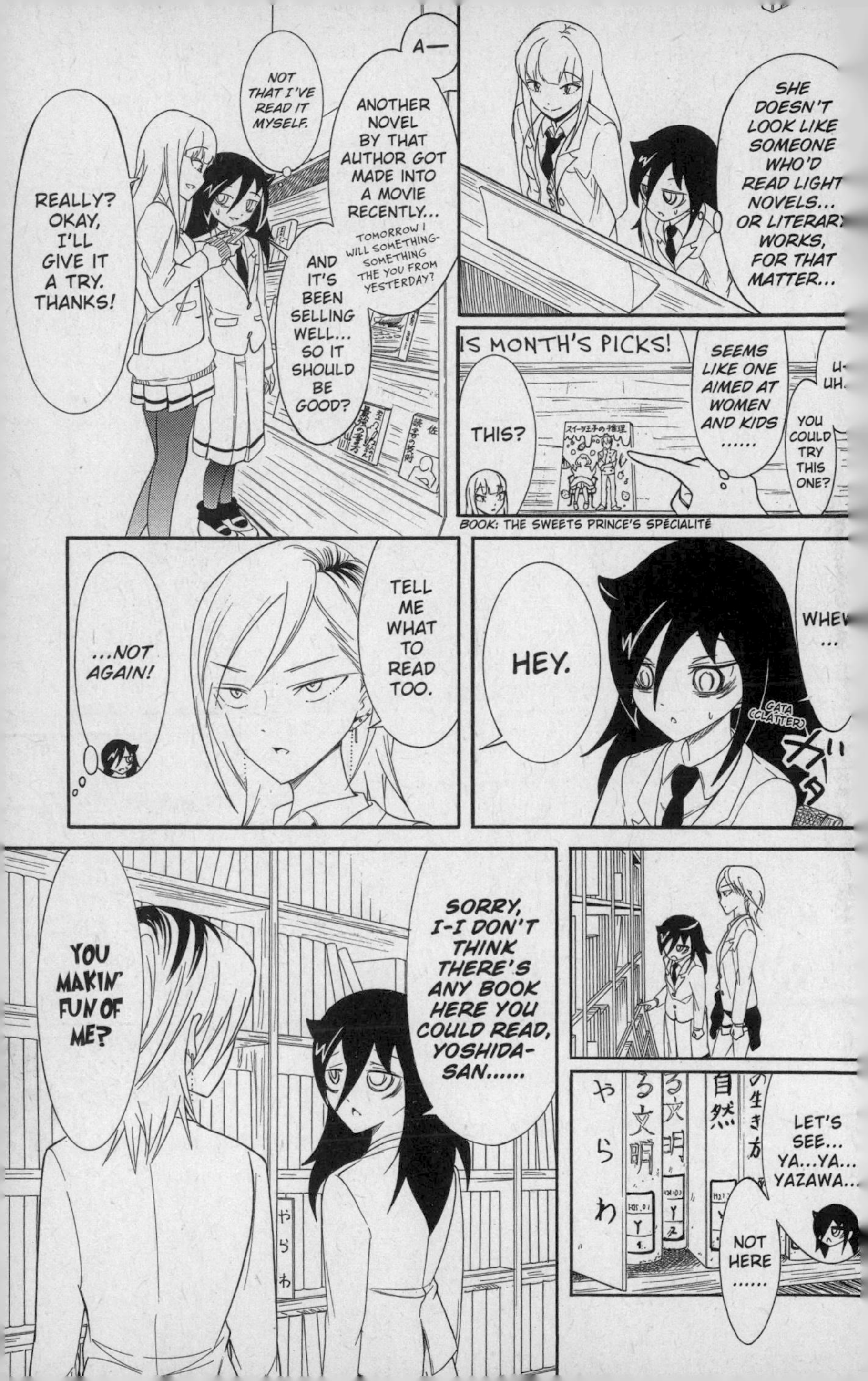
SHE DOESN'T LOOK LIKE SOMEONE WHO'D READ LIGHT NOVELS... OR LITERAR WORKS, FOR THAT MATTER...
IS MONTH'S PICKS!
U-UH.
YOU COULD TRY THIS ONE?
SEEMS LIKE ONE AIMED AT WOMEN AND KIDS ......
THIS?
スイーツ王子の推理
BOOK: THE SWEETS PRINCE'S SPÉCIALITÉ
A—
ANOTHER NOVEL BY THAT AUTHOR GOT MADE INTO A MOVIE RECENTLY...
AND IT'S BEEN SELLING WELL... SO IT SHOULD BE GOOD?
TOMORROW I WILL SOMETHING-SOMETHING THE YOU FROM YESTERDAY?
NOT THAT I'VE READ IT MYSELF.
REALLY? OKAY, I'LL GIVE IT A TRY. THANKS!
WHEW ...
HEY.
GATA (CLATTER)
TELL ME WHAT TO READ TOO.
...NOT AGAIN!
LET'S SEE... YA...YA... YAZAWA...
NOT HERE ......
SORRY, I-I DON'T THINK THERE'S ANY BOOK HERE YOU COULD READ, YOSHIDA-SAN......
YOU MAKIN' FUN OF ME?

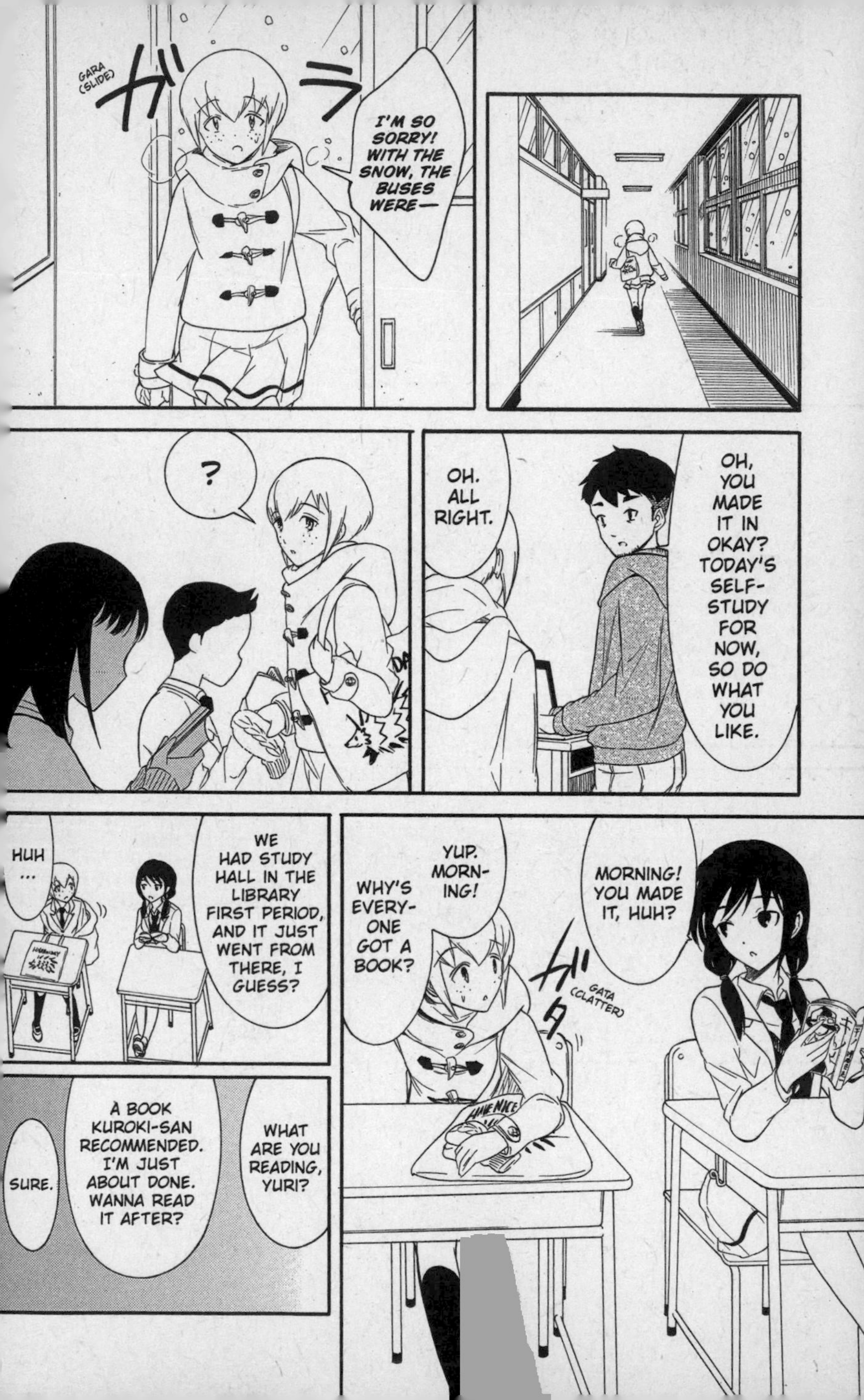
GARA (SLIDE)
I'M SO SORRY! WITH THE SNOW, THE BUSES WERE—
OH, YOU MADE IT IN OKAY? TODAY'S SELF-STUDY FOR NOW, SO DO WHAT YOU LIKE.
OH. ALL RIGHT.
?
MORNING! YOU MADE IT, HUH?
GATA (CLATTER)
YUP. MORNING!
WHY'S EVERYONE GOT A BOOK?
WE HAD STUDY HALL IN THE LIBRARY FIRST PERIOD, AND IT JUST WENT FROM THERE, I GUESS?
HUH ...
WHAT ARE YOU READING, YURI?
A BOOK KUROKI-SAN RECOMMENDED. I'M JUST ABOUT DONE. WANNA READ IT AFTER?
SURE.

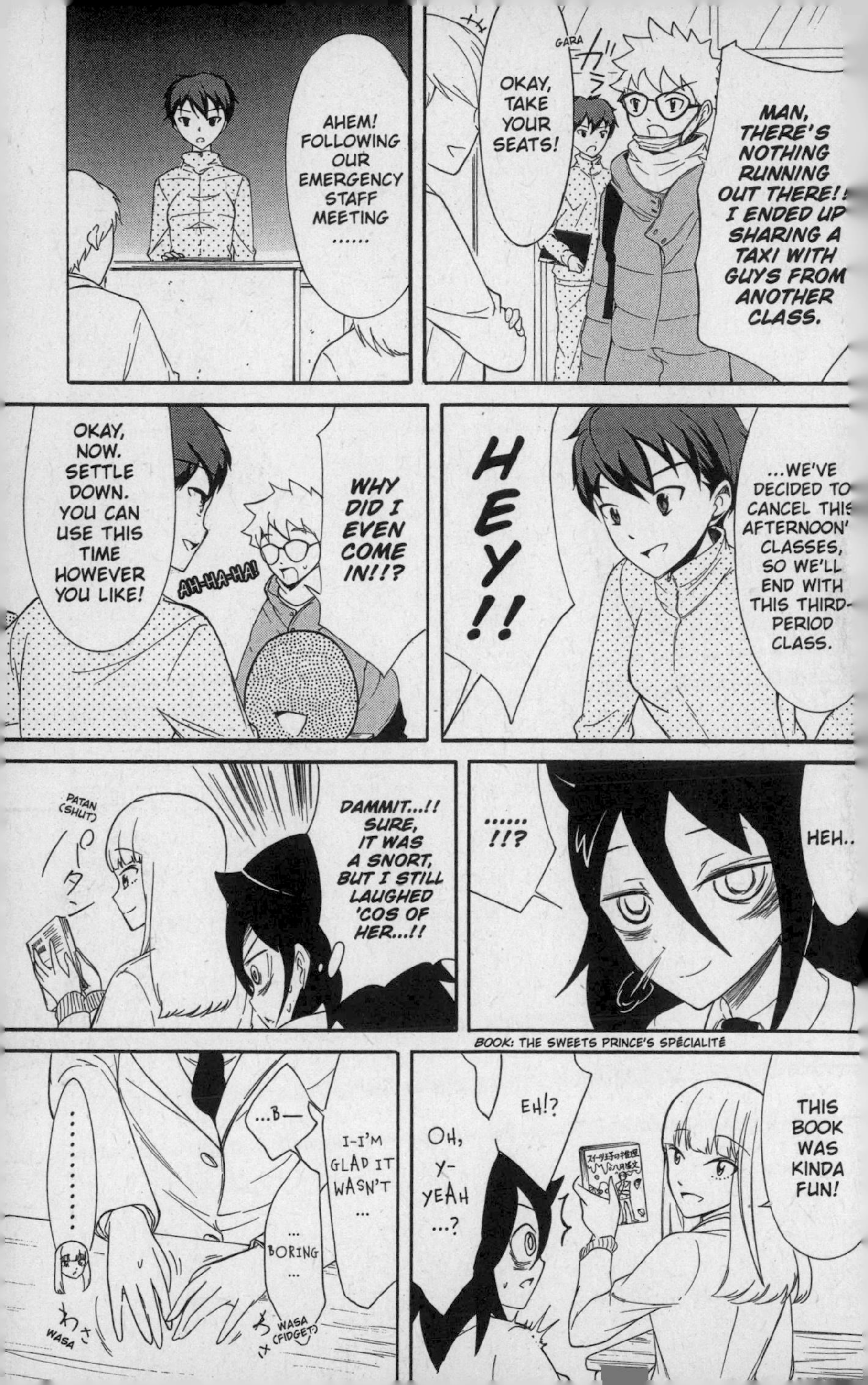
GARA
OKAY, TAKE YOUR SEATS!
MAN, THERE'S NOTHING RUNNING OUT THERE!! I ENDED UP SHARING A TAXI WITH GUYS FROM ANOTHER CLASS.
AHEM! FOLLOWING OUR EMERGENCY STAFF MEETING ......
...WE'VE DECIDED TO CANCEL THIS AFTERNOON' CLASSES, SO WE'LL END WITH THIS THIRD-PERIOD CLASS.
HEY!!
WHY DID I EVEN COME IN!!?
AH-HA-HA!
OKAY, NOW. SETTLE DOWN. YOU CAN USE THIS TIME HOWEVER YOU LIKE!
HEH..
......!!?
DAMMIT...!! SURE, IT WAS A SNORT, BUT I STILL LAUGHED 'COS OF HER...!!
PATAN (SHUT)
BOOK: THE SWEETS PRINCE'S SPÉCIALITÉ
THIS BOOK WAS KINDA FUN!
EH!?
OH, Y-YEAH ...?
...B—
I-I'M GLAD IT WASN'T ... ... BORING ...
....
WASA (FIDGET)
WASA

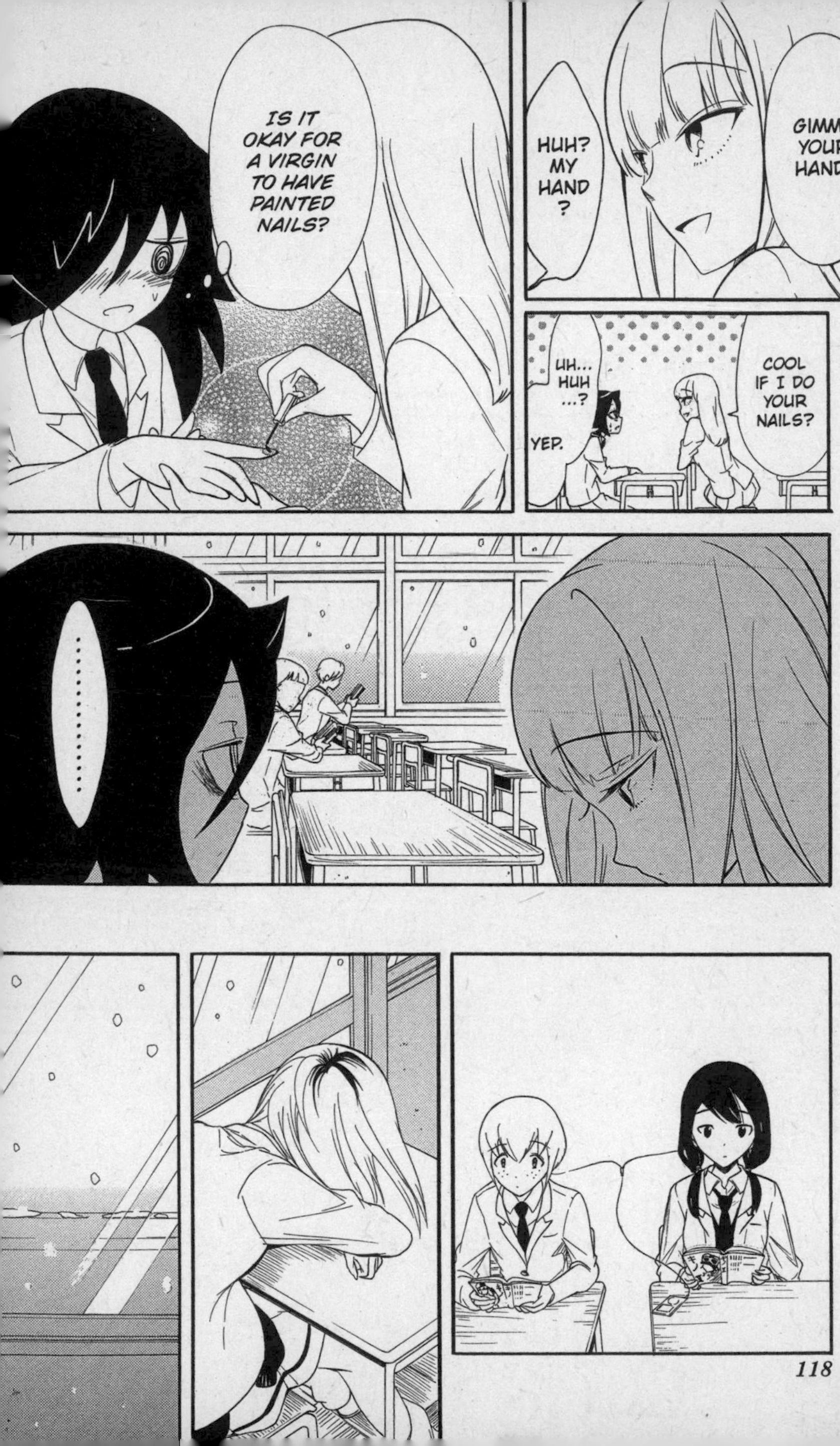
GIMME YOUR HAND.
HUH? MY HAND?
COOL IF I DO YOUR NAILS?
UH... HUH...?
IS IT OKAY FOR A VIRGIN TO HAVE PAINTED NAILS?

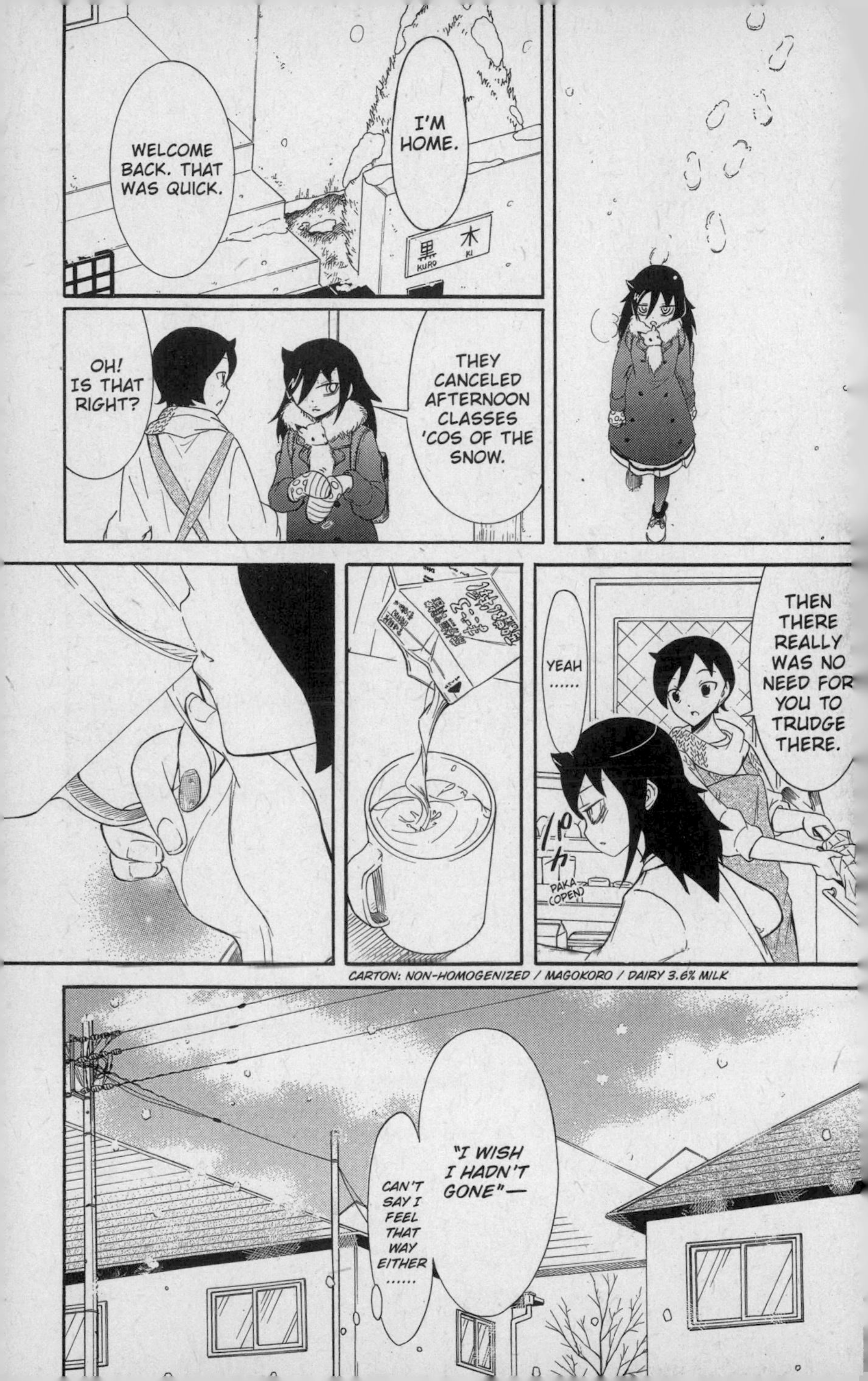
I'M HOME.
WELCOME BACK. THAT WAS QUICK.
黒 木
KURO KI
THEY CANCELED AFTERNOON CLASSES 'COS OF THE SNOW.
OH! IS THAT RIGHT?
THEN THERE REALLY WAS NO NEED FOR YOU TO TRUDGE THERE.
YEAH ......
PAKA (OPEN)
CARTON: NON-HOMOGENIZED / MAGOKORO / DAIRY 3.6% MILK
"I WISH I HADN'T GONE"—
CAN'T SAY I FEEL THAT WAY EITHER ......

No Matter How I Look at It, It's You Guys' Fault I'm Not Popular!

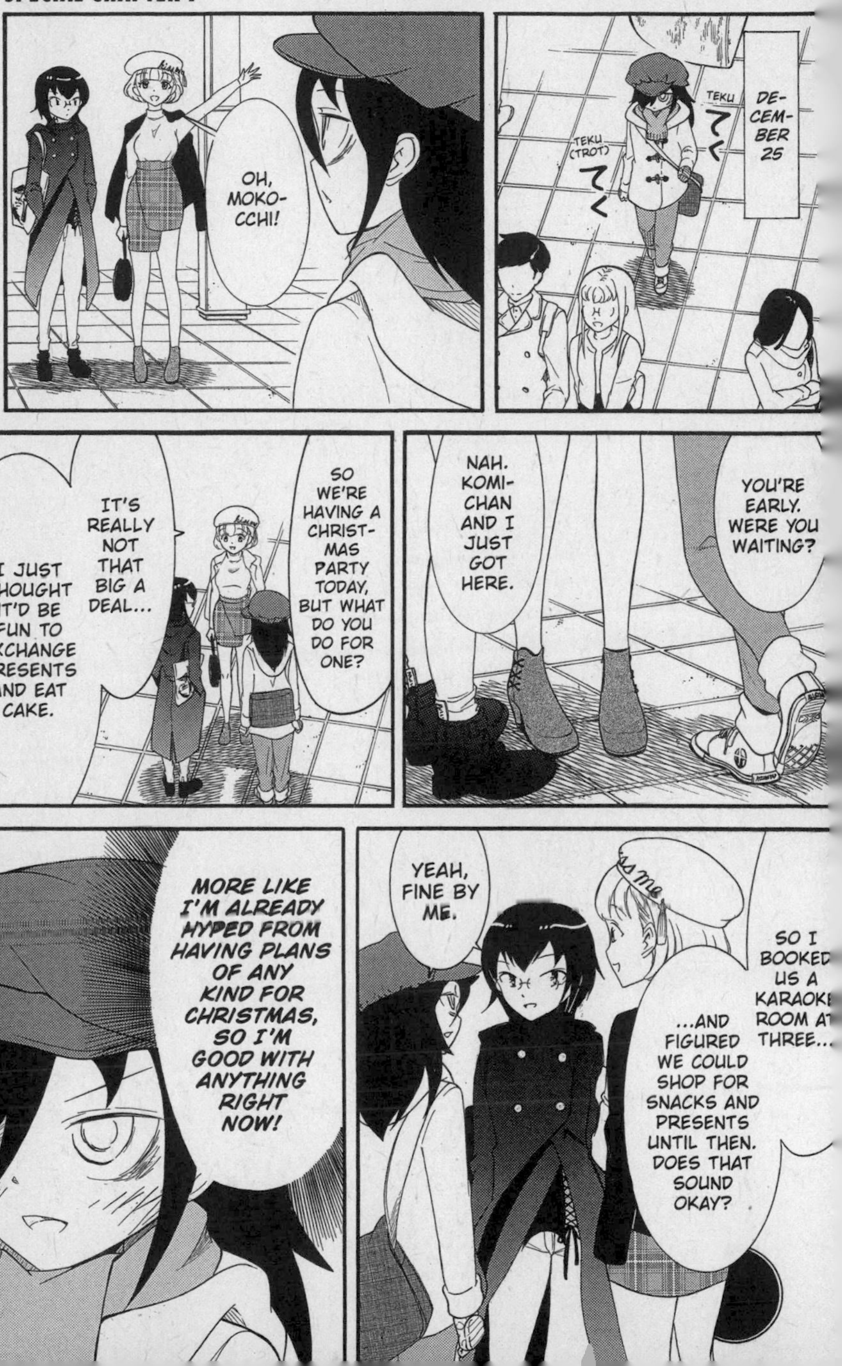
DE-CEM-BER 25
TEKU
TEKU (TROT)
OH, MOKO-CCHI!
YOU'RE EARLY. WERE YOU WAITING?
NAH. KOMI-CHAN AND I JUST GOT HERE.
SO WE'RE HAVING A CHRIST-MAS PARTY TODAY, BUT WHAT DO YOU DO FOR ONE?
IT'S REALLY NOT THAT BIG A DEAL...
I JUST THOUGHT IT'D BE FUN TO EXCHANGE PRESENTS AND EAT CAKE.
SO I BOOKED US A KARAOKE ROOM AT THREE...
...AND FIGURED WE COULD SHOP FOR SNACKS AND PRESENTS UNTIL THEN. DOES THAT SOUND OKAY?
YEAH, FINE BY ME.
MORE LIKE I'M ALREADY HYPED FROM HAVING PLANS OF ANY KIND FOR CHRISTMAS, SO I'M GOOD WITH ANYTHING RIGHT NOW!

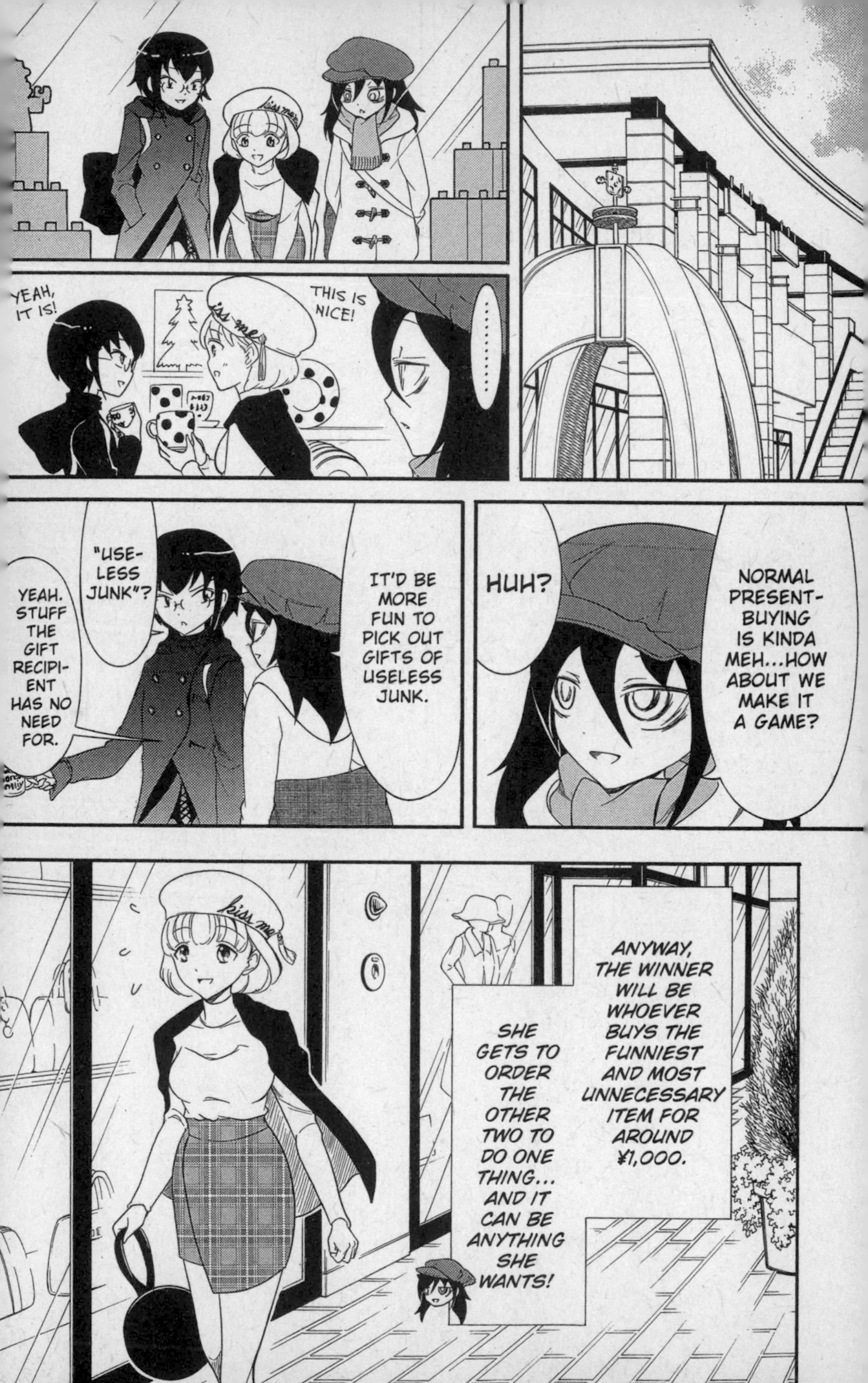
......
THIS IS NICE!
YEAH, IT IS!
NORMAL PRESENT-BUYING IS KINDA MEH...HOW ABOUT WE MAKE IT A GAME?
HUH?
IT'D BE MORE FUN TO PICK OUT GIFTS OF USELESS JUNK.
"USELESS JUNK"?
YEAH. STUFF THE GIFT RECIPIENT HAS NO NEED FOR.
ANYWAY, THE WINNER WILL BE WHOEVER BUYS THE FUNNIEST AND MOST UNNECESSARY ITEM FOR AROUND ¥1,000.
SHE GETS TO ORDER THE OTHER TWO TO DO ONE THING... AND IT CAN BE ANYTHING SHE WANTS!

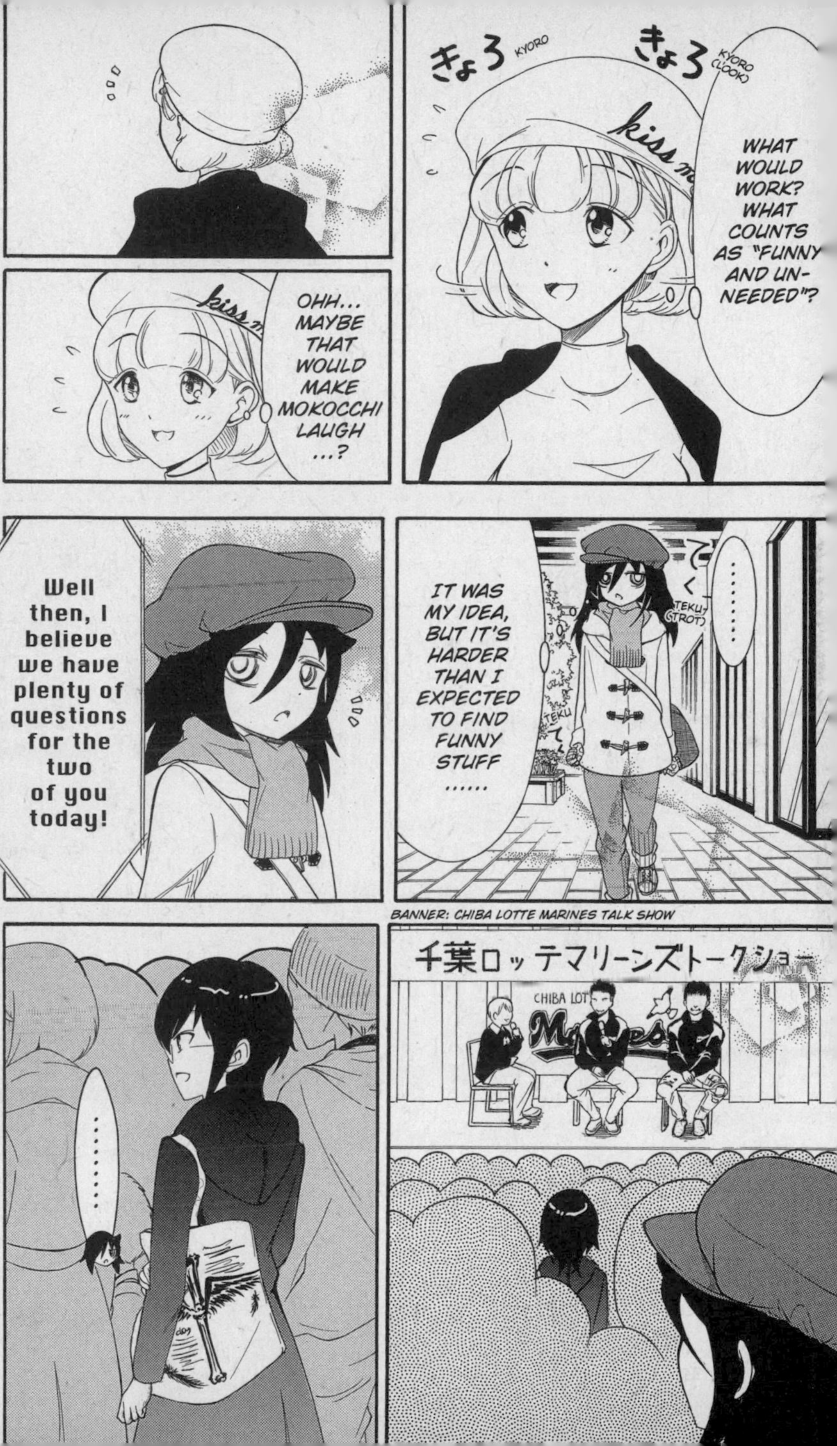
きょろ KYORO
きょろ KYORO (LOOK)
WHAT WOULD WORK? WHAT COUNTS AS "FUNNY AND UN-NEEDED"?
OHH... MAYBE THAT WOULD MAKE MOKOCCHI LAUGH ...?
......
てく TEKU (TROT)
てく TEKU
IT WAS MY IDEA, BUT IT'S HARDER THAN I EXPECTED TO FIND FUNNY STUFF ......
Well then, I believe we have plenty of questions for the two of you today!
BANNER: CHIBA LOTTE MARINES TALK SHOW
千葉ロッテマリーンズトークショー
CHIBA LOTT
......

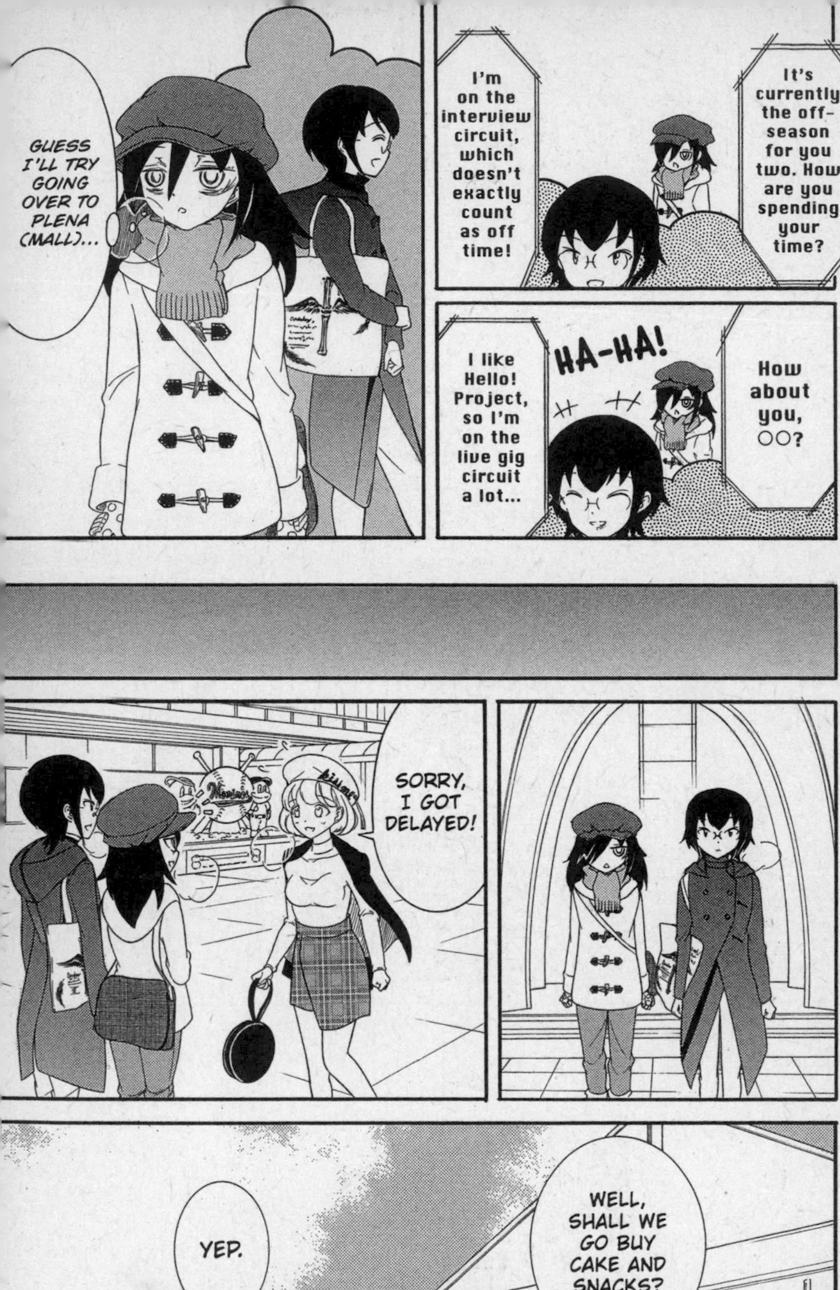
It's currently the off-season for you two. How are you spending your time?
I'm on the interview circuit, which doesn't exactly count as off time!
How about you, OO?
HA-HA!
I like Hello! Project, so I'm on the live gig circuit a lot...
GUESS I'LL TRY GOING OVER TO PLENA (MALL)...
SORRY, I GOT DELAYED!
WELL, SHALL WE GO BUY CAKE AND SNACKS?
YEP.

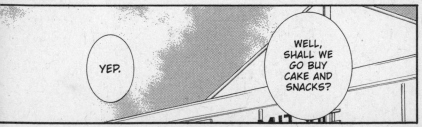

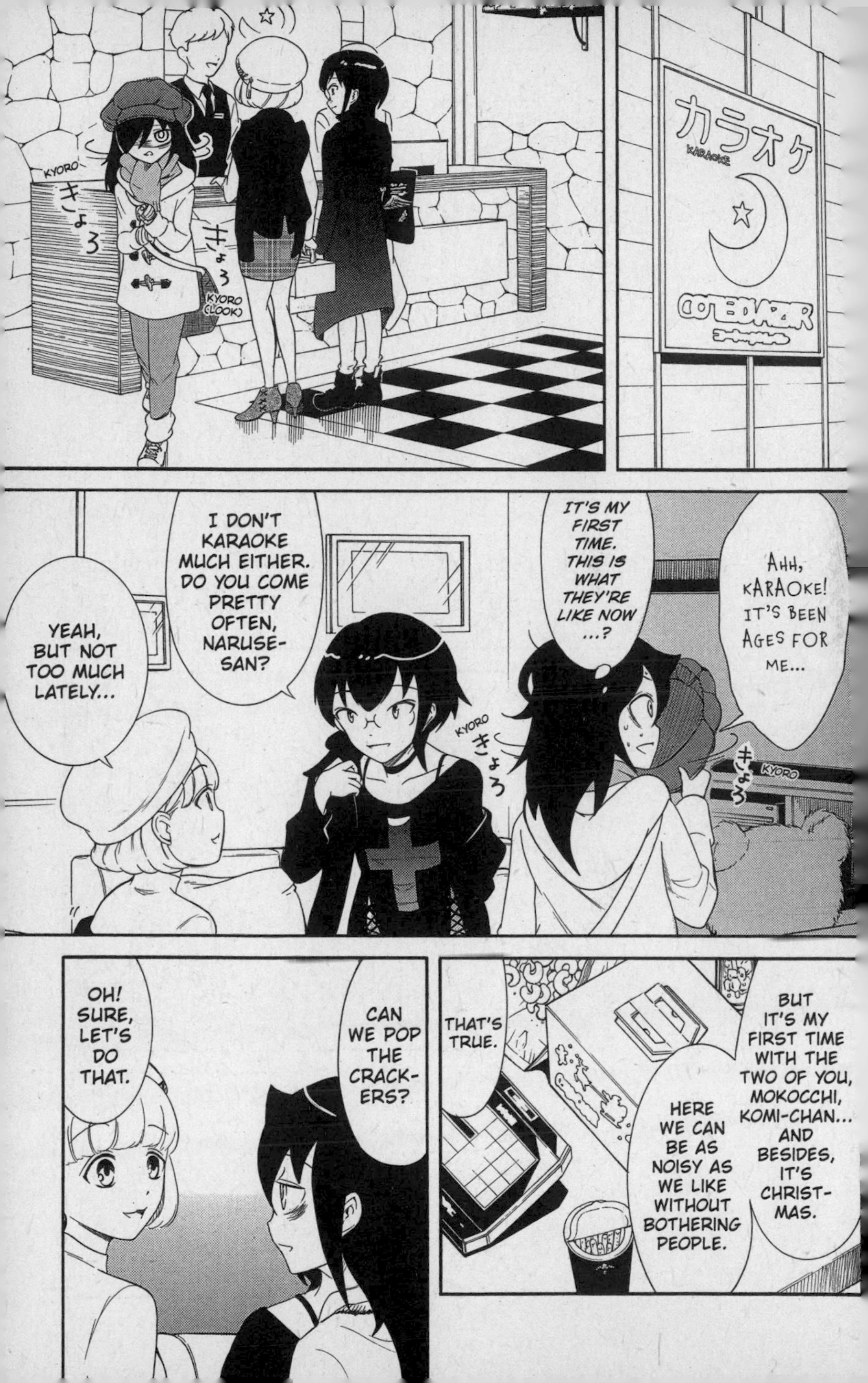
カラオケ
KARAOKE
KYORO
きょろ
きょろ
KYORO (LOOK)
AHH, KARAOKE! IT'S BEEN AGES FOR ME...
きょろ
KYORO
IT'S MY FIRST TIME. THIS IS WHAT THEY'RE LIKE NOW ...?
KYORO
きょろ
I DON'T KARAOKE MUCH EITHER. DO YOU COME PRETTY OFTEN, NARUSE-SAN?
YEAH, BUT NOT TOO MUCH LATELY...
BUT IT'S MY FIRST TIME WITH THE TWO OF YOU, MOKOCCHI, KOMI-CHAN... AND BESIDES, IT'S CHRIST-MAS.
HERE WE CAN BE AS NOISY AS WE LIKE WITHOUT BOTHERING PEOPLE.
THAT'S TRUE.
CAN WE POP THE CRACK-ERS?
OH! SURE, LET'S DO THAT.

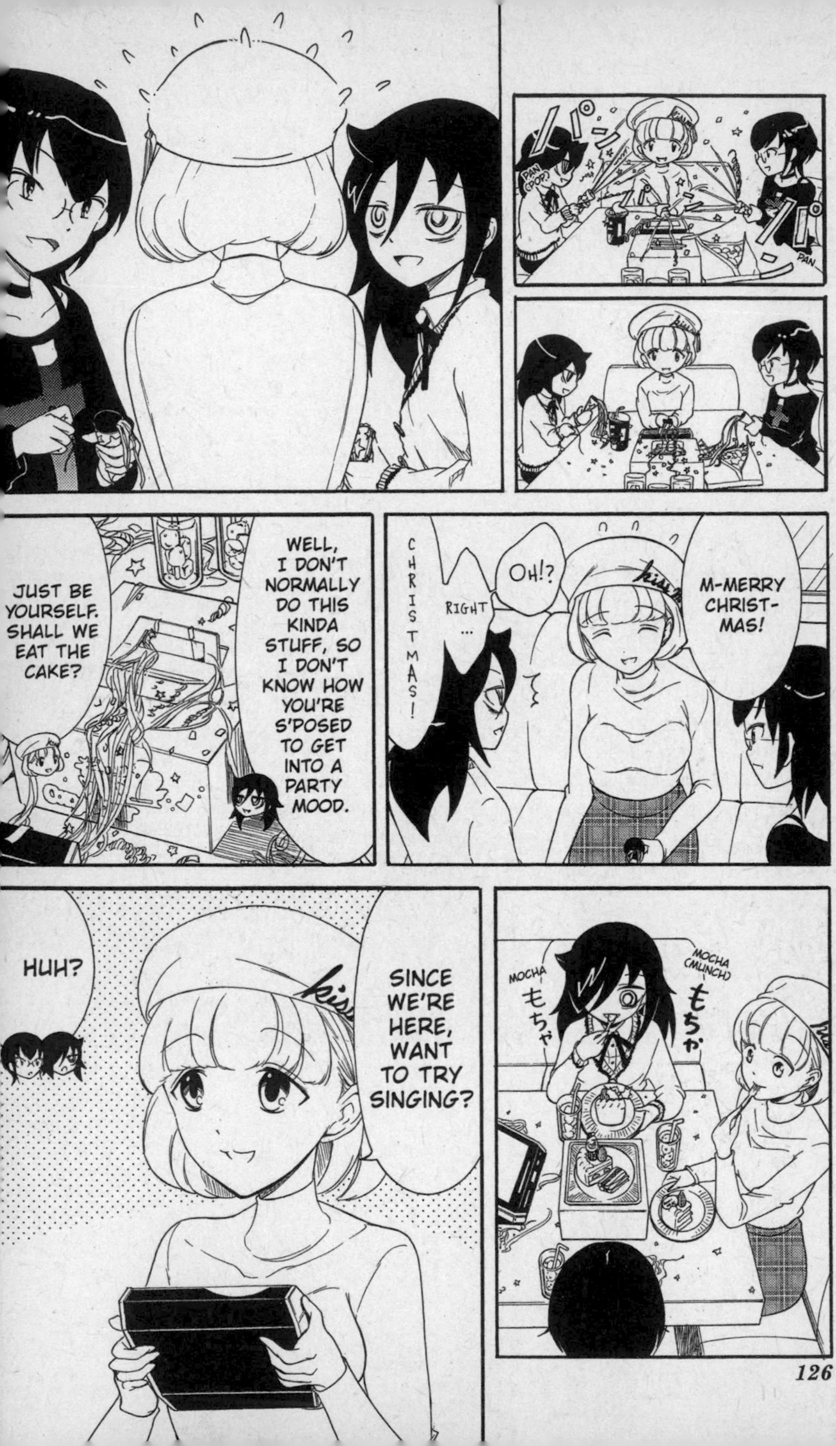
PAN (POP)
PAN
M-MERRY CHRISTMAS!
OH!?
RIGHT ...
CHRISTMAS!
WELL, I DON'T NORMALLY DO THIS KINDA STUFF, SO I DON'T KNOW HOW YOU'RE S'POSED TO GET INTO A PARTY MOOD.
JUST BE YOURSELF. SHALL WE EAT THE CAKE?
MOCHA (MUNCH)
もちゃ
MOCHA
もちゃ
SINCE WE'RE HERE, WANT TO TRY SINGING?
HUH?

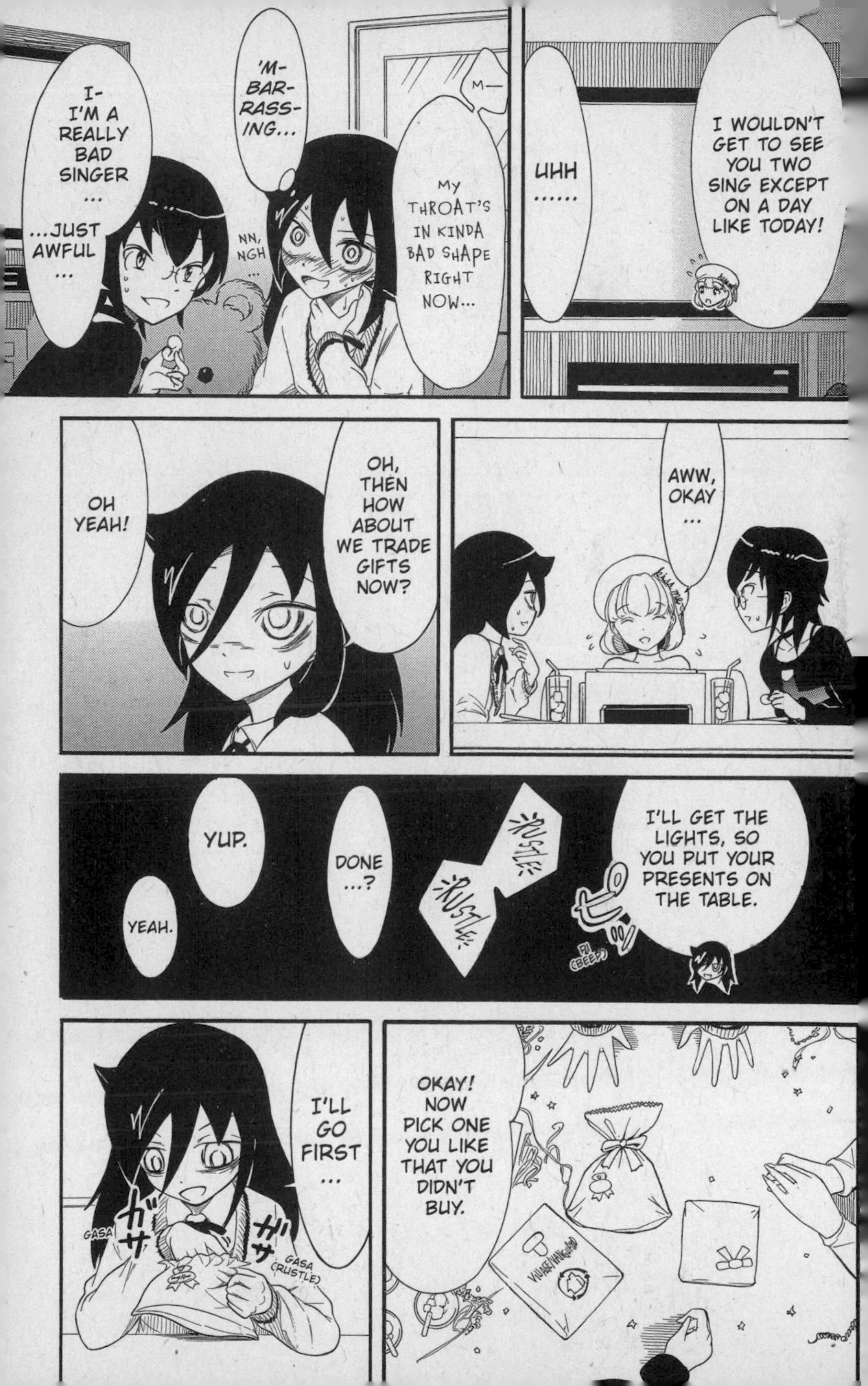
I WOULDN'T GET TO SEE YOU TWO SING EXCEPT ON A DAY LIKE TODAY!
UHH ......
M—
MY THROAT'S IN KINDA BAD SHAPE RIGHT NOW...
'M-BAR-RASS-ING...
NN, NGH ...
I- I'M A REALLY BAD SINGER ... ...JUST AWFUL ...
AWW, OKAY ...
OH, THEN HOW ABOUT WE TRADE GIFTS NOW?
OH YEAH!
I'LL GET THE LIGHTS, SO YOU PUT YOUR PRESENTS ON THE TABLE.
PI (BEEP)
RUSTLE
RUSTLE
DONE ...?
YUP.
YEAH.
OKAY! NOW PICK ONE YOU LIKE THAT YOU DIDN'T BUY.
I'LL GO FIRST ...
ガサ
GASA (RUSTLE)
ガサ
GASA

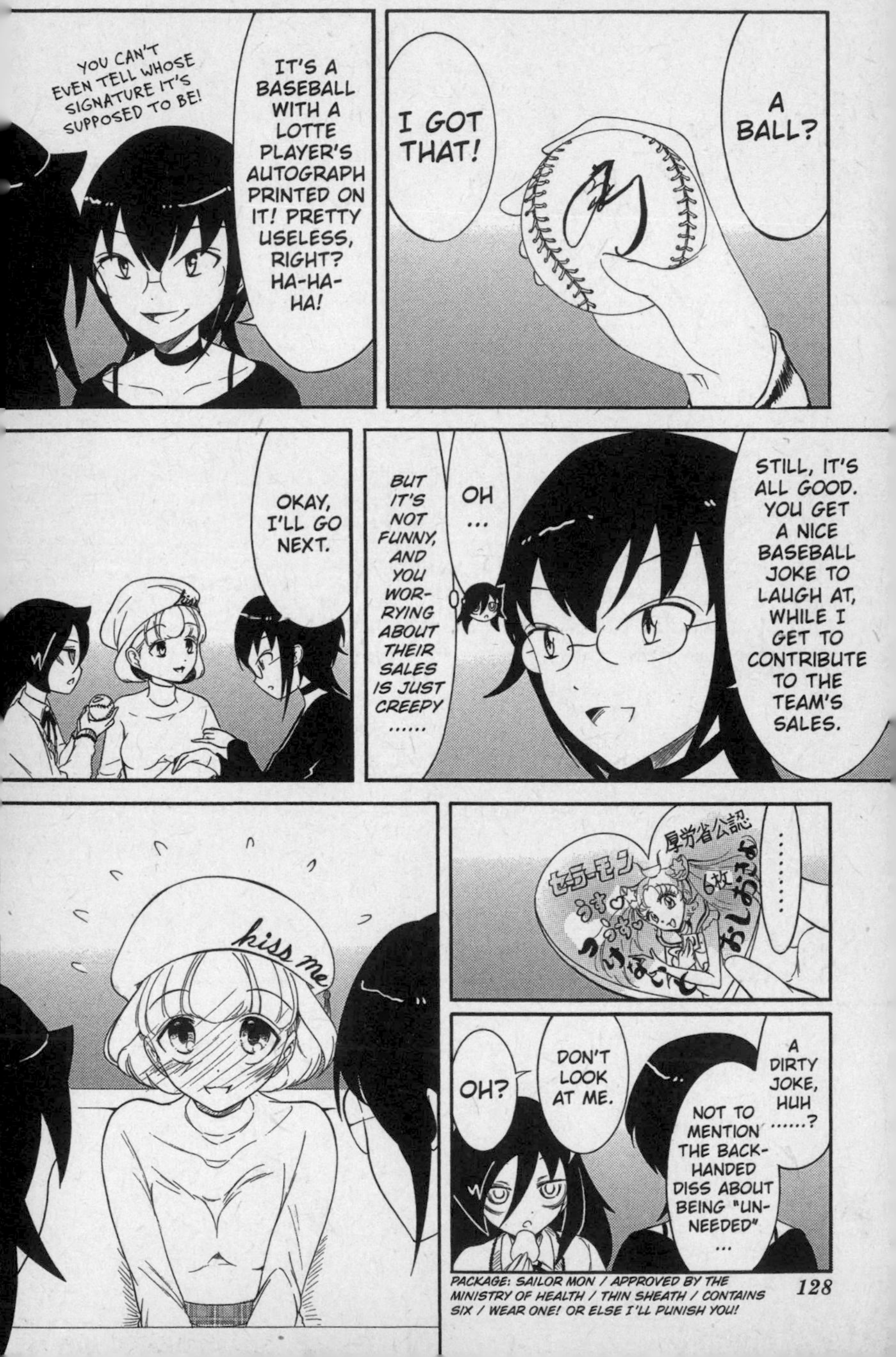
A BALL?
I GOT THAT!
IT'S A BASEBALL WITH A LOTTE PLAYER'S AUTOGRAPH PRINTED ON IT! PRETTY USELESS, RIGHT? HA-HA-HA!
YOU CAN'T EVEN TELL WHOSE SIGNATURE IT'S SUPPOSED TO BE!
STILL, IT'S ALL GOOD. YOU GET A NICE BASEBALL JOKE TO LAUGH AT, WHILE I GET TO CONTRIBUTE TO THE TEAM'S SALES.
OH ...
BUT IT'S NOT FUNNY, AND YOU WORRYING ABOUT THEIR SALES IS JUST CREEPY ......
OKAY, I'LL GO NEXT.
......
厚労省公認
セーラーモン
6枚
A DIRTY JOKE, HUH ......?
NOT TO MENTION THE BACK-HANDED DISS ABOUT BEING "UNNEEDED" ...
DON'T LOOK AT ME.
OH?
kiss me

PACKAGE: SAILOR MON / APPROVED BY THE MINISTRY OF HEALTH / THIN SHEATH / CONTAINS SIX / WEAR ONE! OR ELSE I'LL PUNISH YOU!

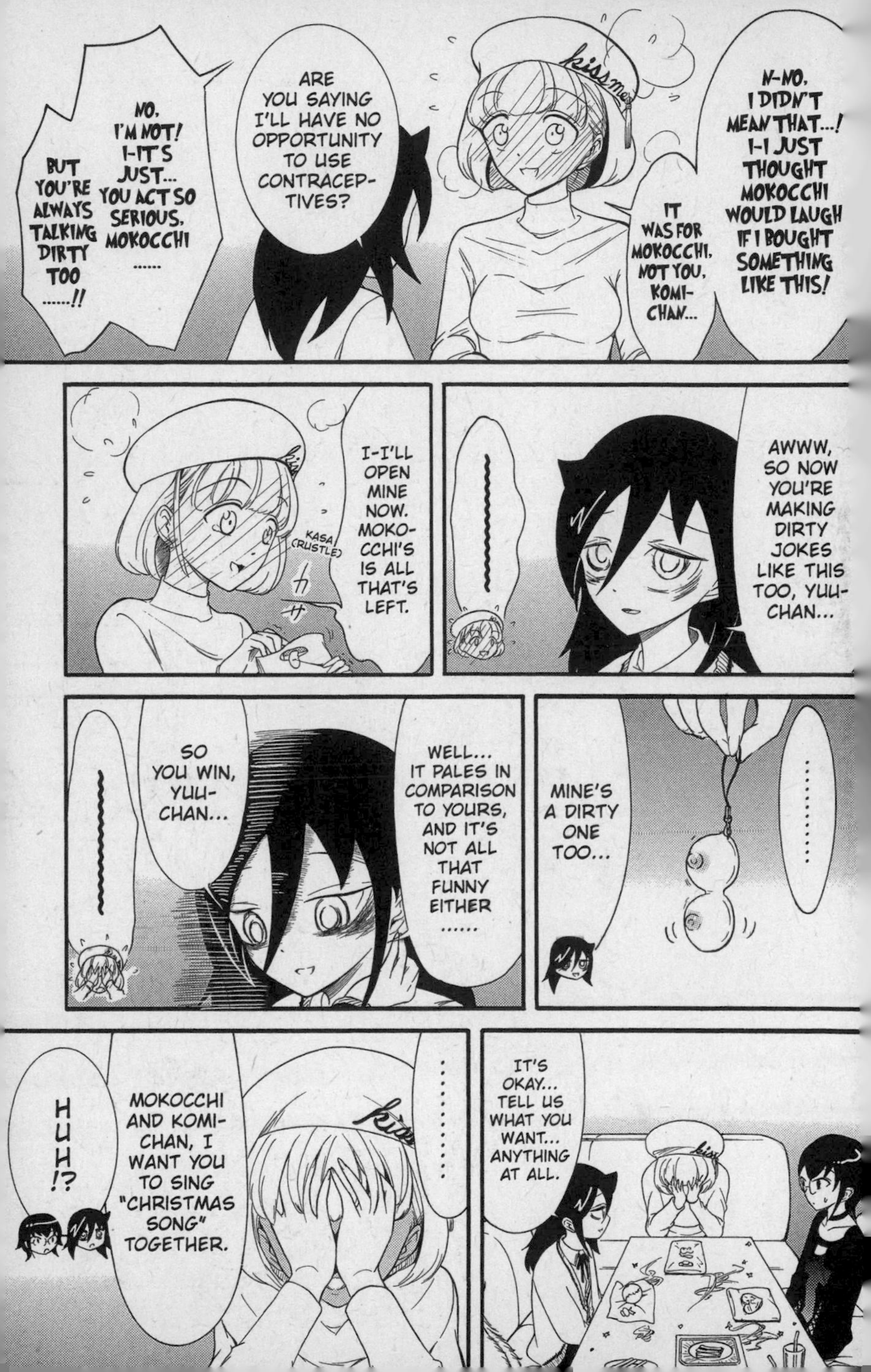
N-NO, I DIDN'T MEAN THAT...! I-I JUST THOUGHT MOKOCCHI WOULD LAUGH IF I BOUGHT SOMETHING LIKE THIS!
IT WAS FOR MOKOCCHI, NOT YOU, KOMI-CHAN...
ARE YOU SAYING I'LL HAVE NO OPPORTUNITY TO USE CONTRACEPTIVES?
NO, I'M NOT! I-IT'S JUST... YOU ACT SO SERIOUS, MOKOCCHI ......
BUT YOU'RE ALWAYS TALKING DIRTY TOO ......!!
AWWW, SO NOW YOU'RE MAKING DIRTY JOKES LIKE THIS TOO, YUU-CHAN...
I-I'LL OPEN MINE NOW. MOKOCCHI'S IS ALL THAT'S LEFT.
KASA (RUSTLE)
....
MINE'S A DIRTY ONE TOO...
WELL... IT PALES IN COMPARISON TO YOURS, AND IT'S NOT ALL THAT FUNNY EITHER ......
SO YOU WIN, YUU-CHAN...
IT'S OKAY... TELL US WHAT YOU WANT... ANYTHING AT ALL.
......
MOKOCCHI AND KOMI-CHAN, I WANT YOU TO SING "CHRISTMAS SONG" TOGETHER.
HUH!?

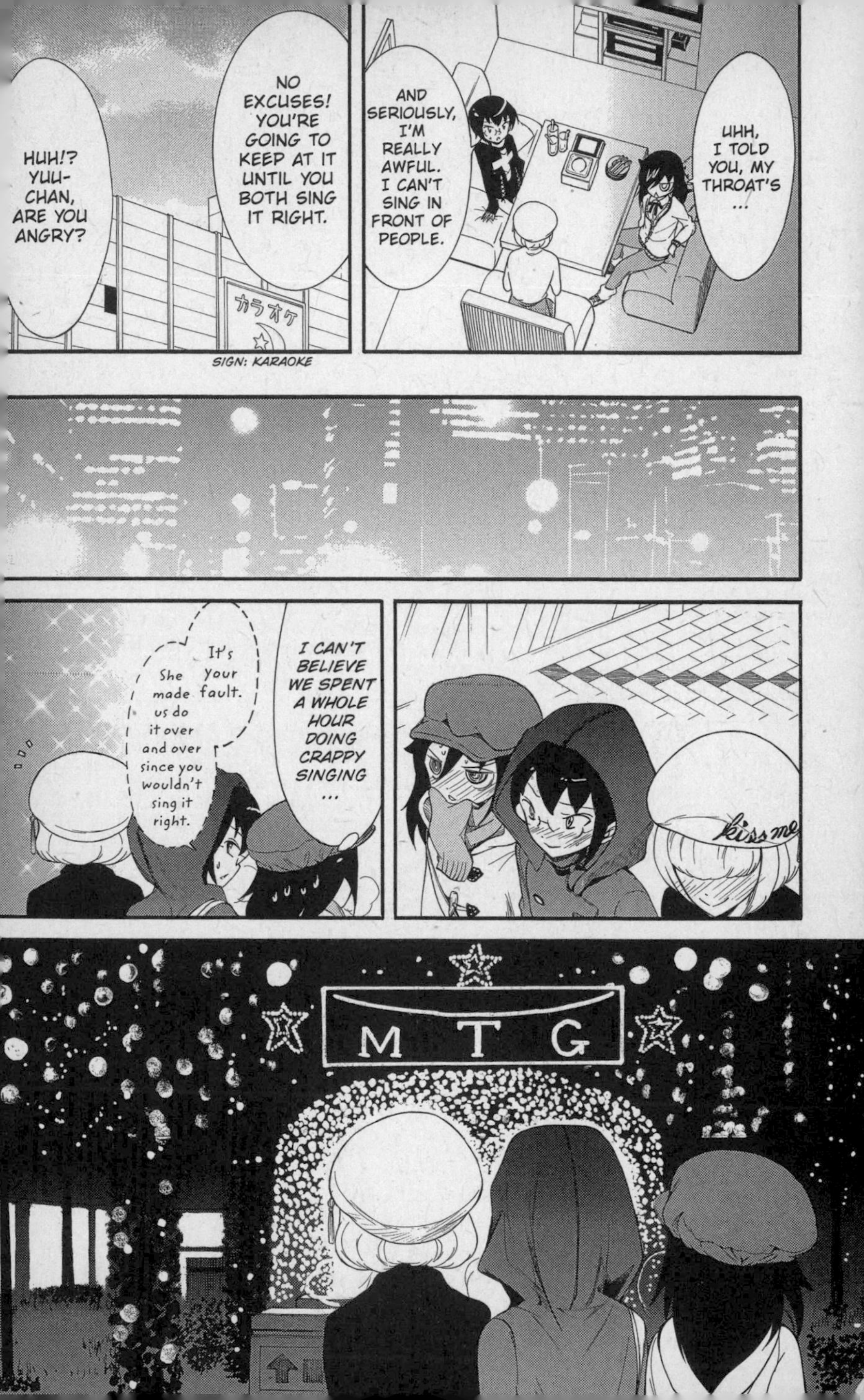
UHH, I TOLD YOU, MY THROAT'S ...
AND SERIOUSLY, I'M REALLY AWFUL. I CAN'T SING IN FRONT OF PEOPLE.
NO EXCUSES! YOU'RE GOING TO KEEP AT IT UNTIL YOU BOTH SING IT RIGHT.
HUH!? YUU-CHAN, ARE YOU ANGRY?
カラオケ
SIGN: KARAOKE
kiss me
I CAN'T BELIEVE WE SPENT A WHOLE HOUR DOING CRAPPY SINGING ...
It's your fault.
She made us do it over and over since you wouldn't sing it right.
MTG

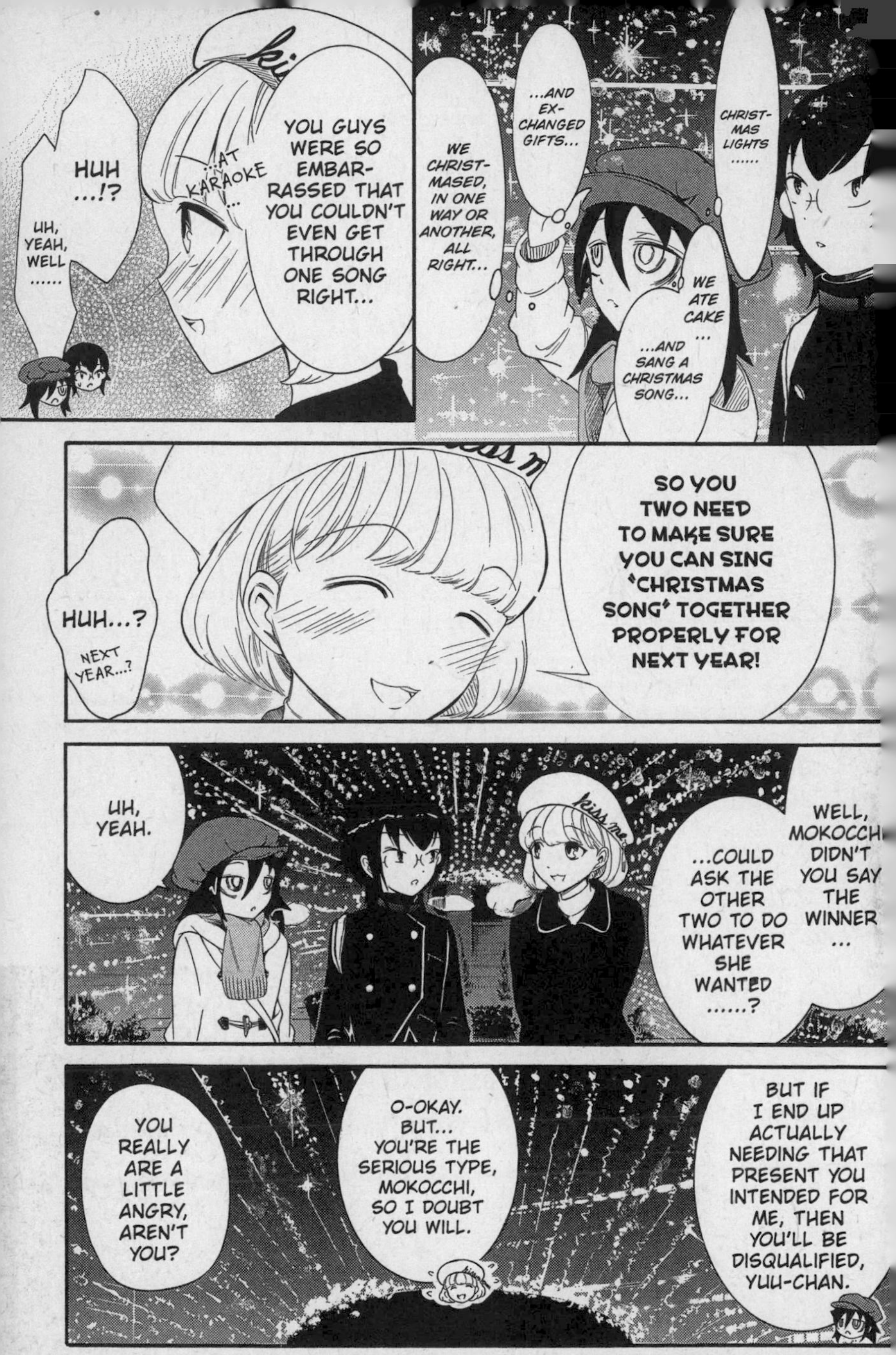
CHRISTMAS LIGHTS......
...AND EXCHANGED GIFTS...
WE CHRISTMASED, IN ONE WAY OR ANOTHER, ALL RIGHT...
WE ATE CAKE...
...AND SANG A CHRISTMAS SONG...
YOU GUYS WERE SO EMBARRASSED THAT YOU COULDN'T EVEN GET THROUGH ONE SONG RIGHT...
...AT KARAOKE...
HUH...!?
UH, YEAH, WELL......
SO YOU TWO NEED TO MAKE SURE YOU CAN SING "CHRISTMAS SONG" TOGETHER PROPERLY FOR NEXT YEAR!
HUH...?
NEXT YEAR...?
WELL, MOKOCCHI DIDN'T YOU SAY THE WINNER...
...COULD ASK THE OTHER TWO TO DO WHATEVER SHE WANTED......?
UH, YEAH.
BUT IF I END UP ACTUALLY NEEDING THAT PRESENT YOU INTENDED FOR ME, THEN YOU'LL BE DISQUALIFIED, YUU-CHAN.
O-OKAY. BUT... YOU'RE THE SERIOUS TYPE, MOKOCCHI, SO I DOUBT YOU WILL.
YOU REALLY ARE A LITTLE ANGRY, AREN'T YOU?

TO BE CONTINUED IN NO MATTER HOW I LOOK AT IT, IT'S YOU GUYS' FAULT I'M NOT POPULAR ⑫!

AFTER FAIL 107... BONUS

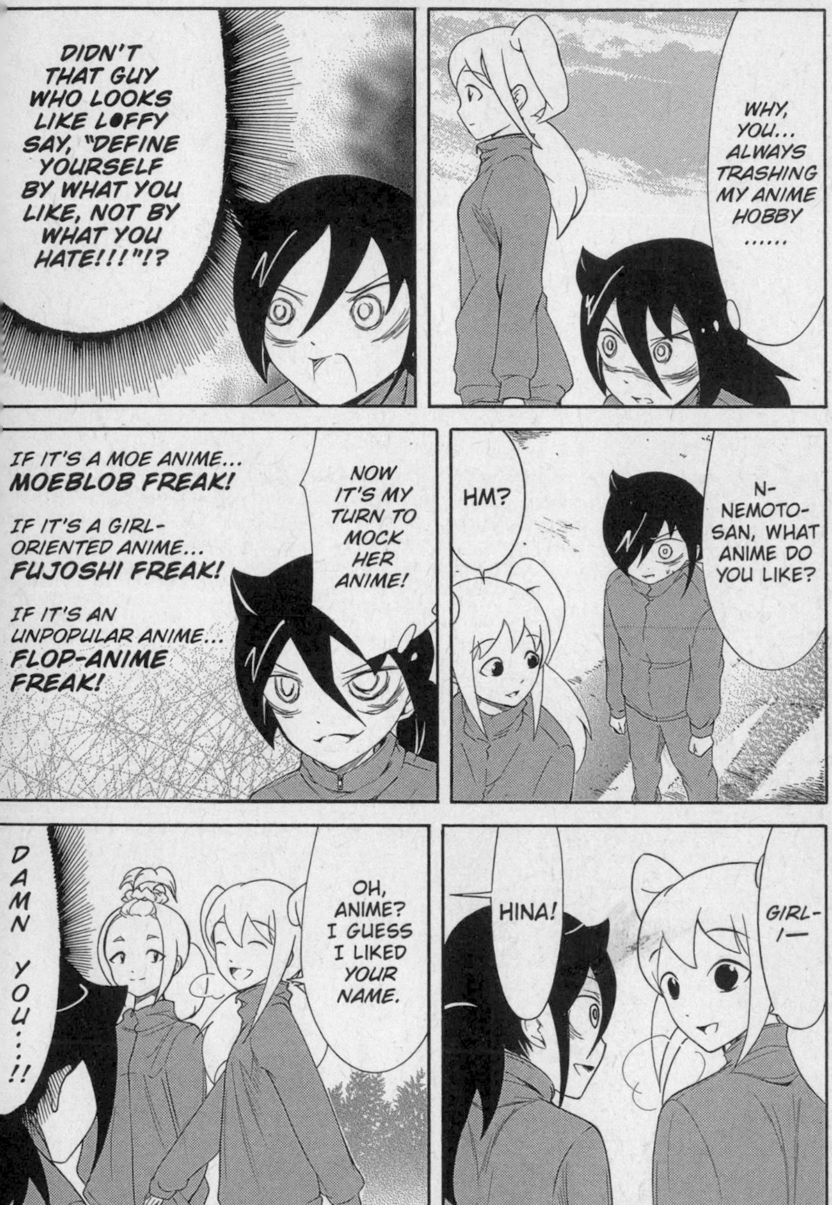
WHY, YOU... ALWAYS TRASHING MY ANIME HOBBY ......
DIDN'T THAT GUY WHO LOOKS LIKE L●FFY SAY, "DEFINE YOURSELF BY WHAT YOU LIKE, NOT BY WHAT YOU HATE!!!"!?
N-NEMOTO-SAN, WHAT ANIME DO YOU LIKE?
HM?
NOW IT'S MY TURN TO MOCK HER ANIME!
IF IT'S A MOE ANIME... **MOEBLOB FREAK!**
IF IT'S A GIRL-ORIENTED ANIME... **FUJOSHI FREAK!**
IF IT'S AN UNPOPULAR ANIME... **FLOP-ANIME FREAK!**
GIRL-I—
HINA!
OH, ANIME? I GUESS I LIKED YOUR NAME.
DAMN YOU...!!

AFTER FAIL 109...

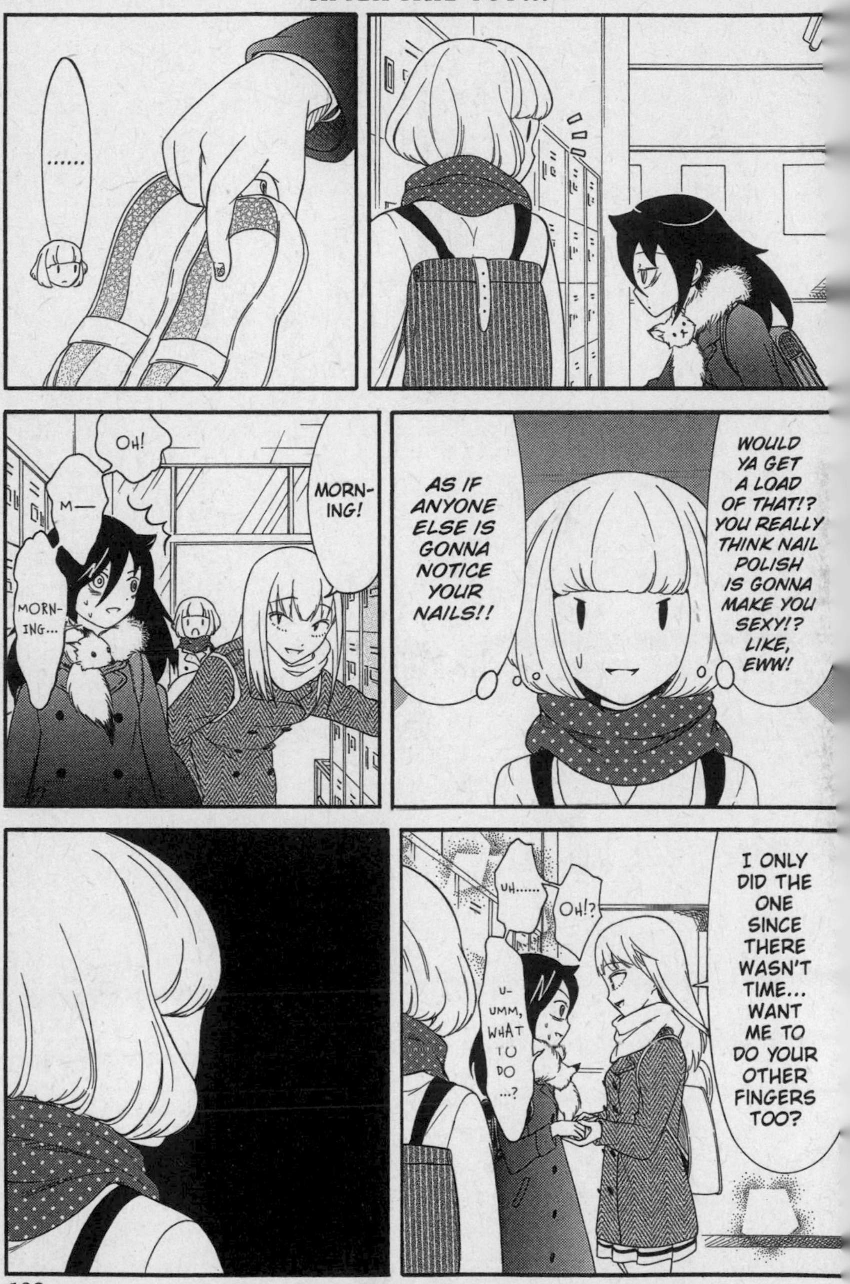
......
WOULD YA GET A LOAD OF THAT!? YOU REALLY THINK NAIL POLISH IS GONNA MAKE YOU SEXY!? LIKE, EWW!
AS IF ANYONE ELSE IS GONNA NOTICE YOUR NAILS!!
MORN-ING!
OH!
M—
MORN-ING...
I ONLY DID THE ONE SINCE THERE WASN'T TIME... WANT ME TO DO YOUR OTHER FINGERS TOO?
OH!?
UH......
U-UMM, WHAT TO DO ...?

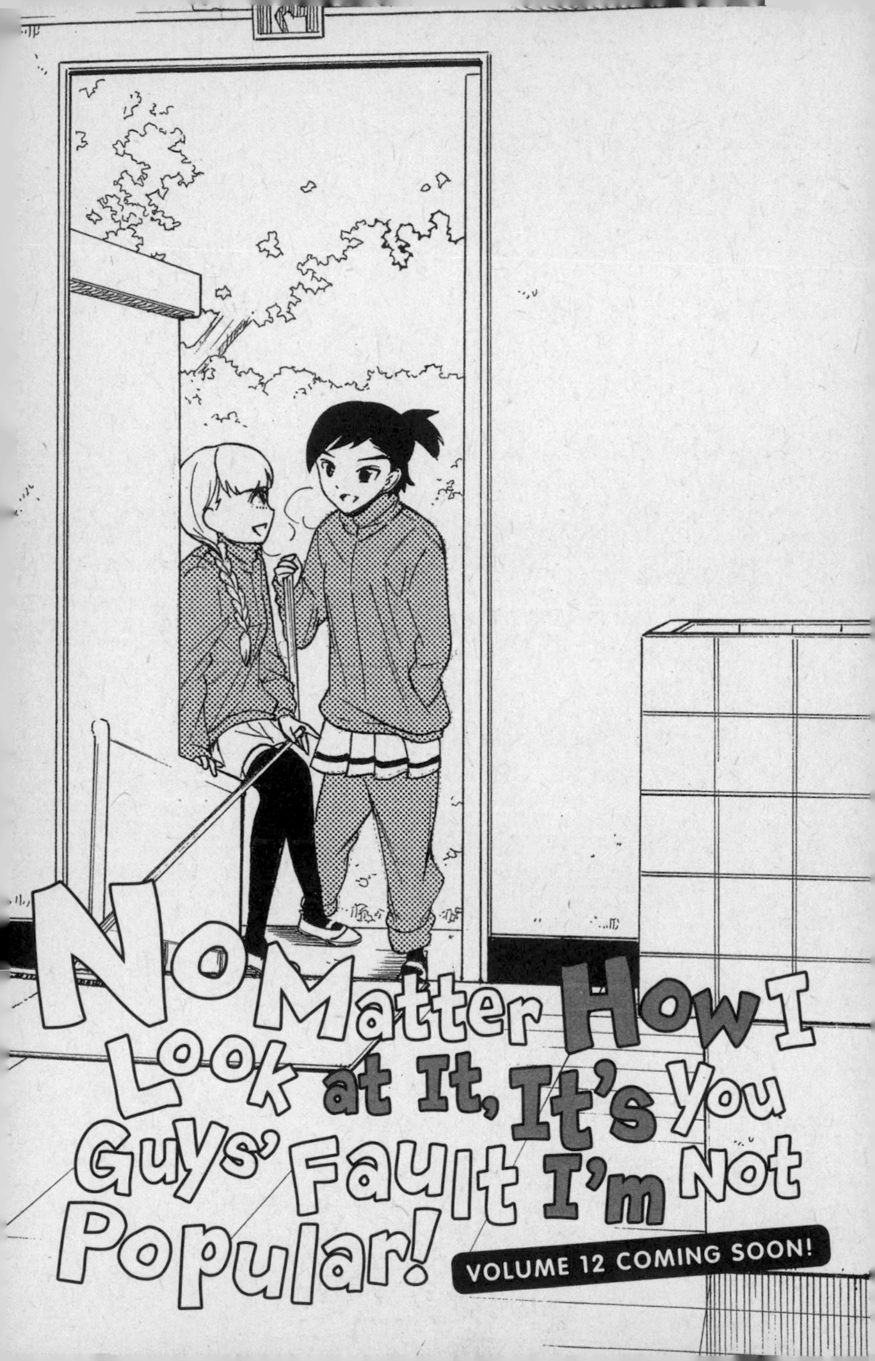
No Matter How I Look at It, It's You Guys' Fault I'm Not Popular!
VOLUME 12 COMING SOON!

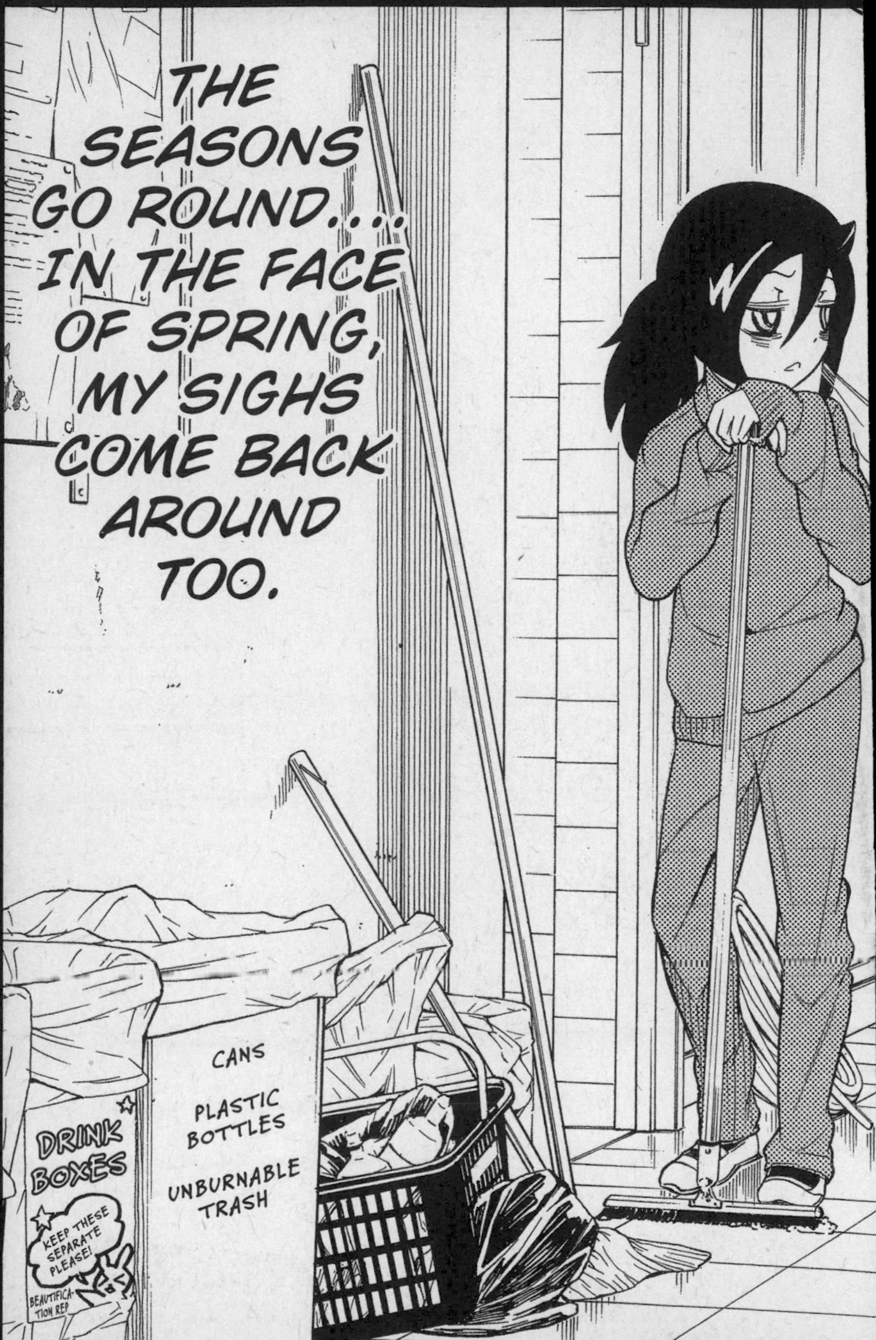
THE SEASONS GO ROUND.... IN THE FACE OF SPRING, MY SIGHS COME BACK AROUND TOO.
CANS
PLASTIC BOTTLES
UNBURNABLE TRASH
DRINK BOXES
KEEP THESE SEPARATE PLEASE!
BEAUTIFICATION REP

THIS HAPPENS A LOT LATELY

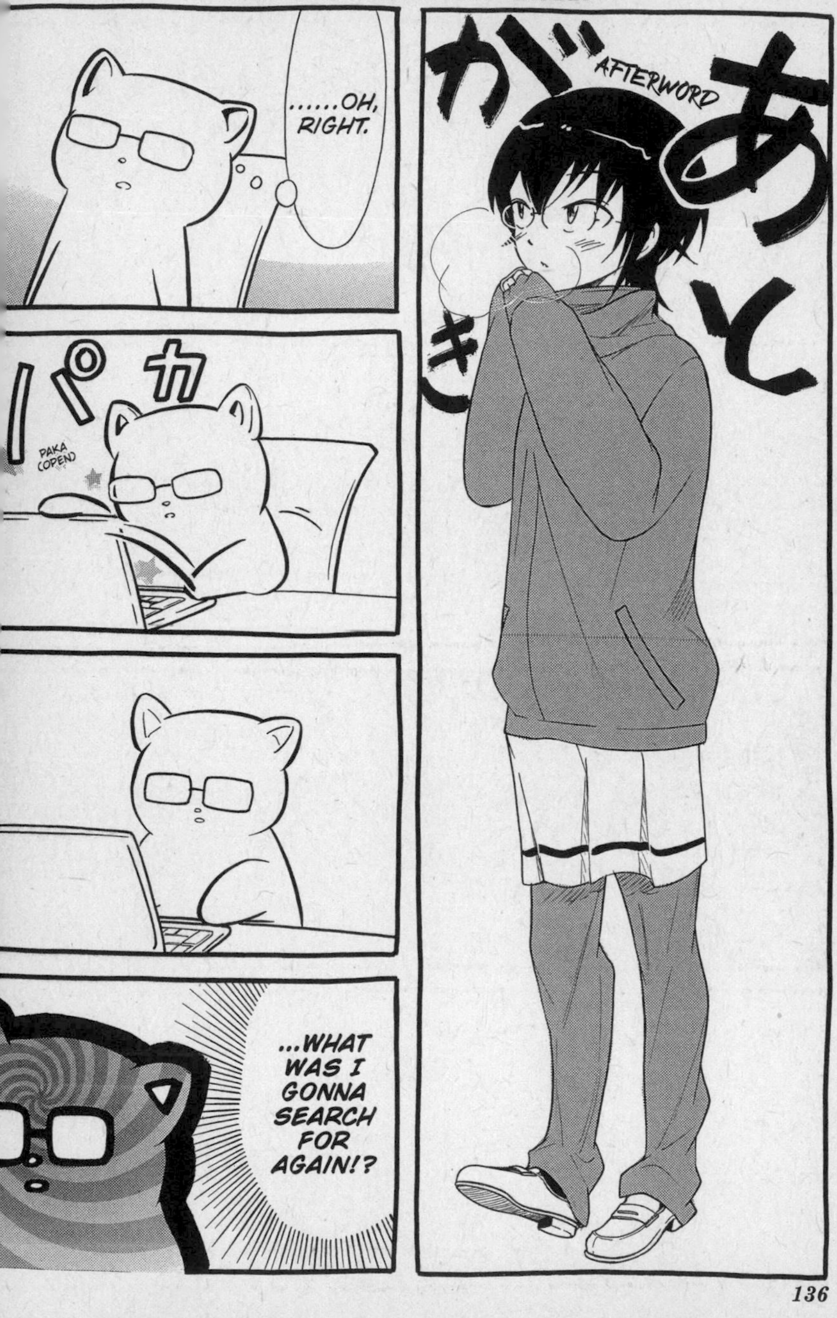
あとがき
AFTERWORD
......OH, RIGHT.
パカ
PAKA (OPEN)
...WHAT WAS I GONNA SEARCH FOR AGAIN!?

THE MATTER I WAS CONCERNED ABOUT

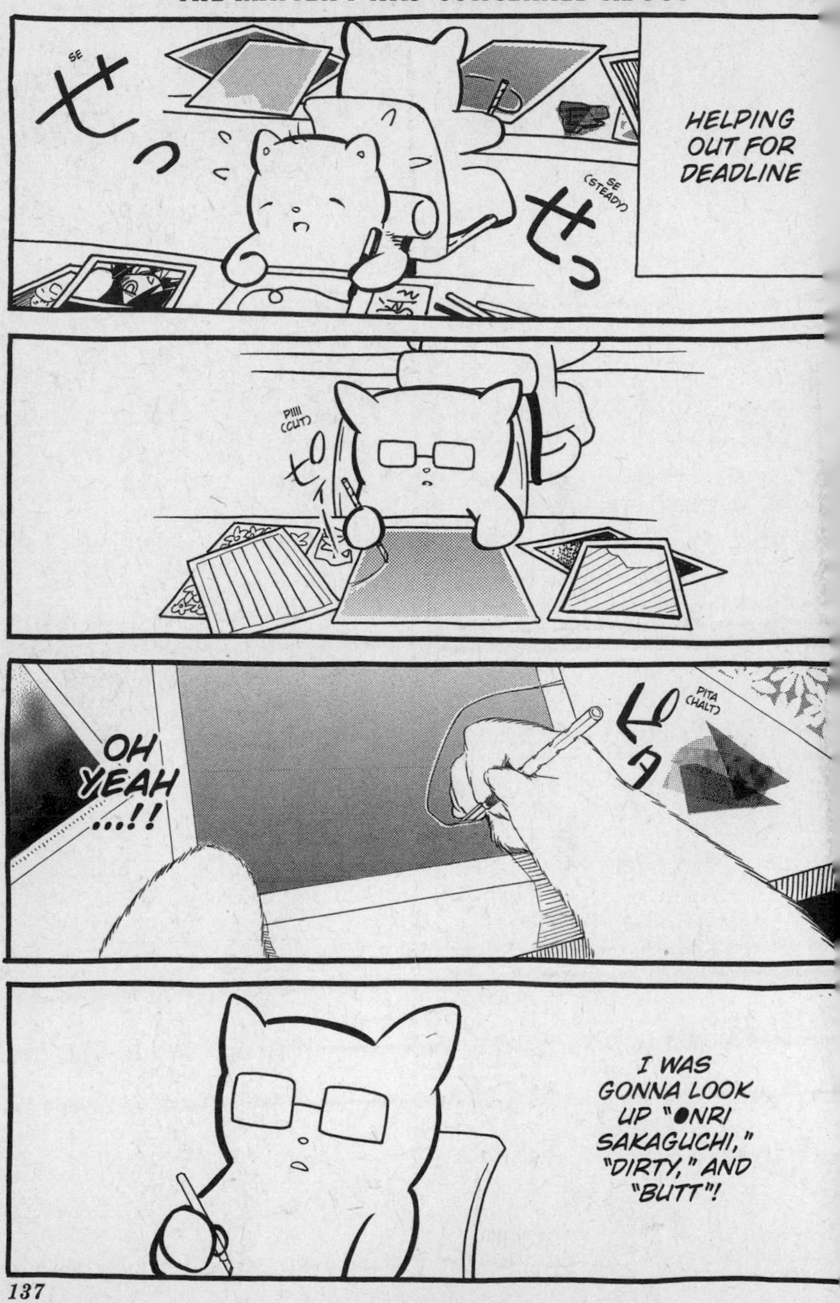
HELPING OUT FOR DEADLINE
せっ
SE (STEADY)
せっ
SE
ピーッ
PIIII (CUT)
ピタ
PITA (HALT)
OH YEAH ...!!
I WAS GONNA LOOK UP "ONRI SAKAGUCHI," "DIRTY," AND "BUTT"!

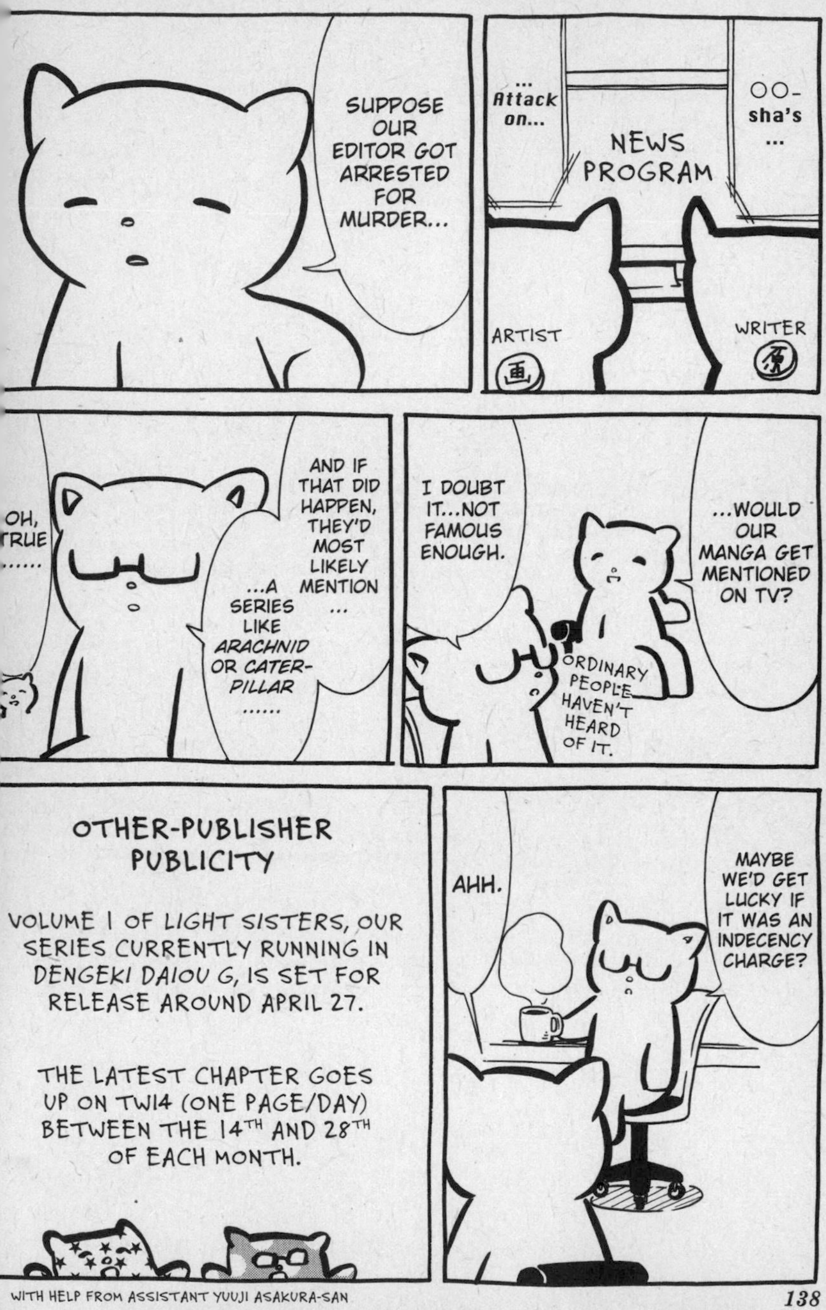

OO-sha's ...
NEWS PROGRAM
... Attack on...
WRITER
ARTIST
SUPPOSE OUR EDITOR GOT ARRESTED FOR MURDER...
...WOULD OUR MANGA GET MENTIONED ON TV?
I DOUBT IT...NOT FAMOUS ENOUGH.
ORDINARY PEOPLE HAVEN'T HEARD OF IT.
AND IF THAT DID HAPPEN, THEY'D MOST LIKELY MENTION ...
...A SERIES LIKE *ARACHNID* OR *CATER-PILLAR* ......
OH, TRUE......
MAYBE WE'D GET LUCKY IF IT WAS AN INDECENCY CHARGE?
AHH.
OTHER-PUBLISHER PUBLICITY
VOLUME 1 OF *LIGHT SISTERS*, OUR SERIES CURRENTLY RUNNING IN DENGEKI DAIOU G, IS SET FOR RELEASE AROUND APRIL 27.
THE LATEST CHAPTER GOES UP ON TW14 (ONE PAGE/DAY) BETWEEN THE 14TH AND 28TH OF EACH MONTH.

WITH HELP FROM ASSISTANT YUUJI ASAKURA-SAN

WE THOUGHT WE
COULD KEEP UP THE
"VIRGIN" JOKES UNTIL
THE VERY LAST VOLUME,
BUT WE'VE RUN OUT
OF MATERIAL...

PAGE 1
The **posters** in the post-graduation information office are advertising entrance exam and open house dates for Japanese colleges. The poster on the right is an actual one from February 2014 for **Chiba Institute of Science** (Chiba Kagaku Daigaku), written as Chiba Gaku Daigaku for copyright reasons.

PAGE 1
Akahon (literally "red book") is a Japanese publisher of guidebooks for college exam takers. There are books about the various universities and their exams, common exam subjects such as English vocabulary, and even stuff like "(Food) Recipes for Exam Success."

PAGE 1
Akiba Foreign Language University is a parody of Kanda Foreign Language University (Kanda Gaigo Daigaku). Kanda Station is on the Yamanote loop railway in Tokyo and is just south of the station for Akihabara (aka Akiba), the neighborhood famous as a center of electronics and other geek interests.

PAGE 3
In Japanese, Tomoko was starting to type *odaiji ni*, which basically means "Take care of yourself." The fully visible options are, in order: *ochinchin* ("weenie"), *oppai* ("boobs"), *otouto* ("little brother"), Ochiai Fukushi (a relatively new voice actor), the polite prefix *o-*, another kanji pronounced *o* ("cord" or "thong"), and finally a kanji that means "hemp" and is only really pronounced *o* at the start of a few surnames and words that have to do with hemp.

PAGE 6
Tomoko is reading 2014's Issue 14 of **Young Champion**, a manga anthology magazine aimed at young men that is published by Akita Shoten. The cover features singer Miori Ichikawa, a member of idol megagroup NMB48 and previously of AKB48.

PAGE 13
Beautiful Boy by MisioisiM refers to the light novel *Beautiful Boy Detective Squad* (*Bishounen Tanteidan*) by NisioisiN. As in volume 10, the parody author name in Japanese uses the word for "east" (*higashi*) instead of "west" (*nishi*).

PAGE 40
The heated table that Tomoko is sitting under is called a **kotatsu**. Japanese homes tend not to have central heating, so a kotatsu is a very popular and cozy way to keep warm in the winter.

PAGE 40
Hot Springs (for) Women, with a slight name alteration, is an actual Japanese travel show featuring hot springs resorts that welcome female travelers and families. They're especially popular places to visit during the colder months.

PAGE 40
The logo above the store Tomoko is visiting, Makuhari Ito-Yokado, is a slightly altered version of the English logo for SEVEN & i HOLDINGS, the parent company in Japan of retail chains 7-Eleven, Ito-Yokado, and Denny's. The swirly line normally looks more like a cursive *i*.

PAGE 41
The snack Tomoko picks up, **Matsutake Hill**, is a stand-in for the actual cookie snack Mushroom Mountain (*Kinoko no Yama*).

PAGE 41
The two bath powder packs Tomoko buys include powder to release carbon dioxide gas and produce bubbles, as seen later in the chapter. The actual brand name for **HABU** is BABU (a riff on "bubble"), and **Travel Hotel** (*Tabi no Ryokan*) is actually Travel Inn (*Tabi no Yado*). **Noboribetsu** is the largest hot springs town in the northern Japanese island of Hokkaido. On the shelf, there are also items with the company name **KNEIPP**, a German maker of nutrient, body care, and bath products.

PAGE 43
Instead of "**My body is ready...for bubbles,**" Tomoko says, "*Babumi o kanjiru,*" in the original. This is a pun on BABU (the actual bath powder brand, the name of which riffs on "bubble"). It also refers to the term *babumi*, which is derived from the Japanese stereotypical baby utterance *babu*, a word used often on social media that means "eliciting motherly affections or feeling such affection."

PAGE 45
Tomoko and Tomoki are watching the anime movie *The Disappearance of Haruhi Suzumiya*, a follow-up to the two anime seasons based on light novel series *The Melancholy of Haruhi Suzumiya* by Nagaru Tanigawa. The plot of *Disappearance* basically revolves around a winter hot pot party, though with unusual complications.

PAGE 47
Radio exercises are a standard set of calisthenic exercises to promote general health, the instructions for which are broadcast every morning on the NHK public radio and television networks and accompanied by piano music. These are often compulsory for students, especially during the summer, when **stamps** are given to prove attendance. This is why young Tomoko was making Tomoki get a stamp for her.

PAGE 47
Nori egg (*nori tamago*) is a rice seasoning made of bits of dried seaweed and dried, cooked egg.

PAGE 49
Tomoko is looking at the **TV guide screen** for a Panasonic VIERA HDTV, and the channels she's checking are TBS 1 and 2, and Fuji TV 1 and 2; letters in those names were either changed or removed, for copyright reasons.

PAGE 50
GameCenter CX, also known as *Retro Game Master* outside Japan, is a biweekly series in which host Shinya Arino tries to beat a retro game in one day. It usually airs on premium channel Fuji TV 1, but a special version airs on the regular Fuji TV broadcast channel roughly twice a year. However, it has no set schedule, which is why it catches Tomoko by surprise. Ice cream is often featured on the show as well.

PAGE 53
In Japan, the night of January 1 is considered to be when you have the **first dream of the new year** (*hatsuyume*), rather than the night of December 31, which is when people make their first shrine visit of the year (*hatsumode*).

PAGE 55
The forest where Tomoko's dream is set is Aokigahara at the northwestern foot of Mount Fuji. It's historically been considered a place where ghosts dwell, and it's become the most popular place in Japan to commit suicide in modern times, so it's already a spooky place.

PAGE 61
Plenty of Japanese names are gender neutral, but **Kouhei** is definitely a boy's name.

PAGE 64
Doki Doki Memorial Female's Side is a parody of *Tokimeki Memorial Girl's Side: 3rd Story*, a version of the classic *Tokimeki Memorial* dating sim, where the player character is a girl instead of a boy. Naturally, they're playing it on a **SOMY PFP** handheld console, instead of a SONY PSP.

PAGE 70
The Japanese terms Tomoko is using for her **furry image search** are 1) *kemona* (*kemoner*), the slang term for people interested in furry creatures, or *kemono*; and 2) *mesukemo*, a slang term for female furry creatures.

PAGE 73
Pure-White Lovers (*Masshiroi Koibito*) is a parody name for White Lovers (*Shiroi Koibito*), a brand of European-style sandwich cookie made by Ishiya Co., Ltd. in Sapporo, Hokkaido, which has become a popular Hokkaido souvenir.

PAGE 78
The Japanese term Tomoko used for Mako, *gachirezu*, is a slang term for "lesbian." When she later describes Ucchi as "jumpy," Tomoko uses the term *kyorojuu*, a slang word for someone who has plenty of friends in real life and gets fearful when they aren't around, so they look around suspiciously (*kyoro kyoro*) at those times.

PAGE 79
Saize is a nickname for the Italian restaurant and café chain Saizeriya.

PAGE 81
The backpack brand, **OUTDOOP**, is a parody of brand name OUTDOOR PRODUCTS.

PAGE 82
Adult Day (*Seijin no Hi*), also known as Coming of Age Day, is an official Japanese holiday on the second Monday of January, when communities hold ceremonies as a rite of passage for young people who've recently turned twenty, the age when a person is considered an adult in Japan.

PAGE 82
The Japanese slang term for **delinquents** used here is *yanki*, which is derived from the old English term "Yankee" for people from the American colonies. A common way for Japanese delinquents to break the rules is to dye their hair lighter (like Yoshida does) and adopt more American-style rebel fashion.

TRANSLATION NOTES 2 ··

PAGE 82
Hakama are traditional Japanese loose-fitting trousers.

PAGE 84
Yoshida's **Di●ney** and **Mi●key** name drops refer to Tokyo Disneyland (home of Mickey Mouse and friends), which is located in the city of Urayasu in Chiba Prefecture, right at the border of Tokyo.

PAGE 84
Yoshida's friend is drinking **BOSS**, a Japanese canned coffee brand.

PAGE 96
The Japanese version of Tomoko's **"What'chu smilin' 'bout!?"** is a reference to a sudden dialect outburst on TV by Tsuyoshi Shimoyanagi, a former pitcher for the Hanshin Tigers baseball team.

PAGE 97
MGRP stands for *Magical Girl Raising Project* (*Mahou Shoujo Ikusei Keikaku*, or *Maho Iku*, for short), an anime which ran October–December 2016 and was adapted from a series of action/survival light novels by Asari Endou.

PAGE 114
A **light novel** is a Japanese style of novels aimed primarily at young adults, which use anime-style illustrations and are often adapted into manga and anime. The term itself is a Japanese-made combination of English words (*raito noberu*).

PAGE 114
The Needs-Friends Union (*Tomodachi Iru Doumei*) is a parody name for the light novel series *The Don't-Need-Friends Union* (*Tomodachi Iranai Doumei*) by Nagi Sonoh.

PAGE 115
The Sweets Prince's Spécialité is a parody of *The Cake Prince's Spécialité* (*Spécialité du prince des gâteaux*) by Takafumi Nanatsuki. The movie-adapted novel Tomoko mentions is *Tomorrow I Will Date the You from Yesterday* (*Boku wa Ashita, Kinou no Kimi to Deeto Suru*).

PAGE 115
The **other books on the shelf**, identified by the rough cover designs and partial titles, are:
1. *I Want to Eat Your Pancreas* (*Kimi no Suizou o Tabetai*), a bestselling young adult novel by Yoru Sumino from 2015 that is getting a movie adaptation in 2017;
2. the second half of *A Man Called Pirate*, a historical novel by Naoki Hyakuta from 2012 that got a ten-volume manga adaptation starting in 2014 and a movie released in December 2016;
3. A parody of *The Strongest Way to Read That We Practice Every Day...* (*Bokura ga Mainichi Yatteiru Saikyou no Yomikata...*), a reading tips guide from 2016 by Akira Ikegami and Masaru Satou; and
4. A riff on *Reading Techniques* (*Dokusho no Gihou*), another reading tips guide by Masaru Satou from 2012.

PAGE 115
The two books on the left side of the Y section are probably *Forest-Preserving Civilizations* (*Mori o Mamoru Bunmei* and *Dominating Civilizations* (*Shihaisuru Bunmei*) by Yoshinori Yasuda, a Japanese geographer and environmental archaeologist.

PAGE 115
The **Yazawa** Tomoko is looking for is likely influential Japanese rock singer Eikichi Yazawa and his 1978 autobiography *Nariagari* (*The Upstart*). He started out in the *bosozoku* (rebel)-style rock band Carol before going solo in 1975, and his music and autobiography were very popular with young Japanese rebels. It has been adapted into two different manga series (1993, 2008) and a TV drama series (2002).

PAGE 116
The book that Yuri's reading is *Kino's Journey* (*Kino no Tabi*), the first volume of a light novel series by Keiichi Sigsawa that has received critical acclaim and anime adaptations. On page 118, she's reading *Kino no Tabi II*, the second volume of the series.

PAGE 124
Hello! Project is a collective of Japanese female idol singers.

PAGE 124
Plena refers to the Plena Makuhari shopping mall. The area they're shopping in is just southwest of Kaihin-Makuhari Station, not far from the Makuhari Messe conference center and the Marines' baseball stadium, and also includes MITSUI Outlet Park Makuhari, the sign for which is shown at the bottom of the page.

PAGE 125
The girls go to karaoke at the Kaihin-Makuhari branch of karaoke chain **COTE D'AZUR**, just northeast of the station.

PAGE 127
VILLAGE/VANGUARD, where Tomoko bought her present, is a Japanese bookstore chain that also sells novelties. The closest branch to the girls is at AEON Mall, about a kilometer away.

PAGE 128
The **autograph** on the baseball Komi bought appears to be by Taiga Hirasawa, an infielder for the Chiba Lotte Marines.

PAGE 128
Komi does indeed unwrap a box of *Sailor Moon* condoms, which actually exist. They were released for sale in November 2016 as part of an effort to reduce sexually transmitted infections in young women. The actual condom boxes were heart-shaped but only had the English text "prevention of STI" on them with a different character drawing. The design shown is actually more like what appeared on the poster from the campaign, which had the slogan *Kensa shinai to oshioki yo!!* ("Get tested, or I'll punish you!"), instead of *Tsukanai to oshioki yo!!* ("Put one on, or I'll punish you!").

PAGE 129
The "**Christmas Song**" that Yuu insists that they sing is most likely the 2015 J-pop song by the group Back Number.

PAGE 130
The **M T G** in the Christmas light display stands for Makuhari Techno Garden, a pair of skyscrapers near Kaihin-Makuhari Station. The square between the buildings features a tunnel of lights as part of their yearly display.

PAGE 132
The **line Tomoko quotes** is by protagonist Kibino Mabiki from Kouhei Nishi's manga *Tsugihagi Hyouryuu Sakka*, a three-volume series that ran in *Weekly Shounen Jump* starting in 2006.

PAGE 132
The anime that Hina was starting to name off was *Girlish Number*, a multimedia series from 2016 about a female voice actress. It was released in serial novel form by Wataru Watari (the author of *My Youth Romantic Comedy Is Wrong, As I Expected*) and in manga form starting earlier in the year, in addition to the twelve-episode anime series from October–December 2016 that Hina watched.

PAGE 132
your name., mentioned by Hina, is the 2016 anime film by Makoto Shinkai that shattered box-office records in Japan and was watched by many people who don't normally watch anime, which is why it's a safe one for Hina to mention in front of her friends.

PAGE 137
Anri Sakaguchi is a relatively new porn actress, and in late 2016, there was gossip about her butt looking dirty in one of her films.

PAGE 138
On January 10, 2017, a deputy editor of Kodansha's *Weekly Shounen Magazine* was arrested on suspicion of having murdered his wife the previous August. Early news reports stated that he was the editor of the popular manga series *Attack on Titan* (*Shingeki no Kyoujin*), which runs in the magazine, but he was only peripherally involved with the series.

PAGE 138
ARACHNID and **CATERPILLAR** are two SquareEnix manga series written by Shinya Murata with different artists; the latter is a spin-off of the former.

NO MATTER HOW I LOOK AT IT, IT'S YOU GUYS' FAULT I'M NOT POPULAR! ⑪

Nico Tanigawa

Translation/Adaptation: Krista Shipley, Karie Shipley
Lettering: Bianca Pistillo

This book is a work of fiction. Names, characters, places, and incidents are the product of the author's imagination or are used fictitiously. Any resemblance to actual events, locales, or persons, living or dead, is coincidental.

WATASHI GA MOTENAI NOWA DOU KANGAETEMO OMAERA GA WARUI! Volume 11 © 2017 Nico Tanigawa / SQUARE ENIX CO., LTD. First published in Japan in 2017 by SQUARE ENIX CO., LTD. English translation rights arranged with SQUARE ENIX CO., LTD. and Yen Press, LLC through Tuttle-Mori Agency, Inc., Tokyo.

English translation ©2017 by SQUARE ENIX CO., LTD.

Yen Press, LLC supports the right to free expression and the value of copyright. The purpose of copyright is to encourage writers and artists to produce the creative works that enrich our culture.

The scanning, uploading, and distribution of this book without permission is a theft of the author's intellectual property. If you would like permission to use material from the book (other than for review purposes), please contact the publisher. Thank you for your support of the author's rights.

Yen Press
1290 Avenue of the Americas
New York, NY 10104

Visit us!
⚹ yenpress.com
⚹ facebook.com/yenpress
⚹ twitter.com/yenpress
⚹ yenpress.tumblr.com
⚹ instagram.com/yenpress

First Yen Press Edition: December 2017

Yen Press is an imprint of Yen Press, LLC.
The Yen Press name and logo are trademarks of Yen Press, LLC.

The publisher is not responsible for websites (or their content) that are not owned by the publisher.

Library of Congress Control Number: 2013498929

ISBNs: 978-0-316-41412-8 (paperback)
978-0-316-44788-1 (ebook)

10 9 8 7 6 5 4 3 2 1

BVG

Printed in the United States of America